C. Faulhaber
11/85

Celestina by Fernando de Rojas:
An Annotated Bibliography
of World Interest
1930-1985

Joseph T. Snow

Madison, 1985

Bibliographic Series, No. 6
Copyright © 1985 by
The Hispanic Seminary of
Medieval Studies, Ltd.

ISBN 0-942260-58-9

Comedia de Calisto y Melibea

Toledo 1500

for
Alan
Dorothy
and
Keith

Contents

General Introduction

When I and two graduate students first began to think that a bibliography which would set out to document worldwide interest in Fernando de Rojas' *Celestina* would be a useful tool for research, there was no idea of just where or how far it would lead, nor of how much time it might take to prepare such a compilation. This was in 1974: the fruits of those first labors were published as "Un cuarto de siglo de interés en *La Celestina*, 1949-75: Documento bibliográfico" [*Hispania* 59 (1976), 610-60; henceforth abbreviated LCDB]. In the introduction to that compilation, I thought it wise to cite the prophetic words of Palau y Dulcet: "la bibliografía completa de *La Celestina* está aún por hacer." His words are even more meaningful and applicable now that I am in a position to offer a more-than-fifty-year bibliographical overview of work in a field that has drawn the interest of scholars, editors, translators, students, musicians, actors, poets, literary historians, bibliophiles and, not least of all, generations of new readers.

Once I had acquired some control over the mass of information, as I seemed to be doing in my teaching of Rojas' masterwork and in my ongoing acquisition of articles and bits of information supplied by users of LCDB, I found it hard to "let go." I now see that it was a reluctance to let go of that control that led me to create a newsletter which would provide a convenient place for LCDB supplements. The result was *Celestinesca*, founded in 1977 at the University of Georgia, and it would come to include not only the envisioned supplements to LCDB but international news concerning almost anything celestinesque as well as articles, notes, reviews and varied illustrations. By May of 1985, seventeen LCDB supplements had appeared and these contained over 450 items, not counting book reviews.

It seemed the time had come to go back to the drawing board and devise a way in which some conflation of the growing bulk of information—now in eighteen separate places—could be effected. One thing led to another and the idea of growing backwards as well as forwards became a feature of the project. How far back to go? Time, assistance, and resources seemed to limit this growth to a mere twenty years. A fifty year span seemed a useful period of time to document—in *Celestina* studies they are crucial years—but the user of this bibliography needs to be aware that I am including items published through mid-1985, i. e., the current moment (and a few still in press). The idea of "documenting" interest over the span of fifty years also provided me with a means—I think legitimate—of including items earlier than 1930 when they appeared in reprinted form within the target period. Thus, even this updated version of the LCDB of 1976 is open to both earlier and more modern additions, a fact which emphasizes its ongoing nature. In some ways, the present work would be volume 2 of, ideally, a complete bibliographical survey of modern *Celestina* studies, in which volume 1 would begin with the 1822 Madrid printing by León Amarita of LC and extend to 1930, where this volume begins. I have many of these materials in my possession but, given the exigencies of time and the limits of my own energies, decided that to include and complete the pre-1930 file would delay too long the publication of the present accumulation.

The main goal of the present work is simply to produce a handy and useful guide to *Celestina* items in which the user can place maximum trust. All but the asterisked items have been seen and the bibliographical information concerning them—let this at least be clear—is not copied from other compilations: all annotated items carry, then, their own verification. The annotations provided are also meant to be a user guide, mostly to content or point of view. In the case of longer items, e.g. monographs and books, truly adequate annotation is impractical but this shortcoming is somewhat countered by the inclusion of the reviews in print, at least those I have been able to locate. Designed to be a further aid—and used whenever possible—are the two types of cross-references included in the annotations: one is the entry number of an item, the other will be to author and year. While no bibliography is free of error, I have attempted to make this one as trouble-free as possible by seeking the aid of machines which make proofreading and electronic correction a painless process. I was privileged to be able to reduce the nitty-gritty work associated with bibliographic compilations by using, at Wisconsin's Hispanic Seminary of Medieval Studies, machine-aided text-editing and formatting techniques developed there over a period of years under continuing grants from the National Endowment for the Humanities.

There are several new features in this expanded LCDB. One is that it is in English and not Spanish, a switch motivated as much by friendly suggestions as by more practical reasons. Another is that I have combined in one list all the items formerly separated by artificial distinctions: theses, monographs, studies in books and miscellanies, etc. It makes a very long list indeed and the most suitable arrangement seemed to be an alphabetical list, by last name of author. However, to facilitate the consultation of this listing there is a Subject Index provided at the end of the volume in which, for example, by looking under "Characterizations: Pármeno," one will find the numbers of the entries which provide a basis for study of this character. This index, while not exhaustive, will provide the user of the bibliography a good starting point for further study.

The section of editions (critical, facsimile and popular) from LCDB has been preserved, expanded and enhanced with information about contents, illustrations and other potentially interesting signposts reflecting modern tastes. The section on translations and adaptations has grown substantially. While it may be of relatively little interest to the literary scholar of either the CCM or the TCM traditions, it will furnish a great deal of detailed information—to students of theatre history—about Rojas' work on twentieth-century stages. Information included in this section has without doubt been the hardest to harvest, and a great deal more assuredly remains to be unearthed. For each of the separate sections, explanatory paragraphs are provided at the beginning as a guide for the user.

Acknowledgments: I have been accumulating materials for this bibliography on *Celestina* for over a decade now and there is a rather large number of people who have contributed in ways great and small. The names of those colleagues who have sent along information, offprints, programs, photos and other materials, and others who have helped me with items in Polish, Hebrew, Chinese, Russian, and Hungarian, make a very long list; although they are too numerous to list, they will know who they are, and it is a pleasure to be able to thank them, even anonymously, at this time. They have helped me make this compilation—however inperfect it may prove to be—as complete as it is.

Another debt of gratitude goes back to 1974-76 and to two students, Jane F. Schneider and Cecilia Castro Lee, who collaborated with me in the Spanish-language *esbozo* of the present work, mentioned above. Their enthusiasm and effort were exemplary, their support and diligence were an inspiration. The technical assistance lent by Diana Rineer and Alison Reeve in the early stages I still recognize as invaluable. Donald Bleznick, then editor of *Hispania*, gave much-appreciated encouragement to the project, supporting it for eventual publication and assigning as editorial overseer Hensley C. Woodbridge, whose considerable talents as a bibliographer gave to the printed form a coherence and logic that it otherwise would not have had.

I have worked the past few summers in Madison, Wisconsin, in space generously provided by both the Hispanic Seminary of Medieval Studies and the Institute for Research in the Humanities. I owe a very large debt of gratitude to Profs. Lloyd A. Kasten and John

J. Nitti of the Seminary, and to Ruth Richards, staff programmer, for their unfailing aid in helping me put my materials into machine-readable form and for guiding me through the typesetting program at the end. I was supported financially in the summers of 1981, 1983 and 1985 by grants from the University of Georgia's Department of Romance Langauges. All along I have had the assistance of capable people in the Inter-Library Loan offices at the Universities of Georgia and Wisconsin. I worked in several libraries in London, Barcelona and (especially) Madrid, in all of which I met with the kindest co-operation.

It would be near-miraculous if human error were totally absent from this bibliography. I have tried hard to keep errors out, but I alone am responsible for any that remain. This has been a vast undertaking, at times daunting, but the co-operation and support I have had had from *celestinófilos* around the world has at all times made any special efforts worthwhile.

Joseph T. Snow
Madison, August 1985

I. Studies On *Celestina*

The following alphabetical listing is inclusive of books dealing specifically with *Celestina*, chapters or studies included in books not specifically about *Celestina*, theses, notes and articles from journals, newspapers, homage volumes, reference tomes, literary histories and other sorts of scholarly productions. Full bibliographical citation has been provided for the items annotated. Only a very few entries have not been seen and these are indicated with an asterisk (*). Abbreviations used are keyed to a masterlist to be found at the end of the text. For works which have been reprinted, the more recent date is usually cited first, with information on the earlier appearance(s) following. When an author is responsible for more than a single entry, the entries are arranged chronologically; when two of these bear the same imprint year, entries are further arranged alphabetically by first significant word (e. g., not to include definite articles).

A

1. ABAD, Manuel. "La ilustración de portadas de LC, en siete ediciones del siglo XVI." *Revista de Ideas Estéticas* 35 (1977), 229-35 [with four plates].

    Shown are the covers of Seville '1502' and 1523, Valencia 1514, Paris 1527, Toledo 1538, Medina del Campo 1530-40(?) and Alcalá 1569. Four of them are discussed in detail because they depict actions which take place in the TCM: the remaining three are different in that they are types and are not linked to any specific action.

2. ABBATE, Gay. "The 'Celestina' as a Parody of Courtly Love." *Ariel* 3, no. 1 (April 1974), 29-32.

    Calisto plays the part of the courtly lover, a role revealed to the reader through the irony of situation. Melibea is also playing a role. Their deaths round out the parody based on Andreas Capellanus' *De amore*.

3. ABRAMS, Fred. "The Name *Celestina*: Why did Fernando de Rojas Choose It?" *RomN* 14 (1972-73), 165-67.

    The name is modeled on a parody of 'infernal' (i. e., 'celestial') suggested by the *Libro de buen amor*.

4. ABRUÑEDA, Angeles, and Manuel ARIZA. "El adjetivo calificativo en LC." ACTAS: 213-28.

    LC shares in the Renaissance taste for the pre-positioning of the adjective (with 1205 occurrences) above post-postioning (with 306 occurrences). Comments range from adjectives grouped by opposed semantic meanings to adjectives especially employed by various of the characters.

5. ACHARD, Paul. "La *Célestine* de Fernando de Rojas (1492)." *La Gerbe* (March 26 1942), p. 6.

    Newspaper publication of three scenes from the author's stage adaptation of LC (see entry 1036.2.): the prologue, spoken by a 'sereno' added by Achard; Pármeno's description of Celestina (scene 2); and the irreverent commentary of the servants during the love scene at Melibea's door (scene 7).

6. ADINOLFI, Giulia. "LC e la sua unità di composizione." *Filologia Romanza* 1 (1954), 12-60.

    Rojas is sole author of LC: the pretense that he is not results from his own fear about the reception of some of the first act's concepts.

7. AGUIRRE, J. M. *Calisto y Melibea, amantes cortesanos.* Zaragoza: Almenara, 1962. 94p. (Col. Ensayos, 1)

    There is in LC an evident criticism of the courtly manner as much in literature as in life.

    a. BHS 41 (1964), 67-68, A. D. Deyermond
    b. BH 69 (1967), 493-95, P. Heugas

8. ALBANESE, Paolo. "LC con aspecto particular de la picaresca." Thesis (Tesina). Messina, Italy. 1975. (*)

9. ALBORG, Juan Luis. *Historia de la literatura española.* Vol. I. Edad Media y Renacimiento (Madrid: Gredos, 1966; revised and enlarged ed., 1970; rpt. 1972 [cited]), 532-615.

    Retraces the history of LC criticism in terms of the major problems; authorship, social reality portrayed, genre, intention of the author and more. There are extensive bibliographical notes.

10. ALCALA, Angel. "Rojas y el neoepicureísmo: Notas sobre la intención de LC y el silencio posterior de su autor." ACTAS: 35-50.

    Reviews differing ideas of Rojas' intentions, the didactic (Bataillon, 1961), the humanistic (Lida de Malkiel, 1962), the philosophic (Gilman, 1956) and, more briefly, others espoused by Berndt-Kelley (1963) and Maravall (1964). Alcalá espouses his own view in the light of these: LC is a manifesto of disillusionment with the world and points the way to an escape from it. At the same time it underscores a basic agreement with then-current Renaissance ideas of Neoepicureanism.

11. _____. "El neoepicureísmo y la intención de LC: Notas para una relección." RF 88 (1976), 224-45.

    With minor changes it is almost identical to the previous entry.

12. ALCINA, Juan. *Fernando de Rojas. La Celestina.* Guías Laia de Literatura, 8, Barcelona: Ed. Laia, 1983. 100p.

    A student guide designed to facilitate a reading of LC and, at the same time, outline the more vexing problems the text presents.

Sections include those on the text, the author(s), the social background of the work, contemporary works, suggestions for study and a final one which recommends four editions and twenty-seven studies.

13. ALLISON, A. F. *English Translations from the Spanish and Portuguese to the Year 1700*. London: Dawsons of Pall Mall, 1974.

On pp. 158-59 there is notice of the partial translation of John Rastell (see entry 1029) and the more ambitious one of James Mabbe (see entries 1008, 1019 and 1024) in the 1631 and 1634 editions.

14. ALMIÑAQUE, Conrado B. *El concepto de la muerte en la literatura española del siglo XV*. Montevideo: Ed. Géminis, 1975.

Certain passages of LC evaluated for their rhetorical flair or their lyrical qualities.

a. REH 10 (1976), 315-16, J. A. Madrigal

15. ALONSO, Amado. "Sobre antecedentes de LC." RFH 4 (1942), 266-68.

He rejects a link between LC and the old woman of the *Historia de los amores de Bayad y Riyad*, supposed source for *Celestina*, according to A. R. Nykl, translator of the Arabic work.

16. ALONSO, Dámaso. "La novela española y su contribución a la novela realista moderna." *Cuadernos del idioma* 1, no. 1 (1965), 17-43.

Rojas rates high praise for his ability to humanize his characters: it is this quality which made the work so popular in Europe.

17. ALONSO HERNANDEZ, José Luis. "De *Buen Amor* a *Celestina*. Estabilidad y evolución de un léxico y sus campos semánticos." *Les Langues Neo-latines* 69 (1975), 3-39.

A study of complex semantic comparisons. After determining certain rules for word choices in the LBA, the author analyzes the behavior of the same words in LC, the principal lexical item being 'alcahueta'. There are both literary and sociological inferences drawn.

18. ALVAREZ, Guzmán. *El amor en la novela picaresca española*. The Hague: Van Goor Zonen, 1958.

The relationship of LC to the picaresque is peripheral, limited to some elements of the characters of the male servants (pp. 120-21).

19. AMEZÚA, Efigenio. "La 'celestinesca española' en la evolución del amor y la sexualidad en Europa occidental." Thesis (Licence). Univ. of Louvain, 1970. V. Heylen. (*)

20. _____. *La erótica española en sus comienzos*. Barcelona: Fontanella, 1974. 221p.

The final two-thirds of the book are useful. A concept of the erotic, derived from a line beginning with the LBA and passing through the Arcipreste de Talavera and Rodrigo de Cota to Rojas, is established and is found to have passed from the stage of pleasantness to one of contentiousness. The author posits that love and sexuality 'a la española' reflect a longing for "Buen Amor".

a. YWMLS 37 (1975), 258, A. A. Heathcote

21. AMÍCOLA, José. "El siglo XV y el teatro castellano." *Filología* 14 (1970), 145-69, especially at 167-69.

LC seen as a clear influence in Encina's *Egloga de Plácida y Victoriano*, in Lucas Fernández' *Egloga o farsa del nacimiento*, and in Torres Naharro's *Comedia himenea*, especially in utilization of types and manner of characterization.

22. ANDERSON IMBERT, Enrique. "*Comedia de Calixto y Melibea*." *Realidad* 3 (1949), 301-08; rpt. in *Los grandes libros de Occidente* with the title "LC" (Mexico: Ed. de Andrea, 1958), pp. 30-44.

Throughout the work it is egoism and individualism that stand out; the dominant tone is very much sexual, a moral is lacking, and the multiple deaths are a sure sign of prevailing chaos. All this finally put LC on the 1640 *Index*.

23. ANGULO IÑIGUEZ, Diego. "Murillo y Goya." *Goya*, nos. 148-50 (January-June 1979), 210-213.

Influence of LC in Murillo's 'Mujeres en la ventana' and in Goya's 'Celestina'. Illustrated.

24. ANON. "1492. Fernando de Rojas crée le théâtre moderne: LC." *Rendez-vous*, no. 9 (1958), n. p. (*)

25. ANON. "*Celestina, tragicomedia de Calixto y Melibea*." *Cel* 6, no. 1 (May 1982), 31-32.

A short piece salvaged from the 19th century [originally in Madrid's *La censura* 1 (1844), 144], interesting for its view that Rojas' work was dangerous reading. A 1793 Holy Office proclamation banned LC even for those licensed to peruse offensive materials.

26. ANTOLIN, Angelika. "Einige Ubersetzungen der 'Celestina' in Kritischen Vergleich." Thesis (Magisterarbeit). Univ. of Erlangen-Nürnberg, 1975. (*)

27. ANTON, Karl-Heinz. "Acerca del saber de Celestina." ACTAS: 193-200.

Two encounters are scrutinized: Calisto and Melibea in the opening scene of Act 1 and Celestina and Melibea in Act 4. Structures of offense and defense are found in them, reflecting the "omnia secundum litem fiunt" cited by Rojas in his introd., and furnishing an insight into the reasons for Celestina's verbal triumph over Melibea.

28. ANZOATEGUI, Ignacio B. "Calisto o el amante," in his *Tres ensayos españoles* (Buenos Aires: Sol y Luna, 1938), 71-115; new ed. Madrid, 1944: 79-124.

Calisto is a quintessentially Spanish lover and sinner, a symbol of an abandonment of self in order to begin to 'be' what one really is. There are interesting comparisons of Calisto to Don Juan and to Don Quijote.

29. ARBEA G., Antonio. "Una fuente latina ignorada del suicidio de Melibea." *Revista Chilena de Literatura*, no. 14 (1979), 55-73.

The work in question is Hugolini Pisani de Parma's *Philogenia*. In the third of its sixteen scenes, the titular heroine threatens to throw herself from the top floor of her house.

30. ARCINIEGA, Rosa. "LC, antelación del *Don Juan*." *Revista de Indias* 6 (New Series, 2) (1939), 258-77.

A version of her epilogue to the book by Ortega (1932), modified to show how and in what ways LC prepares the way for the work by Zorrilla.

31. ARMISTEAD, S. G. and J. H. SILVERMAN. "Algo más sobre 'Lo de tu abuela con el ximio' (LC I): Antonio de Torquemada y Lope de Vega." PSA 69, no. 205 (1973), 11-18.

In an article to complement another by Green (1956), two further examples of apes who were lovers of women are adduced.

32. _____. "A Neglected Source of the Prolog to LC." MLN 98 (1978), 310-12.

With reference to Rojas' comments on conflict in the animal world, there is in the Peninsula's oral tradition a song featuring a series of animals, each pursued by another, which may have provided an additional stimulus for the prologue materials.

33. _____. "Un poema celestinesco en la tradición sefardí moderna." *Cel* 2, i (May 1978), 3-6.

Discusses a poem from Morocco which exists in five variant versions and whose content and metrical form indicate a sixteenth-century origin. LC seems to have provided inspiration for it.

34. _____. "Un poema celestinesco en la tradición sefardí moderna (nota adicional)." *Cel* 2, ii (Fall 1978), 29.

See the entry immediately above. Furnishes additional proofs (from unedited versions) for the poem's celestinesque origin.

35. ARMISTEAD, S. G. and J. T. MONROE. "*Albas, mammas,* and Code-Switching in the Kharjas: A Reply to Keith Whinnom." *LaC* 11 (1982-83), 174-207 (especially 181-82 and 198-199, n. 2).

The *alborada* in Act 19 is adduced as partial proof that this genre deals with engagements and marriages, as distinct from the *alba*, which portrays mostly adulterous affairs.

36. ARTIGAS, Miguel. "El pleito sobre el autor de LC," in *El erudito español: Don Manuel Serrano y Sanz* (Madrid: Nuevas Gráficas, 1935), pp. 146-47.

High praise for the confirmation and identification of the

historical Fernando de Rojas in documentation presented by Serrano y Sanz [*Revista de Archivos, Bibliotecas y Museos* 6 (1902), 245-99].

37. ARTILES, Jenaro. "LC y *Romeo y Julieta*." ACTAS: 325-38.

Resumé of the available evidence—from English translations and possible stage adaptations from about 1525 to the end of the 16th century—for LC influence on Shakespeare.

38. ARTILES, Joaquín. "Sobre el autor de LC," in his *Paisaje y poesía en la Edad Media* (La Laguna: J. Reguló, 1960), 129-50.

Reviews previous criticism dealing with Act 1, Acts 2-16, and the interpolations. As a personal contribution, he notes that the sole passages describing landscapes occur in the latter additions. This may mean either that Rojas waxed poetical as the text evolved or that another hand was at work.

39. ASENSIO, Eugenio. *Itinerario del entremés desde Lope de Rueda a Quiñones de Benavente*. Madrid: Gredos, 1965. 374p.

The influence of Rojas on the 'entremés' is discussed *passim*.

40. ASENSIO, Manuel. "El tiempo en LC." HR 20 (1952), 28-43.

Reviews the commentary on the topic of time in LC since 1535 (Juan de Valdés). The notion of time in LC is intentional, used effectively and artistically and adds a dimension of profundity to the work which must be the concept of a sole author: Rojas.

41. _____. "A Rejoinder." HR 21 (1953), 54-50.

A further espousal of the ideas presented earlier (see entry above) in the light of objection to them presented by Gilman (entry 374). This time, Asensio concentrates on the effect of temporal arrangements in the characterization of Calisto.

42. _____. "La intención religiosa del *Lazarillo de Tormes* y Juan de Valdés." HR 27 (1959), 78-102.

Contains a series of remarks comparing Celestina to the 'ciego' from *Lazarillo*.

43. ASTIAZARAN, Gloria C. "LC vista como obra satírica." ETL 10 (1981), 5-13.

A string of text citations exemplifies forms of satire in LC: incongruencies, irony, etc. All serve Rojas as moral criticism of his social environment.

44. AUSTIN, Karen O. "A Possible Resolution for Some of the Ambiguities and Contradictions in LC." *Southern Quarterly* 12 (1973-74), 335-51.

The most interesting idea is that the confused sense of time in LC may reflect, artistically, the temporal dislocation suffered by its protagonists, a kind of representation of their mood. If so, then the sense of time is not to be seen as poor construction but rather as sensitive art.

45. AYALA CASTRO, Marta Concepción. "Comparación del léxico del primer auto de LC con el de la versificación de Ximénez de Urrea." Thesis (Tesina). Univ. of Malaga, 1981. (*)

46. AYERBE-CHAUX, Reinaldo. "La triple tentación de Melibea." *Cel* 2, ii (Fall 1978), 3-11.

A closely-reasoned analysis of Celestina's psychological triumph over Melibea in Act 4 using parallels with the doctrine of temptation from scholastic writings.

47. AYERBE-POZO, Guillermo F. "Cuatro visiones modernas de LC." Diss. New York Univ. 1978. 426p. DAI 39/6, 3566-67A. No. 7824192. J. R. Stamm.

Covers four major critical approaches to LC: Lida de Malkiel's (1962), Bataillon's (1961), Gilman's (1956) and Maravall's (1964).

48. AYLLON, Cándido. "Pessimism in LC." Diss. Univ. of Wisconsin, 1956. 382p. DA 16/12, 2454-55. No. 00-18370. J. H. Herriott. (See entry 52.)

49. _____. "Death in LC." *Hispania* 41 (1958), 160-64.

Death is omnipresent in LC and in multiple forms, reflected in the conceptualizations of individual characters. It is brought into play by love and avarice, forces normally opposed to each other.

50. _____. "Negativism and Dramatic Structure in LC." *Hispania* 46 (1963), 290-95.

Shows how pessimism is developed gradually in LC and how the work's structure intensifies it.

51. _____. "Petrarch and Fernando de Rojas." RR 54 (1963), 81-94.

Maintains that fundamental ideas of pessimism in Rojas' LC—especially those that deal with life, old age, fortune and death—come from Petrarch's prose works.

52. _____. *La visión pesimista de LC.* Mexico: Ed. de Andrea, 1965. 189p. (Col. Studium, 45)

Studies Rojas' portrayal of the world of LC, its dramatic arrangement and interlacing of plot, motives, characters and themes, and shows how these elements—affected by Christian pessimism, Petrarchan humanism, *converso* bitterness, etc.—project a vision of endless and hopeless conflict in which action and thought are meaningless. The resulting gloom is a product of literary motifs and personal experience.

a. BA 40 (1966), 446, D. W. Bleznick
b. *Stylo*, no. 7 (1968), 213-14, Aguayo Q.

53. _____. "La ironía en LC." RF 82 (1970), 37-55.

Rojas' bitter vision of the world is artistically controlled by his

expert irony in use of language, characterization, situation and, above all, in major structural arrangements.

54. _____. *La perspectiva irónica de Fernando de Rojas.* Madrid: Porrúa Turanzas, 1984. 285p. Paper.

The first chapter treats irony in general and is followed by a reading—in six chapters—of LC which highlights the use of different kinds and levels of irony by Rojas and how they are used to produce a dramatic structure for the work.

55. AZAR, Inés. "Metáfora, literalidad, transgresión: Amor-Muerte en LC y en la *Egloga II* de Garcilaso." *Lexis* 3, no. 1 (July 1979), 57-65.

Rojas manages to deride troubadouresque metaphors by literalizing them in his masterpiece. The result? A chaos, a world without limits, morals, or alternatives, a world dominated by egocentrism. The *amor-muerte* metaphor from the troubadour era becomes, in Rojas' hand, a tragic reality.

56. _____. "Speech Act Theory on Self, Responsibility and Discourse," in *Homenaje a Ana María Barrenechea,* ed. L. Schwartz Lerner and I. Lerner (Madrid: Castalia, 1984), 33-40.

Utilizing the theory of minimal units of dicourse, or 'speech acts', as a guide, the author finds that in LC the intentions declared and the promises made by the characters form a network of motifs—all of which are frustrated or thwarted when it is realized that language in and of itself is incapable of maintaining a concept of reality (analyses are made of Melibea and Celestina in this regard). LC is an eminently self-conscious text: knowing that language is a trap, the characters allow themselves to becomes trapped as they use language in efforts to gain power; all such efforts fail.

B

57. BAADER, Horst. "Melibea conversa? Randbemerkungen zu einem neuen Interpretationsversuch der 'Celestina'." RJ 8 (1957), 287-89.

A brief discussion on 'conversos' in Spain which ends with a rejection of the assertion that Melibea was 'conversa' (see Orozco: 1957).

58. BAGBY JR., Albert I. and William M. CARROLL. "The Falcon as a Symbol of Destiny: De Rojas and Shakespeare." RF 83 (1971), 306-10.

On the possible symbolic value of a hawk as destiny in Act 1.

59. BAHNER, Werner. "LC en el teatro de la República Democrática Alemana."*Beiträge zur Romanische Philologie* 13 (1974 [1976]), 319-22; also ACTAS: 485-89.

Treats of the German adaptation of Hartmann and Fries (see entry 1057.1.) and its staging in Weimar, 1970, with some useful remarks on the departures and shades of meanings suggested in the adaptation.

60. BALDELLI, Ignazio. "Girolamo Claricio editore de LC." *Giornale Storico della Letteratura Italiana* (Torino) 127 (1950), 111-16.

Some comments on Claricio's corrections to the text of *L'amorosa visione* for the first edition of 1521.

61. BALDWIN, Spurgeon W. "'En tan pocas palabras' (LC, aucto IV)." *RomN* 9 (1967-68), 120-25.

These words of Melibea's offer difficulty of interpretation. Some fuller meaning for them is conferred by the proper meaning of 'expresar' in the question: "¿Si esso querías, porqué luego no me lo expresaste?"

62. BARBERA, Raymond E. "Sempronio." *Hispania* 45 (1962), 441-42.

After Celestina, Sempronio is LC's most vital character.

63. _____. "Calisto: The Paradoxical Hero." *Hispania* 47 (1964), 256-57.

Calisto is conventional, an expression of Rojas' pessimism in the form of parody and paradox.

64. _____. "A Harlot, a Heroine." *Hispania* 48 (1965), 790-99.

As Pedro Salinas defines heroism for the picaresque, Celestina becomes a heroine: she allows society to be seen and profiled not in its triumphs but in its failings.

65. _____. "Fernando de Rojas, Converso." *Hispania* 51 (1968), 140-44.

What it was to be a 'converso' and an 'hidalgo' in the sixteenth century. (See also Green, entry 407.)

66. _____. "Medieval Iconography in LC." RR 61 (1970), 5-13.

Symbolic meanings are proposed for a) Calisto's falcon, b) the wall of Melibea's garden and c) the ladder from which Calisto plummets to his death, among others.

67. BARON PALMA, Emilio. "Pármeno: La liberación del ser auténtico. El antihéroe." CHA, no. 317 (November 1976), 383-400.

Citing the studies of Lida de Malkiel (1962), Gilman (1956) and Maravall (1964), this article aspires to greater completeness in the study of Pármeno. It is not Pármeno who changes in LC. Rather, a series of masks are dropped and the real Pármeno is gradually exposed as a vile hypocrite, egotistical and cowardly.

68. BARRICELLI, Juan Pedro. "LC y la naturaleza del Mal." CA 40, no. 2 (March-April 1981), 69-77.

Celestina, as a personification of evil, is contrasted with Shakespeare's Iago, Manzoni's Innominatio (*I promessi sposi*) and Balzac's Vautrin (*Le père Goriot*), among others.

69. BARRICK, Mac Eugene. "A Critical Edition of Gaspar Gómez de Toledo's *Tercera Parte de la Tragicomedia de LC.*" Diss. Univ. of Pennsylvania, 1965. 743p. DA 26/12, 7308A. No. 66-05600. O. H. Green and A. G. Reichenberger. (See below, entry 71.)

70. _____. "Sancho's Trip to El Toboso: A Possible Source." MLN 81 (1966), 222-25.

The model for Don Quijote's questions to Sancho on his return from El Toboso is in LC, although the actual situation is closer to one in *La tercera Celestina* of Gaspar Gómez de Toledo.

71. _____. *Tercera parte de la tragicomedia de Celestina de Gaspar Gómez de Toledo.* Philadelphia: Univ. of Pennsylvania Press, 1973. 597p.

The extensive introd. and bibliography cover almost all topics of interest to scholars of LC and its continuations.

a. BH 76 (1974), 407-11, P. Heugas
b. *Hispania* 58 (1975), 396, R. W. Tyler
c. BHS 53 (1976), 141-42, K. Whinnom
d. *RenQ* 29 (1976), 120-22, E. Berndt-Kelley
e. NRFH 25 (1976), 407-12, D. Eisenberg
f. RR 69 (1978), 348-49, A. Alcalá

72. _____. "Celestina's Black Mass." *Cel* 1, ii (Fall 1977), 11-14.

The goat hair and blood Celestina employs would indicate a deep involvement in magical arts, as documents of the period reveal. These scenes would have had immediate impact on contemporary audiences.

73. _____. "El 446° refrán de *Celestina*." *Cel* 7, ii (Fall 1983), 13-15.

Celestina's comment in Act 9: "Hijos, estará corrupta la letra, por treze tres," is the reflection of a proverbial phrase recorded in many compilations of the sixteenth century and later. Such was the popularity of LC that many later literary works recall Celestina's specific use of the original. There may be several other partial refrain-like expressions imbedded in LC.

74. BARROSO, A., et al. *Introducción a la literatura española a través de los textos (aportación a una metodología del comentario de textos).* Madrid: ISTMO, 1979. (Col. Fundamentos, 65)

The user is asked to confront texts directly: LC is in chapter 9 (pp. 237-59). A brief introd. explains the nature of LC as a transitional work between the Middle Ages and the Renaissance, and then follow excerpts from Acts 9 and 12 (two from the latter). A full explication of the first excerpt follows—based on content, techniques and style, language and critical attitude. Only six works on LC find their way into the bibliography.

75. BASDEKIS, Demetrius. "Romantic Elements in LC." *Hispania* 44 (1961), 52-54.

The author touches on certain of the following elements in the presentation of some of LC's characters: love hand-in-hand with tragedy; emotion dominating reason; the presence of melancholy; sublimation of the supernatural and a strong concept of individuality.

76. BATAILLON, Marcel. "¿Melancolía renacentista o melancolía judía?" *Homenaje a Archer M. Huntington* (Wellesley, Massachusetts, 1952), 39-50; rpt. in *Varia lección de clásicos españoles* (Madrid: Gredos, 1964), 39-54.

Wonders whether certain 'conversos' and Rojas among them should be considered within a Biblical tradition of melancholy (from Jeremiah) or within a Renaissance aesthetic that allows for a degree of worldly bitterness.

77. _____. "Structure et style dans le roman espagnole et portugais du XVI siècle." *Annuaire du Collège de France* 57 (1957), 443-48.

Resumé of a course given by Bataillon in which he explicated the moral nature of LC as perceived by its contemporary audience and as approved by the authorities, by Cervantes, and by its Latin translator, Gaspar von Barth.

78. _____. "Gaspar von Barth: Interprète de LC." RLC 31 (1957), 321-40. Also appears as an appendix to Bataillon, entry 82.

Barth's Latin translation demonstrates the German liking for the moral message of LC, since it is a clearly didactic version.

a. LR 13 (1959), 91-93, P. Groult.

79. _____. "LC primitive." *Studia Philologica et Litteraria in Honorem L. Spitzer* (Bern: Francke Verlag, 1958), 39-55; included in Chapter 2 of Bataillon, entry 82.

Act 1 was composed—as Rojas avers—by another author, one for whom Rojas entertained the highest regard, as his continuation shows. The elements of witchcraft deserve special praise.

a. LR 15 (1961), 167, P. Groult
b. RF 73 (1961), 170-71, E. Müller-Bochat

80. _____. "Pour une histoire exigeante des formes: Le cas de LC." *Proceedings of the International Comparative Literature Association* (Chapel Hill, North Carolina) I, part 1 (1959), 35-44.

The romantic view of LC impedes the proper grasp of its ironies, emphasizing as it will the excess of passion. LC is a moral dramatic work, a fact underscored in its characterizations and its frequent inclusion of proverbs and other bits of wisdom lore.

a. LR 15 (1961), 265, M. Van Oorlé

81. _____. "LC." *Realisme et poésie au théâtre*, ed. by J. Jacquot (Paris: Ed. du Centre National de la Recherche Scientifique, 1960), pp. 11-22. A second ed., illustrated, appeared in 1978.

Having seen in Paris the Escobar staging of LC (see 979.3.),

Bataillon praises it for being based on the CCM. The earlier form of LC makes much more of morality and emphasizes its social realism.

82. _____. *LC selon Fernando de Rojas*. Paris: M. Didier, 1961. 270p. (Etudes de Littérature Etranger et Comparée, 42)

A remarkable and provocative study of the didactic intentions behind the writing of LC. Every effort is spent in placing LC in its period, for it ought to be understood within the context of the times.

a. *Figaro Littéraire* (August 12 1961), M. P.
b. *Cuadernos del Congreso de la Libertad de la Cultura*, no. 55 (1961), 85, C. Bayón
c. BBMP 38 (1962), 179-80, R. Marcus
d. RJ 13 (1962), 371-75, M. Kruse
e. *Insula* 17, no. 182 (January 1962), 1,5, G. de Torre
f. NRFH 16 (1962), 464-72, C. B. Johnson
g. *Symposium* 16 (1962), 233-36, A. D. Deyermond
h. RR 53 (1962), 215-18, C. F. Fraker
i. *RPh* 16 (1962-63), 323-31, E. S. Morby
j. BHS 40 (1963) 35-40, P. E. Russell
k. LR 17 (1963), 90-93, P. Groult
l. *Modern Philology* 61 (1963), 46-49, D. W. McPheeters
m. RLC 37 (1963), 305-11, D. Devoto
n. *Rivista di Letterature Moderne e Comparate* 16 (1963), 150-56, G. Chiarini
o. BH 66 (1964), 396-405, P. Heugas
p. *Filológiai Közlöny* 10 (1964), 441-45, K. Kulin
q. QIA 4, no. 25 (1960-65), 291-95, E. Caldera
r. RF 78 (1966), 170-73, H. Baader
s. ZRP 82 (1966), 9-21, A. Rüegg
t. BICC 23 (1968), 111-12, J. J. Montes Giraldo

83. _____. "Langues et littératures de la péninsule ibérique et de l'Amérique latine." *Annuaire du Collège de France* 64 (1964-65), 479-87.

Notes from a course Bataillon gave in which he meticulously compares points of difference between his view of LC and those of Lida de Malkiel (1962): sources, characterizations and artistic intentions.

84. _____. *Défense et illustration du sens littéral*. Presidential Address before the Modern Humanities Research Association. London: MHRA, 1967. 33p.

Our own failure to understand an author results in our ascribing to the author faults which may not be faults at all. Illustrated with several examples of ambiguous passages from LC which would have been viewed differently by the reading public of the 16th century than by modern critics, because the latter do not take into account Rojas' audience, circumstances or historical moment.

85. _____. "La librería del estudiante Morlanes." *Homenaje a D. Agustín Millares Carlo*, I (Gran Canaria: Caja Insular de Ahorros, 1975), 329-47.

The basically law-oriented library Morlanes inherited (he was a younger contemporary of Fernando de Rojas) contained an unidentified copy of LC.

86. BATTISTESSA, Angel J. "Acotación a un comentario crítico." BAAL 23 (1958), 35-52.

Comments on Croce (entry 209) and LC.

87. BAYO, Marcial José. "Nota sobre LC." *Clavileño* 1 (September-October 1950), 48-53.

On some commonplace conceits LC shares with J. Manrique's *Coplas*.

88. BEARDSLEY JR., Theodore S. "Spanish Literature," in *The Present State of Scholarship in Sixteenth-Century Literature*, ed. W. M. Jones (Columbia/London: Univ. of Missouri Press, 1978), 71-110.

LC studies have been numerous in recent years, although there still remain many points to be clarified, some of which are specified in this study.

89. _____. "The Lowlands Editions of *Celestina* (1539-1601)." *Cel* 5, no. 1 (May 1981), 7-11.

Important notes for the study of the textual transmission of the TCM.

90. _____. "*Celestina*, Act 1, scene 1: 'Ubi sunt'?" *HR* 52 (1984), 335-341.

Agrees with Riquer (entry 756) that the first scene takes place in a church, that Rojas was aware of it but shifted it for purposes of his own, and argues for a possible early staging of LC with a central set containing a church (for the street scenes) and with the protagonists' houses to its right and left.

91. BECKER-CANTARINO, Bärbel. "LC en Alemania: El *Pornoboscodidascalus* (1624) de Kaspar Barth." ACTAS: 377-82.

Notes on Barth's introd. to the Latin version of LC he prepared. The interpretation more closely corresponds to German tastes in moral fiction than to the social reality of Rojas' Spain.

92. BELL, A. Robert. "Folklore and Mythology in LC," in *Medieval Epic to the 'Epic Theatre' of Brecht*, ed. R. P. Armato and J. M. Spalek (Los Angeles: Univ. of Southern California Press, 1968), 47-56.

The proverbs, *sententiae*, and maxims of LC, all folkloric elements, play an artistic role in LC: they are used to build arguments, to foreshadow events and to counsel against falsehood in an immoral world.

93. BELTRAN, Luis. "The Old Woman and Authority: Evolution and Meaning of a Literary Character." Diss. Univ. of Michigan, 1966. 183p. DA 27, 2129-2130A. No. 66-14485. T. Garbaty.

This theme in LC is developed in the final chapter.

94. _____. "La envidia de Pármeno." *LaC* 7, no. 1 (Fall 1978), 4.

Abstract of a paper read at the MLA Meetings, New York, December 1978, which appeared in revised form (see entry immediately below) a year later.

95. _____. "La envidia de Pármeno y la corrupción de Melibea." *Insula*, no. 398 (January 1980), 3, 10.

A reading of the TCM which leads to the conclusion that faith, hope and charity are altogether lacking. The Seven Deadly Sins have the upper hand in Rojas' world, a world devoid of Christian values.

96. BENITEZ, Frank. "Perspectivismo semántico en LC." Diss. Univ. of California, Riverside, 1970. 240p. DAI 31/08, 4111A. No. 71-3870. C. Ayllón.

On ways in which Rojas, through multiple perspective, achieves a semantic distancing designed to undermine the medieval commonplaces of LC and, at the same time, to recharge them with new meanings. Words and concepts are first isolated and then re-contextualized semantically.

97. _____. "Dimensión semántica del acaescer en la palabra celestinesca." ACTAS: 67-73.

Reviews the Petrarchan doctrine centered on idea as reality, emphasizing its platonic source. Petrarchan thought in LC is changed into a defense of the search for the material and the visible good. Rojas is able to convey this shift through semantic distancing, a technique that involves contrasting a traditional meaning of a word with an evolved meaning.

98. BERGAMIN, José. "Rojas, mensajero del infierno: Releyendo LC." *Revista de la Facultad de Humanidades y Ciencias* (Montevideo) 6, no. 9 (1952), 61-74; rpt. in his *Fronteras infernales de la poesía* (Madrid: Taurus, 1959; 2nd ed., 1980), 53-76.

There is in LC an excess of demoniacal and satanic spirituality, the spell created by fate and made physically manifest by such things as love philters. In LC there is also a Senecan presence in the rhetoric, the philosophy and the final tragedies.

99. BERMEJO CABRERO, José Luis. "Aspectos jurídicos de LC." ACTAS: 401-08. Rpt. in his *Derecho y pensamiento político en la literatura española* (Madrid: Autor, 1980), 97-109.

Parts of LC reveal knowledge of law codes, crimes and punishments, legal formulae, etc. Celestina possesses most of this knowledge and her death scene is treated here in some detail, as is the report of the executions of Sempronio and Pármeno.

100. BERNDT-KELLEY, Erna Ruth. "Tratamiento de algunos temas humanísticos en LC." Diss. Univ. of Wisconsin, 1959. 256p. DA 20/06, 2275. No. 59-05748. J. H. Herriott. (See following entry.)

101. _____. *Amor, muerte y fortuna en LC*. Madrid: Gredos, 1963. 206p. (Biblioteca Románica Hispánica. Estudios y Ensayos, 68)

The three themes are placed on a historical-literary continuum with the goal of demonstrating how it was that Rojas transformed traditional material into new and original material.

a. *Cultura Neolatina* 23 (1963), 295-96, E. Scoles
b. *Insula* 18, no. 203 (October 1963), 8, M. Moya Trelles
c. BCB 7 (1964), 1840-41, E. Camacho Guisado
d. BHS 42 (1965), 53-54, A. D. Deyermond
e. *Hispania* 48 (1965), 382, C. Ayllón
f. HR 33 (1965), 401-06, M. E. Barrick
g. *Symposium* 19 (1965), 182-84, M. Scorsone

102. _____. "Popularidad del romance 'Mira Nero de Tarpeya'." *Estudios Dedicados a James Homer Herriott* (Madison: Univ. of Wisconsin Press, 1966), 117-26.

Wonders whether the great popularity of this ballad is not in fact due to its appearance in Act 1 of LC.

a. *RPh* 24 (1970-71), 148-49, A. D. Deyermond

103. _____. "Algunas observaciones sobre la edición de Zaragoza de 1507 de la TCM." ACTAS: 7-28.

A clear demonstration of the editorial importance of Zaragoza 1507 in the text tradition of the TCM. A series of tabulated variants is provided to support these claims.

104. _____. "Peripecias de un título: En torno al nombre de la obra de Fernando de Rojas." *Cel* 9, ii (Fall 1985).

A complete review of the names Rojas' work has had, in and out of Spain, in Spanish and in translation, from 1499 to 1822. Profusely illustrated with title pages and, occasionally, colophons.

105. BERRETTINI, Célia. "Uma interpretação social de LC." *Minas Gerais, Suplemento Literário* (July 17 1976), 4-5.

Follows Garrido Pallardó (1957), Orozco (1957) and Serrano Poncela (1958) in declaring Melibea a 'conversa'. This fact explains all the text's problems: Calisto not wanting to marry Melibea, Pleberio's being unable to avenge his daughter, and much more.

106. _____. "O conflito amor/sociedade em LC." *O Estado de São Paulo, Suplemento Literário*, no. 90 (July 16 1978), 3-4.

Similar arguments to the entry immediately above: the events of LC acquire greater dimension and meaning when Melibea is seen as a 'conversa'.

107. BERSHAS, Henry N. "'Testigo es el cuchillo de tu abuelo' (*Celestina*, I)." *Cel* 2, i (May 1978), 7-11.

Shows that there is a folkloric tradition behind the titular phrase and amply documents it with generous citation of examples. The idea is that, when young, a woman accepts swords as payment for favors and, when old and unattractive, pays for lovers with them.

108. BISTRISKY, N. "Be'ikuot *Ha-Selestina*" (Following the Trail of LC). *Osar Yehudi Sefarad* 6 (1963), 85-87. [In Hebrew]

Suggests that E. Jardiel Poncela, of Jewish ancestry, may have been influenced by Fernando de Rojas.

109. BLANCO WHITE, José María. "LC," in *Antología*, ed. V. Llorens (Madrid: Ed. Labor, 1971), 181-211. (Textos hispánicos modernos, 12)

Republication of the famous essay (1824) considered to be the starting point of modern interest in LC and which proposes Rojas as sole author.

110. BLOUIN, Egla M. "Proceso de individuación y arquetipo de la Gran Madre en LC," in *The Analysis of Hispanic Texts: Current Trends in Methodology*, ed. Mary Ann Beck et al (New York: Bilingual Press/Ed. Bilingüe, 1976), 16-48.

Detailed study of the Great Mother archetype and its hispanicizing into the go-between in a world of changing values. Its has both positive and negative implications in its pure form, but in its manifestation in Celestina, the negative predominates. The 'Madre terrible' created by Rojas opposes the archetype of the 'Padre Celestial' of the Middle Ages.

a. *Hispania* 60 (1977), 613, M. V. Boyer

111. BLÜHER, Karl A. *Seneca in Spanien*. Munich: Francke Verlag, 1969.

This vol. contains an exposition (pp. 122-25) of how LC reflects some genuine *sententiae* of Seneca (especially in Act 3) and even others not Senecan but attributed to him. Examples of both are given.

112. BOASE, Roger. "Imagery of Love, Death and Fortune in the Poetry of Pedro Manuel Ximénez de Urrea." BHS 57 (1980), 17-32.

The text frequently cites parallels with LC. Urrea was an early imitator of LC in an *Egloga* (1513) based on Act 1.

113. BOHIGAS, Pedro. "De la *Comedia* a la *Tragicomedia de Calisto y Melibea*." *Estudios dedicados a Ramón Menéndez Pidal* 7, part 1 (Madrid, 1957), 153-75.

Discusses the evolution of the first act of the CCM into the TCM and discovers a literary unity. The more satifying form is the CCM.

114. BONET, Carmelo M. "El estilo de LC y su relación con el plateresco." *Criterio* 26 (1953), 942-44; rpt. in expanded form in his *Pespuntes críticos* (Buenos Aires: Academia Argentina de Letras, 1969), 179-88.

A brief note on language in LC, on the manner of presenting dialogue.

115. BORING, Phyllis Z. "More on Parody in Valle-Inclán." *RomN* 15 (1973-74), 246-47.

There are two passages from *Divinas palabras* which may be direct parodies of LC.

116. BOUGHNER, Daniel C. *The Braggart in Renaissance Comedy*. Minneapolis: Univ. of Minnesota Press, 1954. 328p.

Remarks on Centurio's role in LC (pp. 178-84), which is basically for humorous purposes, and also on the possible influence of this figure on Italian theatre through the Italian translation of LC (1506).

   a. *RenN* 7 (1954), 101-02, J. G. Fucilla
   b. CL 7 (1955), 88-89, W. P. Friedrich
   c. MLN 70 (1955), 205-06, L. Bradner
   d. *Shakespeare Quarterly* 6 (1955), 342-43, V. B. Heltzel
   e. HR 24 (1956), 151-53, J. E. Gillet

117. BOULLOSA, Virginia H. "La concepción del cuerpo en LC," in *La idea del cuerpo en las letras españolas (siglo XIII a XVII)*, ed. Dinko Cvitanovic (Bahia Blanca, Argentina: Univ. Nacional del Sur, 1973), 80-117.

The body in LC is shown to be vulnerable to the ravages of time, and love is discussed in this framework.

a.NRFH 25 (1976), 129-30, B. Damiani

118. BRANCAFORTE, Benito. "LC y *La Mandragola*: La razón como medio de corrupción." BHS 47 (1970), 201-09.

Machiavelli may have read Hordognez' 1506 Italian translation of LC and this possibility provides a base for speculations about influences, especially in the area of virtue seen as corrupted by intelligence.

119. _____. "La estructura moral de LC y *El infierno* de Dante." PSA 66 (1972) 5-21.

Aspects of LC which suggest a relationship to Dante's *Inferno* include: its conception of evil; passion in conflict with reason; the chaos of the world; and its restless, violent and rebellious characters. The moral structure is similar, too, with incontinence, fraud and violence being links worthy of further study.

120. BRAULT, Gerard J. "English Translations of LC in the Sixteenth Century." HR 28 (1960), 301-12.

From Rastell, c. 1530 to Mabbe, 1631. Until Mabbe, LC was better known in England in the original or in French translation. There is commentary on the curious *The Delightful History of Celestina the Faire* (London, 1596), based on *Palmerín de Oliva* and not LC.

121. _____. "Interpretations of LC, Old and New." *Bulletin of the Pennsylvania State Modern Language Association* 46 (1967-68), 3-8.

Traces the history of LC translations and goes into some of the alterations suffered by a few of them.

122. _____. "Textual Filiation of the Early Editions of LC and the First French Translation." HR 36 (1968), 95-109.

Herriott's (1964) and Whinnom's (1966) studies are complementary. The 1527 French translation claims to be based on an Italian version but is based on a Spanish text linked to Herriott's stemma IV. Still the best texts for an *editio princeps* are Rome 1506, Zaragoza 1507 and Valencia 1514.

123. BRAVO-VILLASANTE, Carmen. "Otra interpretación de LC." *Insula* 14, no. 149 (1959), Suplemento, 1-2.

Melibea is not a 'conversa' as claimed by Orozco (1957). His logic is assailed and a different picture emerges.

124. BRELUM, Mauricio. "Egoísmo y no amor en LC." *Lectura* 176, no. 3 (April 1 1968), 93-96.

Love should mean desiring good for others. Concupiscent love is self-serving and pure egoism, and this is all we see in the TCM.

125. BRIESEMEISTER, Dietrich. "Zu Christoph Wirsungs deutschen *Celestina*-Übersetzungen (1520 und 1534)," in *Sprache, Literatur, Kultur, Romanistische Beiträge* (Frankfurt a. M., 1974), 50-57.

W.'s first version emphasizes LC's dramatic qualities while the second shows that the translator has shifted his views towards the didactic message LC purportedly transmits. This is shown in a number of ways: in the new subtitle, in textual changes, in new lexical selections to replace the old, etc. The second version is more faithful to the Italian original on which W. based his translations. The two translations bear witness to the strong humanist trend in early sixteenth-century Germany.

126. _____. "La difusión europea de la literatura española en el siglo XVII a través de traducciones neolatinas." *Iberoromania*, no. 7 (1978), 3-17.

Discusses respect for LC in remarks by the Catholic Doergank (1614; his introd. to the *Institutiones in Linguam Hispanicam*) and by the Protestant von Barth (1624; the prologue to his Latin translation of LC).

127. BURKE, James F. "Calisto's Imagination and his Grandmother's Ape." *LaC* 5, ii (1977), 84-90.

The ape is a symbolic reference to unclean thoughts by a woman with child, which inclination appears in the offspring. Sempronio's allusion implies that Calisto's desire to have an illicit affair shows a predisposition to a 'loco amor' which is inherited.

128. _____. "Metamorphosis and the Imagery of Alchemy in LC." *Revista Canadiense de Estudios Hispánicos* 1 (1977), 129-52.

Calisto and Melibea are two materials that need a catalytic agent to make them one, the agent being Celestina. In a reversal of traditional alchemical lore, the result, instead of positive, is fully tragic. Rojas avails himself of the imagery since it serves to explain some changes in his characters, as when 'materia' seeks 'forma'.

C

129. CAMON AZNAR, J. "LC, obra gótica." *ABC* (May 21 1957), 3.

Remarks on LC after seeing the Escobar stage version (see entry 979.2.), presented with a naturalism proper to the Middle Ages as seen in the diabolical attributes given to Celestina and in the tension of contraries projected in the adaptation and staging.

130. CAMPOS, Jorge. "LC, tragedia social." *El Nacional* (Caracas) (April 17 1958), Suplemento Literario, n. p.

A review of recent assessments of the Jewish element in LC, with emphasis on Garrido Pallardó (entry 349) and Orozco (entry 683).

131. CANET VALLES, José Luis. "La *Comedia Thebayda* y *La Seraphina*, in *Teatros y prácticas escénicas. I: El Quinientos Valenciano,* coord. M. V. Diego Moncholí (Valencia: Institució Alfons el Magnànim, 1984), 283-300.

Thebayda (a courtly novel), *Seraphina* (meant for the stage), and *Celestina* all have roots in Terence. There are many differences separating the first two and LC in the development and use of scenic time and space, asides, and character function. In fact, these two works seem closer to the first LC imitation, Pedro Manuel de Urrea's *Penitencia de amor*, than to *Celestina*.

132. CANO, Vicente. "La función dramática del engaño en LC." *Káñina* 8, nos. 1-2 (1984), 77-82.

Reviews different kinds and levels of deceit in LC and concludes that they tend to accelerate the dramatic action, intensifying the sense of haste with which almost everything is done in the work.

133. CANTALAPIEDRA EROSTARBE, Francisco. "Pour une analyse sémiotique de la *Célestine*." Thèse de Troisième Cycle, La Sorbonne, 1979.

The basis of the work published later and recorded below, in entries 134-142.

134. _____. "Por un análisis semiótico de la *Celestina*: los anagramas" (resumen de tesis doctoral). Granada: Univ. of Granada, 1981. 46p. (Tesis de la Univ. de Granada, no. 334)

Focus on analyses of modes of discourse, lexical items, verse types, the preliminary and posliminal materials and the woodcuts used in the illustration of the Seville texts. All converge in showing that one author is responsible for acts 1-12 of the CCM and another (Rojas) for acts 13-16, as well as for the additions of the expanded TCM.

135. _____. *Semiótica del objeto: la 'Celestina'.* Number 5 of *Investigació teatrològica*. Barcelona, 1983. 84p. Illus.

Possibilities for textual interpretation of LC based on a semiotic analysis of the multiple functions of objects. Even though the reader unaccustomed to the use of formulas and equations may be at first disheartened (these are explained on pp. 3-5), the analyses are revealing in that they tend to confirm earlier conclusions of critics approaching the text from other angles (e. g., the more complex treatment of the character of Pármeno, the multifaceted symbolic sequence yarn-girdle-chain). The author

wants to show that there is a theoretical-scientific base for the study of literature.

136. _____. *Semiótica del espacio: la 'Celestina'.* Number 6 of *Investigació teatrològica*. Barcelona, 1983. 108p. Illus.

LC on pp. 1-76 (the remainder is on Mira de Amescua). A scientific approach to spatial arrangements in LC (complete with formulas and symbols whose key is on pp. 7-9), neatly subdivided (high vs low; interior vs exterior, and so on). Differences in usage show that there is a pattern obtaining for the first twelve acts (one author) and another for the remaining nine of the TCM (Rojas).

137. _____. "Los refranes en *Celestina* y el problema de autoría." *Cel* 8, i (May 1984), 49-53.

An act-by-act scheme of refrain use in LC (the CCM compared with the TCM) shows a change of pattern after act 12. This tends to confirm the author's view that Rojas wrote only the final nine acts of the TCM and that a single hand is responsible for the first twelve.

138. _____. *Lectura semiótica formal de LC.* Kassel: Ed. Reichenberger, 1985. Forward by J. T. Snow.

The first part furnishes a detailed explication of these three aspects of LC: characters, objects, and spatial relationships, and especially explores their role in the several narrative levels of the work. The second part of the study is more statistical and develops the theory that encoded in the formal aspects of the text (and its printing and iconographical features) are messages that show that the work Rojas continued had twelve acts, not just a bit more than one, as previously established. Many of these themes have been treated by the author (see preceding entries) but are here better-integrated.

139. _____. "Los rasgos pertinentes del espacio: la *Celestina*." *Actas del Congreso Internacional sobre Semiótica e Hispanismo (1983),* (Madrid: CSIC, 198?). (*)

140. _____. "Las calificaciones de los actores." *Actas de las VI Jornadas de Teatro Clásico Español, Almagro 1983.* (*)

141. _____. "Las calificaciones extereoceptivas de los actores." *Actas del I Simposio de la Asociación Española de Semiótica (Toledo 1984).* (*)

142. _____. "Celestina, retrato de un mito." *Actas de las VII Jornadas del Teatro Clásico Español (Almagro 1984).* (*)

143. CANTARINO, Vicente. "Didactismo y moralidad de LC." *ACTAS*: 103-109.

A new look at Rojas' intentions in writing LC. Offers clarification of the Medieval and Renaissance approaches to didacticism, i.e. an absolutist and a relativist one, respectively. The TCM is a moral work but is of the Renaissance and not particularly of the Middle Ages.

144. CARAVAGGI, Giovanni. "Apostilla al 'Testamento de Celestina'." RL, no. 86 (1981), 141-51.

A comparison of three versions of this 16th-century satirical poem: those of Rome (edited here for the first time), Munich and Naples.

145. CARDIEL SANZ, Estrella. "La cuestión judía en LC," in Actas de las Jornadas de Estudios Sefardíes, ed. A. Viudas (Cáceres: Servicio de Publ. de la Univ. de Extremadura, 1981), pp. 151-59.

An exposition of the state of the question which evaluates a range of critical opinion: Lida de Malkiel, Rodríguez-Puertolas, Serrano Poncela, Gilman, Castro, Forcadas, Maeztu and others.

146. CAREAGA, Luis. "Investigaciones referentes a Fernando de Rojas en Talavera de la Reina." RHM 4 (1938), 193-208.

History of the discovery of the remains of Rojas.

147. CARO BAROJA, Julio. "La magia en Castilla durante los siglos XVI y XVII," in his Algunos mitos españoles (Madrid: Ed. Nacional, 1941; 2nd ed., 1944), 185-303.

Presents the broad European-Spanish context in which magic practices thrived, especially in the hands of women. Appropriate sections for LC are V-VI (pp. 235-249).

148. _____. "La Celestina como arquetipo," in his Las brujas y su mundo (Madrid: Revista de Occidente, 1961), 151-53; English translation is The World of The Witches (Chicago/London: Univ. of Chicago Press, 1965), 101-02.

Presents Celestina as an admixture of literary antecedents against a Renaissance urban backdrop of vivid realism.

149. CARRASCO, Félix. "La ausencia de honra en Pleberio y el 'Contrato de veredicción'." Segismundo 12, nos. 23-24 (1976), 9-26.

In Pleberio's Act 21 lament there is no trace of traditional Spanish 'honra'. Thus, Pleberio's participation seems to lack verisimilitude. The author reconstructs very carefully the entire process of Rojas' presentation of Pleberio to show that, in fact, Pleberio is a very human part of the LC world which, while not avowedly Christian, does not have to be seen as Jewish or 'converso' either.

150. _____. "Diálogo, antidiálogo y conciencia de clase en LC." Idéologie et pratiques discursives. Imprévue (Montpellier: C. E. R. S., 1979), 103-18.

An attempt to come to terms with the dialogic form in LC through a close analysis of Areúsa's long speech in Act 9.

151. CARROLL, William, and Albert BAGBY JR. "A Note on Shakespeare and The Celestina." REH 5 (1971), 79-93.

Essentially the same arguments the authors present in the article printed in RF (see entry 58) this same year.

152. CASA, Frank P. "Pleberio's Lament for Melibea." ZRP 84 (1968), 20-29.

Rojas was not, in Pleberio's lament, rounding out a moral lesson for the reader; rather, he was detailing a tragic vision of the human condition.

153. CASALDUERO, Joaquín. "Parodia de una cuestión de amor y queja de las fregonas." RFE 19 (1932), 181-87.

The second note (185-87) compares the complaints of Areúsa in Act 9 with those of Cristina in Cervantes' La entretenida.

154. _____. "La señora de Cremes y el dolor de muelas de Calisto." ACTAS: 75-79.

Observes the good fortune of Celestina in being admitted to Pleberio's house and the amorous meanings of a toothache in the context of the TCM.

155. CASONA, Alejandro. "De la gran Celestina al gran Galeoto." El Universal (Caracas) (January 17 1956), primera sección, n. p.

The Celestina type in the West is an incarnation of witch, go-between, and evil spirit. Examples are cited from Dante to Echegaray but are not explored.

156. CASSUTO, M. D. "From the Poetry of Joseph b. Samuel Zarfati: The First Hebrew Comedy," in Jewish Studies in Memory of George A. Kohut, ed. S. W. Baron and A. Marx (New York: The Kohut Memorial Foundation, 1935), Hebrew Section, 121-28. [In Hebrew]

A transcription of the 62-line poem inspired by a reading of LC, probably in Italian translation. It dates from about the mid-16th century.

157. CASTANIEN, Donald G. "La Segunda Celestina: XVIIIth and XIXth Centuries." Hispania 43 (1960), 559-64.

Solís adapted, according to neoclassic precepts, the play by Salazar y Torres (El encanto es la hermosura y el hechizo sin hechizo), titling it La Segunda Celestina. A few comments on its celestinesqe ascendancy.

158. CASTELLANOS, José. Diez obras maestras. Barcelona: Ed. Mateu, 1962.

A detailed act-by-act resumé of the action of LC (pp. 155-82).

159. CASTELLANOS, Luis Arturo. "El 'ergo' andaba por las cocinas." ACTAS: 397-400.

Claims to detect in the vague atmospheric setting the definite track of Salamanca, especially in the speech of both Pármeno and Celestina.

160. CASTILLO DE LUCAS, A. "Refranes de interés médico en LC." Actas do Congresso Internacional de Etnografia 3 (1965), 147-66.

A gloss of medically-oriented refrains used by Celestina, and of sayings that deserve status as refrains. Foremost in LC are those which are closely associated with human psychology.

161. CASTRO, Américo. "El problema histórico de LC," in his *Santa Teresa y otros ensayos* (Santander: Historia Nueva, 1929), 193-215. Published the same year in *La Nación* of Buenos Aires, issue for February 14-17.

Profiles the historic moment in Spain which produced, straddling two different approaches to life, a new feeling of personal autonomy. This freedom spawns the contentiousness and contradictions that make of LC such a vital and dynamic literary work.

162. _____. *LC como contienda literaria (castos y casticismos)*. Madrid: Revista de Occidente, 1965. 180p.

The first part of the volume is a re-statement of Castro's theory of the conflict between the 'castas españolas' in the 15th and 16th centuries. His view of the TCM follows: it is a work forged from the destructive animus of Rojas and manages at one and the same time to both react against previous literary forms and to document the 'vivencias' of life and death for the 'converso' of those times. An Appendix records data comparing LC and *Amadís*.

    a. CHA 62, no. 186 (June 1965), 601-03, E. Miró
    b. *Est Lit*, no. 314 (1965), 14, E. Aguado
    c. PSA 38 (1965), 319-26, A. Agustini de del Río
    d. BA 40 (1966), 316, J. Angeles
    e. BCB 9 (1966), 1385-91, E. Cortés Ahumada
    f. *Estudios Generales* (San Juan), no. 16 (1966), 126-36, R. A. González Torres
    g. *Revista de Literaturas Modernas* 6 (1966), 169-70, E. Zuleta
    h. *RenQ* 21 (1968), 118-34, A. A. Parker

163. CASTRO GUISASOLA, Florentino. *Observaciones sobre las fuentes literarias de LC* (rpt. of the Madrid 1924 edition). Madrid: CSIC, 1973. 194p.

Sources for LC are classical, ecclesiastic, Italian, Spanish. Some are labeled as 'indiscutibles' and others as 'de autenticidad dudosa'.

    a. RO 8 (1925), 139-40, M. Fernández Almagro
    b. *Humanitas* (La Plata) 10 (1925), 474-76, A. Marasso
    c. *La rassegna* 33 (1925), 151, U. G.
    d. *Revista de la Universidad de Buenos Aires*, Second Series, 2 (1925), 242-44, A. J. Battistessa
    e. BH 28 (1926), 288-89, G. Cirot
    f. *Literaturblatt für Germanische und Romanische Philologie* (Leipzig) 68 (1927), col. 384-86, L. Pfandl

164. CASTRO Y CALVO, J. M. "LC, encrucijada renacentista," in *Valores universales de la literatura española* (Barcelona: Ed. SAYMA, 1961), 25-43.

Some commentary on: Rojas' prologue and Act 1; the invocation to Plutón of Act 3; the death of Celestina in Act 12; and, finally, the scene in Melibea's garden of Act 19.

165. CAUZ, Francisco A. "Aspectos de la novelística de Salas Barbadillo." Diss. Rutgers Univ., 1972. 199p. DAI 33/4, 1717A. No. 72-27533. E. Nagy.

A considerable debt of Salas Barbadillo to Rojas is profiled in these pages. Especially celestinesque are *La hija de Celestina, Escuela de Celestina* and "La madre".

166. _____. "Salas Barbadillo y LC." BCB 14, no. 3 (1973), 104-08.

The protagonist of *La hija de Celestina* is inspired by LC.

167. *CELESTINA, LA. Sumario de la obra y estudio sobre el autor y su época*. Barcelona: Ed. Vosgos, 1977. 82p. Paper (Compendios Vosgos, 4).

The introd. presents basic data about early editions to 1520. Topics treated are the life of Rojas and the authorship problem in LC. A synopsis of the work follows with separate commentary for each act. At the end, there is a useful summary of each character. Doubtless designed for students, as a memory aid.

168. CERRO GONZALEZ, Rafael. "LC y el arte médico." *Medicamenta* 39, no. 389 (1963), 166.

Focuses on Celestina's medical wisdom in the treatment of her patient, Melibea.

169. CHAMORRO FERNANDEZ, María Inés, ed. *"Segunda comedia de Celestina" de Feliciano de Silva*. Madrid: Ed. Ciencia Nueva, 1968. 527p.

The introd. explores some points of contact between LC and this continuation.

    a. CHA, no. 229 (1969), 237-42, M. Mayoral

170. CHEVALIER, Maxime. "LC según sus lectores," in his *Lectura y lectores en la España del siglo XVI y XVII* (Madrid: Turner, 1976), 138-66.

The inherent ambiguities of the language of the TCM creates two main groups of readers and critics: one which praises and one which condemns the work.

    a. CHA 108, nos. 320-321 (1977), 515-18, W. Casanova
    b. BH 79 (1977), 578-84, M. Gendreau-Massaloux
    c. *Insula*, no. 376 (March 1978), 9, J. Ares Montes

171. CHIARENO, Oswaldo. *Note e recensioni su scrittori spagnoli*. Geneva: M. Bozzi, 1966.

Observations on the modernity of Melibea (pp. 15-19).

    a. BH 70 (1968), 232, R. Ricard

172. CHIARINI, Giorgio. "LC di Fernando de Rojas." *Arena: Rassegna di Studi Teatrali* (Rome) 2 (1955), 240-54.

Too few stage adaptations have kept LC relatively unknown in Italy. There are general bits of information on its date, authorship, sources, genre (he believes it is essentially dramatic), etc. Note is taken of its pagan spirit, pessimism and so forth, even as a denial is made of any satanic feeling in the work.

173. CHICHARRO, Dámaso. *Orígenes del teatro. La Celestina. El teatro prelopista.* Madrid: Cincel, 1979. 95p. Paper (Cuadernos de estudio, 4).

A study guide (relevant pages are 45-63). LC is placed between Lucas Fernández and the pre-Lopean dramatists. Briefly outlines problems of authorship, genre and editions. The interpretative remarks lean heavily on the 'converso' criticism (Serrano Poncela, Orozco Díaz and Gilman) and the social critics (Maravall, Rodríguez-Puértolas, van Beysterveldt). An analysis of Act 1, scene 1 is offered to substantiate the importance of the race question.

174. CH'I-FEN, Liu. "Lung Hung-Niang yu Hsi-niang: Hsisiang yu LC" (La crítica de Hung Niang y Celestina). *Chung Wai Literary Monthly* (Taipei) 6, no. 5 (1977), 56-72. [In Chinese]

Celestina compared with Hung Niang, the go-between of a famed Chinese masterwork. The Chinese counterpart is honest and generous and this results in a different link between herself and her clients, Ying-Yang (Melibea figure) and Chang Cheng (Calisto figure).

175. CHIODI, Olga D. "Pasado y futuro en los personajes de LC: causa y efecto." Diss. Univ. of California-Los Angeles, 1981. 210p. DAI 42/01 (1981-82), 206A. No. 8113831. Enrique Rodríguez-Cepeda. [Abstract also in *Cel* 5, ii (Fall 1981), 60-61.]

The past of each character is studied for its formative influence on present behavior (the textual action and dialogue) and for its role in the determination of cause and effect responses to life throughout LC.

176. CIPLIJAUSKAITE, Birute. "Juegos de duplicación e inversión en LC," in *Homenaje a José Manuel Blecua* (Madrid: Gredos, 1983), 165-173.

There are many character pairs and parallel scenes in LC and, on occasion, truly surprising inversions. Special attention is given over to Areúsa/Melibea (seduction scenes), Pármeno/Calisto, and Pármeno/Lucrecia (others are mentioned also). Rojas uses such devices to enhance and project his ironic vision of the world.

177. CLARKE, Dorothy C. *Allegory, Decalogue and Deadly Sins in LC.* Berkeley, California: Univ. of California Press, 1968. ix + 136p. (UCPMP, 91)

Explores the literary presentation of the Deadly Sins in LC in the light of previous tradition, in order to elucidate the role they play in the moral and aesthetic vision of Fernando de Rojas.

a. *RenQ* 22 (1969), 170-71, J. H. Herriott
b. *Hispania* 53 (1970), 146-47, J. F. Burke
c. *RPh* 25 (1971-72), 479-80, D. S. Severin
d. HR 40 (1972), 312-15, D. W. McPheeters
e. NRFH 21 (1972), 418-21, R. Kersten
f. BH 76 (1974), 202-04, P. Heugas

178. CLEMENS, J. T. W. "A Curious LC Edition." RLC 34 (1960), 245-50.

The ed. discussed is Venice 1553, prepared by G. Giolito di Ferrari.

179. CLOSE, Anthony. "Characterization and Dialogue in Cervantes' 'Comedias en prosa'." MLR 76 (1981), 338-56.

In terms of dialogic art and utilization of popular language, LC is seen as an important precedent for the conversational episodes that are a large part of Cervantes' art. Three or four annotated examples are provided.

180. CONDE JR., Guerra. "Gil Vicente y LC." *Est Lit*, no. 343 (1966), 8-9.

LC as an influence on Gil Vicente's *Barca do inferno*, written just eighteen years after LC.

181. CORFIS, Ivy A. "The 'Primer entremés de Selestina': An Edition, with an Introduction, Notes and a Reading Text of an Anonymous Celestinesque Work of the Sixteenth Century." *Cel* 6, i (May 1982), 15-29.

Edited here is Biblioteca Nacional MS 14612(9), a farse with five characters. In it, the only Rojas-inspired character, Selestina—a less dominant and fearsome figure than her namesake—, is outwitted by a student.

182. _____. "Juan de la Cueva's Sonnet on *Celestina.*" *Cel* 7, ii (Fall, 1983), 21-22.

The sonnet (ca 1603), "La que encendió los pechos mas elados," reflects the Celestina of the TCM rather than any of the later ones.

183. _____. "Fernando de Rojas and Albrecht von Eyb's *Margarita Poetica. Neophilologus* 68 (1984), 206-213.

It seems probable that the *Margarita* was a source for LC; it was certainly part of Rojas' library. It is further cited by the jurist and commentator of the *Celestina comentada*, a Rojas contemporary. The study contains parallel passages that show some probable points of contact between the two texts.

184. CORNEJO, Rafael E. "Bibliografía de LC." ACTAS: 553-82.

Useful only to a point. C. is not aware that Zaragoza 1507 is available or that Norton (1966) has revised the '1502' dates given for several editions in Penney (1954), which he uses. The rest is very partial and copies errors from earlier listings.

185. CORONADO, Juan. "Celestina: imagen de una batalla en campo de plumas." *Plural*, no. 118 (1981), 28-31.

A poetic description and evocation of Eros triumphant in LC.

186. CORRALES EGEA, J. "A propósito de la presentación de LC." *Insula*, no. 140 (1958), 11.

Critique of the French adaptation and staging of Achard (1942, see entry 1036.2) as well as a commentary on the significant structural values of Rojas' work. Rejects the 'converso' approach to understanding LC. Affirms that Calisto and Melibea represent the real centerpiece of the TCM.

187. CORREA, Gustavo. "Naturaleza, religión y honra en LC." PMLA 77 (1962), 8-17.

Traditional religious and social values are diabolically perverted by Celestina in an alliance with anarchic forces whose god is Plutón. This inversion is a structural characteristic of LC.

188. COSTA FONTES, Manuel da. "Celestina's 'Hilado' and Related Symbols." Cel 8, i (1984), 3-13.

Celestina's "hilado" is important on the symbolic level for its rich sexual nuances. Traditional folktales from the Portuguese Azores, here recounted, show that oral tradition was an important carrier of such symbolic values and suggests that Rojas may have had both oral and literary sources for the chain of associations set in action by the "hilado."

189. _____. "Celestina's 'Hilado' and Related Symbols: A Supplement." Cel 9, i (May 1985), 33-38.

See preceding entry. Expands the base of the survey of oral literature in Portuguese with themes current in LC to include the area of Tras-os-Montes in Northeastern Portugal.

190. CRIADO DE VAL, Manuel. "Melibea y Celestina ante el juicio de Don Quijote." Anales Cervantinos 4 (1954), 187-98.

Presents a scheme of evolution from Endrina to Melibea to Dulcinea, and from Trotaconventos to Celestina.

191. _____. Indice verbal de LC. Madrid: RFE, 1955. 266p. (Anejos de la RFE, 64)

Analyzes more than 10,000 verbal forms and concludes—agreeing with Rojas' own statements—that Acts 2-16 (and the later interpolations) are attributable to Rojas, but not Act 1.

a. ASNS 193 (1956), 250-51, H. Bihler
b. NRFH 10 (1956), 71-73, J. M. Lope
c. Revue Belge de Philologie et d'Histoire 34, no. 2 (1956), 472-76, R. Renard
d. BHS 34 (1957), 108-10, F. W. Hodcroft
(See Criado's reply in RFE 40 (1956[1957]), 238-40)
e. HR 25 (1957), 130-32, J. E. Gillet
f. MLR 52 (1957), 122-23, A. I. Watson
g. LR 12 (1958), 203-05, P. Groult
h. Bollettino dell'Istituto di Lingue Estere (Genoa) 6 (1961), 135-36, G. Chiareno

192. _____. "La celestinesca," in his Teoría de Castilla la Nueva (Madrid: Gredos, 1960), 308-30. A second, revised ed. appeared in 1969.

General treatment of the locale of LC and its characters.

193. _____. "Celestina en Flandes." ABC (December 11 1960), n. p.

LC was as popular in the Low Countries as was the romancero. It left pictoral traces in works by Jan Steen, P. G. van Roestratem, Honthorst and others. Five illustrations. This material was included in the author's De la Edad Media: 1965.

194. _____. "Arquetipos españoles: Centurio." ABC (April 4 1961), n. p.

In all ways, Centurio is a caricature, a literary relative of the squire Lazarillo will serve. Deep down he owns a philosophical skepticism. Two illustrations. This material was later incorporated in the author's De la Edad Media: 1965.

195. _____. "Melibea." ABC (June 18 1961), n. p.

Melibea is the first modern, real woman of Renaissance literature (Shakespeare's Juliet is still theatrical). Her failure to marry Calisto is not owing to any Jewish blood she may or may not have, but rather to social conventions, the envy of others, and the presence of a mad passion and a convenient go-between. Four illustrations. Some of this material was included in the author's De la Edad Media: 1965.

196. _____. "Arquetipos españoles: La 'hija' de Celestina." ABC (May 25 1962), n. p.

Treats of Elena, from Salas Barbadillo's Hija de Celestina, of the use of double-edged lexical items, and is illustrated with paintings by Murillo and Goya. Parts were later included in the author's De la Edad Media: 1965.

197. _____. "LC y la pornografía en nuestros clásicos." Est Lit, no. 269 (1963), 5-6.

The possible pornography in LC is attenuated by the clever mask of the argot with which it is presented. Very little is clear-cut.

198. _____. "Elogio y vejamen de Lope de Vega." CHA, nos. 161-162 (1963), 371-79.

Lope surpasses other dramatists of his era—notably Cervantes—but he never achieved the creation of universal characters like those of LC.

199. _____. "Siguiendo a la Celestina," in his Campo literario de Castilla la Nueva (Madrid: Publicaciones Españolas, 1963), 45-47.

Two cities, Salamanca and Toledo, could have been the ideal setting Rojas conceived for LC. Two illustrations.

200. _____. "Calixto, Don Quijote, Segismundo: 'locos amadores'." ABC (July 26 1964), n. p.

Each of the three has in common with the others his being an idealist/ dreamer immersed in a world full of 'pícaros', muledrivers and out-and-out materialists. Illustrated. Material later incorporated in the author's De la Edad Media: 1965.

201. _____. "La celestinesca," in his De la Edad Media al Siglo de Oro (Madrid: Publicaciones Españolas, 1965), 65-87.

Concentrates on discussing Rojas' characters and the impact of LC on later authors.

202. _____. "'La puente es llevada...': Historia de la farsa." ABC (November 24 1965), 42-45.

Act 3 of LC may have as a partial source the chronicle of Pero Carrillo, falconer to Juan II. An account of 1434 is possibly recalled in LC.

203. _____. *El verbo español*. Madrid: Saeta, 1969. 457p.

LC is one of the works cited often throughout this study.

204. _____, ed. *LC y su contorno social* [Actas del Primer Congreso Internacional Sobre LC]. Barcelona: Borrás, 1977.

Record of most of the 'ponencias' presented at the Congress, which was celebrated in Madrid, June 17-22 1974. They are listed separately in this bibliography [= ACTAS: with corresponding page numbers].

a. *Sovremennaya Khudozhestvennaya Literatura za Rubezhom* (Contemporary Fiction Abroad) (Moscow: Progress, 1980), 59-63, A. Osmanova

205. _____. "LC, tratado del 'amor impervio'." *Yelmo*, no. 30 (October-December) 1976, 5-9.

Used as an adjective and attribute of 'love', *impervio* is found only in LC. Since love in LC is always inaccessible, impossible to attain, Rojas' use of the etymological meaning of the word is something new in the love literature of his day.

206. _____. "'Amor impervio' (LC I, 48): What Does It Mean?" *Cel* 1, ii (Fall 1977), 3-6.

An English version of the main portion of the above entry.

207. _____. "Las condiciones de la redacción juglaresca en función de la edición de textos medievales españoles," in *Actele celui de-al XII-lea Congres International de Lingvistica şi Filologie Romanica* (Bucharest, 1971 [1977]), 43-51.

The idea is that works are elaborated by successive authors (here 'juglares') and that the end product ought to serve us in the preparation of editions. Examples: the *Cid*, the LBA and LC.

208. _____. "*El Guitón Honofre*: Un eslabón entre 'celestinesca' y 'picaresca'," in *La picaresca*, ed. M. Criado de Val (Madrid: Fundación Universitaria Española, 1979), 539-46.

Some of the interest in refrains, in introductory materials (letters, prologues, etc.), and in some stylistic excesses link LC to *Guitón*. The latter has characteristics which link it also to *Lazarillo* and to *Guzmán de Alfarache*.

209. CROCE, Benedetto. "Studi su poesie antiche e moderne. XVI. Antica poesia spagnuola. I. LC," in *La critica* (Naples) 37 (1939), 81-91; rpt. in his *Poesia antica e moderna; interpretazioni* (Bari: G. Laterza, 1941; 2nd ed. 1943; 3rd ed. 1950), 209-22.

LC for Croce is fundamentally a poetic creation as seen in its portrait of eternal passion, its conception and its use of language. For him, this invalidates much of the discussion of its nature as a moral or immoral work, as a Medieval or as a Renaissance creation, etc. There is a particularly detailed commentary of Act 1, scene 1, and another on the character of Celestina.

210. CUSTODIO, Alvaro. "LC y la literatura estatal del Siglo de Oro." CA 70, no. 4 (1953), 262-75.

LC reflects the three essential elements of 15th-century Spanish literature and thus summarizes them: the joy of living, an obsession with death and an ascetic sensibility.

211. _____. "Sobre el secreto de Melibea." CA 17, no. 6 (1958), 209-13.

A letter about articles by Orozco (1957) and Serrano Poncela (1958) which make a 'conversa' of Melibea. Such assertions are not necessary to the understanding of LC.

212. _____. "Las adaptaciones escénicas de LC." *Excélsior* (February 7 1960), 1, 4.

Begins with two English versions (Mabbe 1631 and Stevens 1707) which we do not know were staged. Early Spanish versions of this century by Pedrell and Miranda y Carnero were definitely not staged. With some comments, staged versions by F. Fernández Villegas (1909), Achard (1942, entry 1036) and a few others are discussed.

213. _____. "Mi adaptación escénica de LC." *Excélsior* (February 14 1960), 1.

Reveals the genesis of his adaptation and discusses the modifications made of the 1953 Mexico City staging, as well as the subsequent one of 1957 and of this one for 1960. A scene by scene summary is included, showing how Rojas' text has been accomodated to the stage.

214. _____. "LC en el Teatro Reforma." *Notas y comentarios del Teatro de México*, no. 20 (February 1968), 1-2.

A panorama of the Custodio production from 1953-1968, the small changes in it, the era of stage censorship of this version for its being 'inmoral' and 'indigna' (1960-1968), and a description of the features of the newest production (1968).

215. _____. "La belleza actual de LC." ACTAS: 471-83.

A defense of the natural dramatic unfolding of LC. Excesses belong to literary passages and not to dramatic structure. A feature of this presentation is a call for an annual LC festival to look into its dramatic trajectory and its impact on later works.

216. _____. "LC como experiencia teatral." *Cel* 3, i (May 1979), 33-38.

Notes on his own production of LC in both Spanish and English for a Los Angeles repertory company (see entry 994). Includes comments on staging difficulties and on audience reaction.

217. _____. [Interview with Domingo Miras.] *Primer Acto*, no. 201 (Nov.-Dec. 1983), 29-34.

On p. 33, there are data for the history of the staging of LC with regard to Custodio's own production (see 978).

D

218. DAMIANI, Bruno. *Francisco Delicado*. New York/Boston: Twayne, 1974. (TWAS, 335)

Reprises Delicado's role in Venice 1531, the importance of LC in the future of picaresque fiction and connections—especially of structure and characterization—linking LC and *La lozana andaluza*. See also the edition of this work prepared by Damiani and Giovanni Allegra (Madrid: Porrúa Turanzas, 1975).

219. _____. "Las fuentes literarias de *La pícara Justina*." BICC 36 (1981), 44-70.

Of the article's four sections, only the last one (Renaissance and Baroque) mentions LC and without much detail (pp. 60-62). Celestinesque imitations are also included in the discussion.

220. DAMONTE, Mario. "Edizioni antiche della *Celestina* esistenti a Genova." *Studi di Letteratura Spagnola* (1967), 279-81.

Two Spanish eds.—Toledo 1538 and Antwerp 1595—and one Italian ed.—Milan 1514—have been discovered, further clarifying aspects of the textual transmission of LC.

221. DARDON DE TADLOCK, Gisela. "El ensanchamiento temporal en LC y su antecedente en el *Liber Panphili*." ACTAS: 291-98.

Rojas and the Latin author of the *Panphili* both felt a need to expand the time that lapses between the lovers' first encounter and the first scenes of love in order to provide psychological verisimilitude for the growth of the heroine's passion.

222. _____. "*Lesedrama*: El género de LC." Diss. Univ. of Arizona, 1976. 144p. DAI 37/02, 1006A. No. 76-18248. H. Iventosch and D. A. Nelson.

The history of the reading-text genre from the early Christian era to the Renaissance, a genre written to delight the theatre of the mind. It discusses LC, its continuations and imitations, and the modern stage versions of Achard (1942), Pérez de la Ossa (1959) and Alvaro Custodio (1953).

223. DAVALOS, Balbino. "Las dos elegías que engendraron LC." *Letras de México*, no. 9 (1939), 7-8.

The two elegies are an early one by Propertius and one modeled on it by Ovid, both sources for LC according to the author. He offers his Spanish translation of both in order to strengthen his assertion.

224. DeARMAS, Frederick A. "The Demoniacal in LC." *South Atlantic Bulletin* 36, no. 4 (1971), 10-13.

The relationship between 'loco amor' and the demoniacal underscores the strong morality of LC.

225. _____. "LC: An Example of Love Melancholy." RR 66 (1975), 288-95.

A consideration of the *Malleus maleficarum* (earlier than LC) and Burton's *Anatomy of Melancholy* (later than LC) as important for understanding the love entanglements of LC as they were understood in the 16th century.

226. DeGOROG, Ralph P., and Lisa S. DeGOROG. *La sinonimia en LC*. Madrid: Real Academia Española, 1972. 169p. (Anejos de la RAE, 25)

With synonymy as a measure, the authors conclude that Act 1 represents an earlier stage of the language and that Rojas was LC's second author.

227. DELMONTE, Alberto. "Il giardino, la scala, la notte." *Annali della Facoltà di Filosofia dell'Università Stadale di Milano* 23 (1970), 109-15; rpt. with small changes in his *La sera nello specchio* (Milan/Varese: Istituto Editoriale Cisalpino, 1971), 25-33.

LC has a thematic-symbolic structure in which Melibea's garden is Paradise, the ladder is the Ascent and night is Sin. This structure emphasizes the moral shape of the work.

228. DELOGU, Francesco M. "*La Tragicomedia di Calisto e Melibea*," in *Cervantes* (Messina/Milan: Ed. G. Principato, 1939), 225-90.

Interesting remarks on the historical Rojas and the 'Rojas' author of LC, the very early criticism of LC (Vives, Valdés, Cintio, Cervantes, Moratín, Schack, Menéndez y Pelayo, Savj-Lopez, DeLollis, Fitzmaurice-Kelly, Cejador, Montoliu, Maeztu and Vossler), the process of textual formation and an annotated reading of the work which emphasizes the artistic successes that endow LC with a unity of feeling. Discussion of the characterizations of Melibea, Celestina and, to a lesser extent, Pármeno.

229. DELPY, G. "Les profanations du texte de LC." BH 49 (1947), 261-75.

Rojas as author of the entire CCM, but the additions leading to the TCM mar the work and are probably Proaza's doing. Illustrated with eleven examples of such disfigurations (from the interpolations).

230. D'EMIC, Michael T. "LC and the Medieval Didactic Tradition." M. Litt. Trinity College-Dublin, 1975. 202p. K. Adams. (*)

231. DEVLIN, John. *LC: A Parody of Courtly Love. Toward a Realistic Interpretation of the TCM*. New York: Anaya-Las Américas, 1971. 87p.

An essay which centers on courtly love in LC and uses selected passages to demonstrate the parody of it reflected in Rojas' text.

232. DEVOTO, Daniel. "Un ingrediente de Celestina." *Filología* 8 (1962), 97-104; rpt., slightly revised, in his *Textos y contextos* (Madrid: Gredos, 1974), 150-69.

The phrase 'mantilla de niño' (Act 1) is explained.

233. DeVRIES, Henk. "Sobre el mensaje secreto de Calysto y Melybea." ACTAS: 135-51.

[The original, in Dutch, was presented as a paper in Nijmegen, 1974.] This is a numerological argument based on the names of the thirteen main characters of LC. A connection is established between this 'human' *Comedia* and Dante's 'divine' *Commedia*. Celestina is perceived as a depraved *Ecclesia*. DeVries posits that Rojas planned all this.

234. _____. "LC, sátira encubierta: el acróstico es una cifra." BRAE 54 (1974), 123-52.

The author proposes a new interpretation of LC based on numerological allegory which will prove the satiric intent of LC.

235. DEYERMOND, Alan D. "The Index to Petrarch's Latin Works as a Source of LC." BHS 31 (1954), 141-49.

Certain groups of borrowings indicate a definite influence of the *Indice* on Acts 2-16 and show, at the same time, specific interests of the author(s) of LC.

236. _____. "Petrarchan Borrowings and Reminiscences in LC." B. Litt. Oxford Univ. (Pembroke College), 1957. 206p. P. E. Russell.

237. _____. *The Petrarchan Sources of LC*. London: Oxford Univ. Press, 1961. 160p. Rpt. with a new Preface and a Supplementary Bibliography, Westport, Connecticut: Greenwood Press, 1975. 164p.

A detailed espousal of the great use Rojas made of Petrarch's Latin works, especially the *De remediis utriusque fortunae* and the index (Basle 1496) to them. The manner of the incorporation of the Petrarchan material into the context of LC leads to illumination of Rojas' style. The pessimistic view of Rojas might have surprised Petrarch had he been able to see to what uses his works were put.

a. ABC (November 9 1961), 3; (November 10 1961), 1, 3, M. Aznar
b. YWMLS 23 (1961), 172, N. D. Shergold
c. *Regesten van Aanwinsten van het Instituut voor Vergelijkend Literatuur onderzoek* 6 (1961), 5-6, J. T. W. Clemens
d. *Arbor* 48, no. 184 (April 1961), 545-47, M. de Riquer
e. BHS 38 (1961), 293-95, R. B. Tate
f. *MAe* 30 (1961), 138-40, J. Fucilla
g. MLN 76 (1961), 931-34, S. Gilman
h. TLS (August 11 1961), 535, Anon.
i. *Latomus* 31 (1962), 442, L. Bakelants
j. ASNS 199 (1962), 134-37, B. König
k. *Modern Philology* 59 (1962), 306-08, J. Mallo
l. MLR 57 (1962), 615-16, G. D. Trotter

m. RLC 36 (1962), 596-600, M. Bataillon
n. *RenN* 15 (1962), 135-37, R. Lievsay
o. *Symposium* 16 (1962), 237-38, C. L. Penney
p. *RPh* 16 (1962-63), 499-500, R. Lida and M. R. Lida de Malkiel
q. *Brotéria* 77 (1963), 616-17, M. Martins
r. RR 54 (1963), 286-88, D. W. McPheeters
s. HR 31 (1963), 153-59, J. H. Herriott
t. *Revista de Letras* (São Paulo) 5 (1964), 290-94, F. Mendonça
u. *Revista de Literaturas Modernas*, no. 6 (1967), 119-20, C. O. Nallim
v. BH 70 (1968), 147-51, P. Heugas

238. _____. "La crítica de LC de Jacques de Lavardin." *Hispanófila*, no. 13 (1961), 1-4.

Lavardin, when he was preparing towards 1560 a French version of LC, introduced a new character into Act 21, an Ariston, brother to Alisa, who disputed with Pleberio his pessimistic views.

239. _____. "The Text-Book Mishandled: Andreas Capellanus and the Opening Scene of LC." *Neophilologus* 45 (1961), 218-21.

Posits a certain comical attitude in the opening scene based on the proposition that Calisto is 'mishandling' his role as lover, at least in the terms prescribed in manuals (Capellanus' was such a one in circulation). Calisto is disconcerted when Melibea does not respond as the manuals say she should, and the scene plays for humor.

240. _____. *A Literary History of Spain: The Middle Ages*. London: Ernest Benn, 1971.

LC (pp. 166-70) is treated as a prose work in dialogue with many novelistic characteristics. Some discusion of sources, of the author's intentions and of the summary pessimistic view projected by LC.

a. MLR 67 (1972) 670-71, D. W. Lomax
b. *Choice* 9 (1972), 1137, Anon.
c. CL 26 (1974), J. M. Sobré
d. *Hispania* 57 (1974), 370-71, S. Hess

241. _____. *La Edad Media*. Spanish version by Luis Alonso López. Barcelona: Ariel, 1973. (Col. Letras e Ideas. Instrumenta, 1)

The LC section is somewhat amplified for the Spanish translation (pp. 301-13).

a. *Est Lit*, no. 534 (1974), 1617, L. Azancot

242. _____. "The Coherence of Pleberio's Lament." *LaC* 3, ii (1975), 20-21.

Abstract of a paper read at the MLA meeting, New York, December 1974.

243. _____. "Lyric Traditions in Non-Lyrical Genres." *Studies in Honor of Lloyd A. Kasten* (Madison, Wisconsin: Hispanic Seminary of Medieval Studies, 1975), 39-52.

LC treated specifically at pp. 46-47. It deals with Rojas' use of the traditional *alba* or dawn song to satirize the perverted values of his society. Passages contrasted are Calisto-Melibea (Act 19) and Pármeno-Areusa (Act 7).

244. _____. "Hilado-Cordón-Cadena: Symbolic Equivalence in LC." *Cel* 1, i (May 1977), 6-12.

The author establishes a series of linking images that join the idea of captivity to the three objects mentioned in his title. The devil, conjured into the first of them, is then transferred symbolically to the others in turn, the self-interest of the individuals on the receiving end feeding its power. In the end all are trapped. Thus does Rojas make both magic and his own perception of human psychology harmonize into one literary whole.

245. _____. "Symbolic Equivalence in LC: A Postscript." *Cel* 2, i (May 1978), 25-30.

(See the entry immediately above). Deyermond adds here reflections on Rojas' use of snake imagery, imagery he would have inherited both directly and indirectly from bestiaries and popular oral tradition.

246. _____. "LC," in *Historia y crítica de la literatura española*, vol. 1: Edad Media, gen. ed. F. Rico (Barcelona: Ed. Crítica, 1980), 485-528. Paper (Col. Páginas de Filología).

An essay on LC and its critics, presented in a bibliographically useful introd. to a small anthology of pages from major critical writings on LC: Lida de Malkiel (1962), Green (1963; Sp. translation 1969), Russell (1963), Maravall (1964), Bataillon (1961), Gilman (1972) and Castro (1965).

247. _____. "Divisiones socio-económicas, nexos sexuales: la sociedad de *Celestina*." *Cel* 8, ii (Fall 1984), 3-10.

The desires and relationships that transcend social classes in LC make an interesting study and the focus here is on the lower classes' sexual desires for members of the upper class.

248. _____. " '¡Muerta soy! ¡Confesión!': Celestina y el arrepentimiento a última hora," in *De los romances-villancicos a la poesía de Claudio Rodríguez: 22 ensayos ... en homenaje a Gustav Siebenmann,* ed. J. M. López de Abiada and A. López Bernasocchi (Madrid: J. Esteban, 1984), 129-140.

In the change from CCM to TCM, the number of characters asking for absolution upon dying increases from one to three. This study wonders whether Rojas might not have had in mind a deliberate plan to force his readers to review the whole matter of last minute repentance.

249. DIAZ PETERSON, Rosendo. "El mundo de LC." BRAE 56 (1976), 359-68.

The Renaissance conception of world order is more chaotic than the medieval view, reflected in the development from a Christian Aristotelianism to a pessimistic Neoplatonism. LC is just between these two and its art reflects that fact.

250. DIAZ-PLAJA, Guillermo. "Revisión de mitos: LC." *La Nación* (Buenos Aires) (February 9 1964), Section 4, p. 1.

A limited treatment which introduces and summarizes two works and some new views: those of Bataillon (1961) and Lida de Malkiel (1962).

251. _____. "Lo mítico en LC," in his *Los monstruos y otras literaturas* (Barcelona: Plaza y Janés, 1967), 123-30.

A general presentation of the mythical dimension of situation and characterization in LC.

252. DIAZ-SOLIS, Ramón. *Tarde en España: de LC y otros renacientes*. Bogotá: Ed. Tercer Mundo, 1980. 201p.

a. *Cel* 6, i (May 1982), 39-40, E. W. Naylor

253. DiFRANCO, Ralph. "Hispanic Biographical Criticism: The 'Converso' Question." *Michigan Academician* 12 (1979-80), 85-96.

A presentation of the critical—and sometimes polemical—approaches to the life and works of Juan de Mena and Fernando de Rojas.

254. DILLE, Glen F. "A Critical Edition of the *Comedia Serafina* (1521)." Diss. Tulane Univ., 1973. 260p. DAI 34/08, 5164-65A. No. 74-299. D. W. McPheeters. (See below, entry 256.)

255. _____. "The *Comedia Serafina* and Its Relationship to LC." *Cel* 1, ii (Fall 1977), 15-20.

Although the *Serafina* is an imitation of LC and owes much to it—examples are provided—,it is still an independent literary creation in other important ways.

256. _____. *"La Comedia Llamada Serafina"; An Anonymous Humanistic Comedy of 1521.* Carbondale-Edwardsville: Southern Illinois Univ. Press, 1979. xxxvii + 114p.

The editor's introd. and notes explore the links between this imitation and the original *Celestina*.

a. *Cel* 3, i (May 1979), 39-41, J. T. Snow
b. *Cel* 4, ii (Fall 1980), 35-37, J. Lihani
c. REH 16 (1982), 141-42, R. J. Nelson

257. DODDIS MIRANDA, Antonio, comp. *LC: Estudios*, 2 vols. Santiago de Chile: Ed. Universitaria, 1957. 436, 566p.

Contains forty-two articles on LC all published between 1900-1956. Reproduced in offset; designed as a student anthology.

258. DOYON, René-Louis. "LC." *Mercure de France*, no. 309 (May-August 1950), 462-69.

A portrayal of Rojas' Jewish conscience is reflected in LC only in subtle ways in order better to disguise his opposition to the surrounding world. Some examples cited are Calisto's blasphemies, Celestina's dealings with clerics, the attitude toward suicide, and the final stoic pose.

259. DRYSDALL, Denis L. "LC en France de 1521 à 1812." 2 vols. iv + 535p. Diss. (Troisième Cycle, Lettres). Paris, 1970. (*)

260. _____. "LC dans l'édition bilingue de 1633." RLC 45 (1971), 208-21.

Seemingly a student edition. He proposes that the 1633 Spanish text be compared with M. Gast's (Salamanca 1570).

261. _____. "Two Notes on LC." RomN 14 (1972-73), 589-92.

The words 'la moça que esperava al ministro' are a verbal code for the presence of Crito. The phrase 'abatióse el girifalte' is given its due in the Italian translation of Hordognez and in the English version of Mabbe.

262. _____. "Molière and Spain: A Bibliographical Survey Together With a Note on Molière and the Figure of the Go-Between." *Journal of the Australasian Universities Language and Literature Association* 39 (1973), 94-112.

Is LC a possible influence on Molière's *entremetteuse* Frosine? Although Drysdall proves that it was circumstantially possible, he thinks the French figure owes her existence to long literary tradition.

263. _____. "The Guillaume Chaudière Edition of Jacques de Lavardin's *Célestine*." Cel 5, ii (Fall 1981), 49-50.

The first confirmation of the existence of this edition.

264. _____. "The French Version of the *Penitencia de Amor*." Cel 9, i (1985), 22-31.

The Spanish original of 1514, inspired by LC, was translated and published in French in the 1530s. It proves to be based also on some works by Juan de Flores (*Grisel y Mirabella, Grimalte y Gradissa*). The translator makes his version more didactic, moves the locale to Italy, and effects other modifications in order to make his work more popular to contemporary audiences, apparently with only moderate success.

265. DuBRUCK, Edelgard. "The Emergence of the Common Man in Fifteenth-Century Europe: A Probe of Literary Evidence," in *Fifteenth Century Studies*, ed. G. Mermier and E. DuBruck (Ann Arbor, Michigan: Univ. Microfilms International for The Medieval Institute, 1978), 83-109.

In the third section, social reality in LC comes up in connection with the work's purported antifeminism. Celestina takes advantage of this situation (as lived in Spain) to mobilize the female proletariat, a class produced by the social history of the West.

266. DULICK, Michael G. "LC and Chaucer's *Troilus*: A Comparative Study." Diss. St. Louis Univ., 1979. 227p. DAI 40/11, 5852A. No. 80-10723. R. R. Mazza.

A study of common sources and a comparison of characters. While there is no direct contact, it is understandable how—on the historical continuum— Chaucer's love story should eventually erupt in Rojas' tale of passion.

267. DULSEY, Bernard. "LC, ¿versión larga o corta?" *Hispanófila* 11 (1961), 23-28.

The CCM is preferable to the TCM: it is more believable, has greater dramatic thrust and a justified brevity of action and climax.

268. DUNN, Peter N. "'Materia la mujer, el hombre forma': Notes on the Development of a Lopean Topos." *Homenaje a William L. Fichter* (Madrid, 1971), 189-99.

Notes that the topos was taken up also in LC.

269. _____. *Fernando de Rojas*. New York/Boston: Twayne, 1975. 193p. (TWAS, 368)

A compendium of differing considerations relative to the textual problems and interpretations of LC. It has a resumé of critical treatments of each major problem (e.g., authorship, early editions, imitations, thematic unity, genre, and characterization). The last chapter is an explication of the TCM, act-by-act.

   a. *Hispania* 60 (1977), 161-62, H. T. Sturcken
   b. MLR 72 (1977), 471-72, M. E. Beeson
   c. MLN 94 (1979), 416-18, D. S. Severin

270. _____. "Pleberio's World." PMLA 91 (1976), 406-19.

Dunn recapitulates several interpretations of Pleberio and of the meaning of his lament of Act 21. He studies in some detail the whole characterization of the man and his world and finds there a somewhat different person from the one who ends the work.

   a. PMLA 92 (1977), 130-31, S. Gilman. But see also the response by Dunn, ibid., 131-32.

271. DUQUE DIAZ DE CERIO, Pedro Juan. "La presencia de España en *Romeo y Julieta*." *Letras de Deusto* 9, no. 18 (1979), 63-94.

Exploration of the literary connections between the two works (63-79). He relates a history of the tale that Shakespeare knew, and gives a resumé of LC in English translations to Shakespeare's time. There is—examples are presented—some acquaintance with LC reflected in the work by Shakespeare.

272. DURAN, Manuel. "La solución de LC," in *La ambigüedad en el Quijote* (Xalapa, Mexico: Univ. Veracruzana, 1960), 61-73.

Cervantes has frequent recourse to LC: in characterization, depiction of social forms, samples of irony, perspectivism and in the whole area of human communication. Other relevant pages dealing with some of these themes are 103-08 and 175-83.

273. DUTTON, Brian, "Huri y Midons: el amor cortés y el paraíso musulmán." *Filología* 13 (1968-69), 151-64.

The mixture of religious and erotic images in works like *Cárcel de amor* and LC enjoys a long history in Romance territories, and especially in areas once dominated by the Arabs whose literary Paradise is similar.

E

274. EARLE, Peter G. "Don Juan y Calisto: un estudio literario sobre el amor." Thesis (Tesina). Mexico City College, 1951. 63p. (*)

275. _____. "Four Stage Adaptations of LC." *Hispania* 38 (1955), 46-51.

The ones discussed are Rastell's English printing (c. 1530), the Madrid production of 1909, the Paris production of Achard (1942) and A. Custodio's Mexico City staging (1953).

276. _____. "Love concepts in *La cárcel de amor* y LC." *Hispania* 39 (1956), 92-96.

LC belongs to the tradition of the sentimental novel (*La cárcel de amor*) but it surpasses it in scope and value.

277. EATON, Katherine. "The Character of Lucrecia in LC." AION-SR 15 (1973), 213-25.

An analysis of the role of Lucrecia throughout LC which produces a complete picture of her world.

278. EBERWEIN, Elena, "Zur Bedeutung der erweiterten Celestina-fassung," in her *Zur Deutung mittelalterlicher Existenz* (Bonn and Cologne: Röhrscheid Verlag, 1933), 54-79.

The rationale for the expanded TCM is attributable to the force of personality with which Celestina is endowed and to the intensity of the actions she initiates. Her "theme" dominates the last two-thirds of the long first act and thereafter her presence, real or magical, is the work's fulcrum. The turning point in her personal fortunes is her entry into the world of Calisto and Melibea. In the TCM, the lovers die as compensating revenge for the bawd's own death at the hands of Calisto's servants. Thus, her fate is dependent on the outcome of the actions of others, a particularly Renaissance trait of the work.

279. EESLEY, Anne. "The Third Person in *Celestina*." Diss. State Univ. of New York at Stony Brook, 1983. 315p. *DAI* 44/02 (1983-84), 485A. No. DA8315083. E. Rivers. [Abstract in *Cel* 7, i (May 1983), 45-46.]

280. _____. "Four Instances of '¡Confession!' in *Celestina*." *Cel* 7, ii (Fall 1983), 17-19.

Finds that the addition of a call for confession by Calisto in the

TCM adds ambiguity to the notion that last-minute contrition was a guarantor of salvation.

281. ELLIS, Deborah. "'Calle It Gentilesse': A Comparative Study of Two Medieval Go-Betweens." *Comitatus* (Univ. of California-Los Angeles) 8 (1977), 1-13.

Celestina and Chaucer's Pandarus (from *Troilus*). A study of the spatial imagery and in particular of their respective houses leads to interesting observations on their social ambience. Pandarus is part of a firm, secure and stable environment; Celestina faces an uncertain, hostile, chaotic world.

282. _____. "The Image of the Home in Early English and Spanish Literature." Diss. Univ. of California-Berkeley, 1981. xxv + 229p. DAI 43/04 (1982-83), 1141A. No. DA8211918.

Chapter Two, at pp. 62-90, 113-126, deals with the title theme. See also following entry.

283. _____. "'¡Adios, paredes!': The Image of the Home in *Celestina*." *Cel* 5, ii (Fall 1981), 1-17.

Investigation of related images in the TCM which establishes close analogies among them, on the one hand, and among individual destinies of the characters, on the other.

284. EMBEITA, María. "LC, obra del renacimiento." ACTAS: 125-34.

Explores the parallels between Renaissance painting techniques and forms of verbal expression in LC. Both chronicle the social and literary changes taking place in Rojas' era.

285. ERNOUF, Anita Bonilla. "Proverbs and Proverbial Phrases in LC." Diss. Columbia Univ., 1970. 743p. DAI 33/07, 3641-42A. No. 72-33417.

286. ESCOBAR, Luis. "Place de LC dans le théâtre européen." *Rendez-vous,* nos. 14-15 (September 1958), n. p. (*)

287. ESTREMERA GOMEZ, Juan. "Celestina o la seducción y persuasión por la palabra." *Estudios Literarios dedicados al profesor Mariano Baquero Goyanes* (Murcia, 1974), 99-114.

Celestina's genius is revealed through her use of language. It gives her control over people from all classes.

288. EYER, Cortland. "Juan Cirne and the *Celestina*." HR 5 (1937), 265-68.

The death of Dido in Cirne's *Tragedia de los amores de Eneas y de la reyna Dido* has Melibea's suicide as its model.

F

289. FAULHABER, Charles. "The Hawk in Melibea's Garden." HR 45 (1977), 435-50.

Reviews previous interpretations of the opening scene of LC. Notes the echoes of Andreas Capellanus' *De amore* and of Boncompagno de Signa's *Rota veneris*. There follows a clever view of how the first author (i. e., of Act 1) conceived of the encounter in the garden (the lovers had previously met) and how and why Rojas changed this conception (to present a more passive Calisto). Rojas as second author exercised great artistic control over his material.

290. FERNANDEZ, Dario. "La narración corrompida." *Est Lit*, no. 269 (1963), 3-4.

On pornography in various works. Compares LC with Christine Rochefort's *Le repos du guerrier*.

291. FERNANDEZ, Dominique. "Retour à LC." *Nouvelle Revue Française* 10, no. 111 (1962), 518-21.

Celestina as an incarnation of evil, one of the most completely successful in all of literature.

292. FERNANDEZ, Sergio. "El amor condenado" and "El amor transferido," in his *Ensayos sobre literatura española de los siglos XVI y XVII*. Mexico: Univ. Nacional Autónoma, 1961. (Facultad de Filosofía y Letras, 54)

The first of the essays (5-22) concludes that Rojas does not condemn the lovers, since they have no metaphysical concept of condemnation. Death for them is recompense and the agent of their reunion. The second essay (23-42) is a study of how Celestina dispenses love by transferring the kind she has known to others.

293. _____. "La comunicación del bien," in his *Las grandes figuras españolas del renacimiento y el barroco* (Mexico: Ed. Pormaca, 1966), 1-10.

Love in LC is the communication of a vital, not a moral, good; the idea of success which permeates LC requires continual indulgence of a delight which is pure hedonism, and which becomes a kind of mysticism of evil.

294. _____. "Melibea," "Areúsa," "Celestina," in his *Retratos del fuego y la ceniza* (México: Fondo de Cultura Económica, 1968), 43-47, 65-68 and 292-305.

Textual commentaries based on the art of characterization. Melibea is perceived as two figures (the one seen by Calisto; the other by Celestina). Areúsa comes to symbolize the orthodoxy (within the work) of the glorification of sexual love. Celestina, discussed in the context of acts 9 and 12, is viewed in light of her thoughts on old age and death.

295. FERNANDEZ MARQUEZ, Pablo. *Los personajes de LC*. Mexico: Finisterre, 1970.

No pagination (but about 130p). A general essay on character presentation in LC.

296. FERNANDEZ-SEVILLA, Julio. "Creación y repetición en la lengua de LC," in *Actas del II Simposio Internacional de Lengua Española (Las Palmas 1980)*.(*)

297. _____. "Presentadores de refranes en el texto de LC," in *Serta Philologica F. Lázaro Carreter* (Madrid: Cátedra, 1983), 209-18.

A study of the many formulas used in LC to introduce proverbial and refrain materials, both of an obvious and non-obvious nature. So pervasive are the proverbial expressions at all levels of the text that they become structural supports for it.

298. FERRAN, Jaime. "La encrucijada de LC." ACTAS: 89-101.

The metaphor of the crossroads extends beyond the time of LC's writing to linguistic considerations, intellectual content and depiction of society. Rojas, in a personal 'encrucijada' takes an ambivalent line and offers a gamut of possibilities for interpretation of both external and internal structures.

299. FERRE, Rosario. "Celestina en el tejido de la 'cupiditas'," *Cel* 7, i (May 1983), 3-16.

Using as a basis an analysis of primary and secondary groupings of image patterns associated with Celestina's 'hilado', this study develops 1) the idea that Rojas bitterly attacks the self-serving 'cupiditas' that infects his world, and 2) that the image patterns provide clues to Rojas' own aesthetic concerns.

300. FERRECCIO PODESTA, Mario. "Una edición nueva de LC." *Boletín de la Facultad de Filología* (Santiago de Chile) 12 (1960), 259-71.

Prescriptive comments for preparing a critical edition.

301. _____. "La formación del texto de LC." *Anales de la Universidad de Chile*, no. 136 (1965), 89-122.

The author proposes a comprehensive history of external LC matters based on a close investigation of the 'carta-prólogo', the 'argumentos' to the acts and the testimony of the variants from Valencia 1514.

302. _____. "Un caso aleccionador: *zurrio* (LC, aucto XIX)." *Boletín de la Facultad de Filología* (Santiago de Chile) 22 (1971), 37-44.

Presentation of an etymological study of the word's possibilities which leads the author to posit a meaning of 'zumbido' or 'susurro'—an onomatopoetic value for the word in the TCM.

303. _____. "Haba morisca, ¿haba marisca?" *Cel* 8, ii (Fall 1984), 11-16.

A philological explanation of the term (an element of Celestina's 'laboratorio' mentioned in Act 1). It is suggested that Rojas mis-read the manuscript he was working from and, in so doing, created a ghost word.

304. FERRER CHIVITE, Manuel. "Unos momentos en la vida de Fernando de Rojas." *Cel* 5, ii (Fall 1981), 39-47.

From a passage in the section, "El autor a un amigo," there emerges in this study the possibility of a Rojas who portrays himself in an attitude ("retraído en mi cámara, acostado sobre mi propia mano") iconographically associated with intellectual Jews.

305. FERRERAS SAVOYE, Jacqueline. *LC ou la crise de la société patriarcale*. Paris: Ed. Hispano Americanas, 1977. 224p.

Begins with a general introd. to the period. The discussion of LC centers on the low esteem in which women were held and the role money played in the socio-political realities of the epoch. An appendix of 15th-century poems reflects attitudes which, the author claims, substantiate her conclusions.

a. CHA, no. 340 (October 1978), 154-65, A. Castro Díaz
b. *Cel* 4, no. 2 (November 1980), 31-34, A. D. Deyermond

306. FIGUEROA DE AMARAL, Esperanza. "Conflicto racial en LC." *Revista Bimestre Cubana* 71, no. 2 (1956), 20-68.

Melibea as a 'conversa'. The conflict between Christians and Jews which is portrayed in LC is typical of the period's racial problems.

307. FINCH, Patricia S. "Religion as Magic in the *Tragedia Policiana*." *Cel* 3, ii (Fall 1979), 19-24.

Ostensibly religious practices in the TP are disguised magical operations on the part of Claudina, the celestinesque figure. The comparison made of the two works underlines the superior human dimension distinguishing LC.

308. _____. "Magic and Witchcraft in the *Celestina* and Its Imitations." Diss. Catholic Univ. of America, 1981. 224p. DAI 42/6, 2669A. No. 8127531. B. Damiani. [Abstract also in *Cel* 5, ii (Fall 1981), 59-60.]

An historical survey of the nature and significance of magic precedes the question of its role in LC and seven imitations: the *Segunda* and *Tercera Celestinas, Lisandro y Roselia, Tragedia Policiana, Comedia Salvaje, La lozana andaluza,* and *La Dorotea.* The social, aesthetic and moral functions of magic are topics treated.

309. _____. "Gerarda como figura celestinesca," in *Lope de Vega y los orígenes del teatro español*, ed. M. Criado de Val (Madrid: Edi-6, 1981), 617-21.

Discusses ways in which Celestina and Gerarda are alike and not alike. The latter is clearly modeled on Celestina even though she does not dominate in *La Dorotea* as does Celestina in Rojas' work.

310. _____. "The Uses of the Aside in *Celestina*." *Cel* 6, ii (Fall 1982), 19-24.

Rojas' use of the *aparte*—limited to the low-life characters in *Celestina*—is a device associated with the portrayal of reticence, duplicity and hypocrisy. It is occasionally played for comedic effects, but is more often used to advance the plot or to reveal character. Examples of all these types are taken up.

311. FINK, Jacob H. "*Ha Selestina* u'mehabrah ha-yehudi" (LC and Its Jewish Author). *Jahadut Tsorfat* (Paris: Editions Polyglottes, 1951), 168-86. [In Hebrew]

LC, the first realist work of world literature, is the result of Jewish genius: this can be seen in the theme and in the presentation of the work's characters.

312. FITZPATRICK, Juan José. "LC: el proceso de la creación literaria visto a través de una tragicomedia." *La Torre* 3 (October-December 1955), 139-52.

Varied comments on the prefatory materials and the interpolated passages. The author feels they have been overlooked in the past.

313. FLASCHE, Hans. "LC," in his *Geschichte der Spanischen Literatur. I: Von den Anfängen bis zum Ausgang des fünfzehnten Jahrhunderts* (Bern/Munich: Francke Verlag, 1977), 407-41.

Devotes this space to a resumé of the art of LC and to both internal and external problems faced by critics and students.

a. MLR 75 (1980) 676-77, M. Sleeman
b. BHS 57 (1980), 239, E. von Richthofen
c. *Comparative Literature Studies* 17 (1980), 341-42, A. Porqueras-Mayo

314. FLIGHTNER, James A. "Pleberio." *Hispania* 47 (1964), 79-81.

Pleberio is important to the structure and themes of LC. There is a parallel between him and Celestina seen in their age and in their desire for both material acquisitions and power.

315. FOLCH JOU, Guillermo, Pedro GARCIA DOMINGUEZ and Sagrario MUÑOZ CALVO. "La Celestina: ¿hechicera o boticaria?" ACTAS: 163-67.

Celestina is seen as an authentic para-professional in pharmaceutics. Her house and laboratory are accurate reflections of then-current medical knowledge and Rojas must have known such places first-hand.

316. FORCADAS, Alberto M. "'Mira a Bernardo' y el judaísmo de LC." *Boletín de Filología Española*, nos. 46-49 (1973), 27-45.

Both the first author and Rojas must have been 'conversos' and well-versed in their legal knowledge. One aspect of being Jewish in the period was the need to communicate cryptically and the title phrase of this article is a coded message that signals a desire to criticize Christianity by making St. Bernard (the allusion is to him, according to this author) a misogynist.

317. _____. "Otra solución a 'lo de tu abuela con el ximio' (Aucto I de LC)." *RomN* 15 (1974-75), 567-71.

Sempronio's words must have had the intention of defaming

Calisto's claim to having pure Spanish blood, as suggested earlier by Menéndez y Pelayo.

318. _____. "El 'Planto de Pantasilea' en LC." *RomN* 19, no. 2 (1978-79), 237-42.

The 'Planto,' now attributed to Rodríguez del Padrón, is one of that author's amorous poems that doubtless exerted an influence over LC. The high rate of coincidence of lexical terms—especially from Act 6 of LC—supports this contention.

319. _____. "'Mira a Bernardo' es alusión con sospecha." *Cel* 3, i (May 1979), 11-18.

Again takes up the arguments of an earlier piece (see entry 316), under attack by E. M. Gerli (entry 362), regarding the identification of the Bernardo mentioned in Act 1 of LC. He adduces many examples which tend to show that St. Bernard of Clairvaux was considered to oppose the Immaculate Conception and was, therefore, seen as antifeminist. He rejects Gerli's candidate, the Catalan Bernat de Cabrera.

320. _____. "Sobre las fuentes históricas de '...eclipse ay mañana, etc.' y su posible incidencia en acto I de *Celestina*." *Cel* 7, i (May 1983), 29-37.

An analysis of the wonders Sempronio describes in Act 3 shows that each may be linked with events of the second third of the 15th century (see also Rozemond (entry 773). The theory is that Rojas, having employed an earlier text (= Act 1) for the CCM, enhanced—in his own section of the CCM—its archaic flavor with allusions to the earlier time period.

321. _____. "Implicaciones de la 'Afinidad de los opuestos' entre acto I de LC y el *Triunfo de las donas*, in *Josep Maria Solà-Solé: Homage, Homenaje, Homenatge* (Barcelona: Puvill, 1984), 251-265.

Affirms Rojas' familiarity with the works of Juan Rodríguez del Padrón whose presence—strongly felt in Act 1—Rojas was able to extend to the rest of the CCM and TCM. The author claims that Rojas knew perfectly well who the author of Act 1 was but did not disclose his identity for special reasons.

322. FOSTER, D. W. "Some Attitudes Towards Love in LC." *Hispania* 48 (1965), 484-92.

Calisto represents courtly love, Sempronio Ovidian love, Melibea a Christian love and Celestina a hedonistic variety of love. Rojas' pessimism makes them all come to tragic ends.

323. FOTHERGILL-PAYNE, Louise. "LC como esbozo de una lección maquiavélica." *RF* 81 (1969), 158-75.

The *Principe* offered as a possible source of influence on the thought and formation of LC.

324. _____. "La cambiante faz de la Celestina: Cinco adaptaciones de fines del siglo XVI." *Cel* 8, i (May 1984), 29-41.

The five texts all contain allegorizations of LC with two ends in view: to act as a shield for critical attacks (of moral, religious, and political nature)—all perceived by the trained reader—and to help in educating the less well-versed reader to appreciate such abstractions. The works commented upon are: *Comedia intitulada Doleria* (1572) de P. Hurtado de la Vega; *Comedia décima de El Infamador* (h. 1579) de Juan de la Cueva; *General Auto de la Esposa, en los Cantares* (h. 1579) de López de Ubeda; *Comedia Salvaje* (1582) de J. Romero de Cepeda, y *Quinta comedia y auto sacramental de los amores del Alma con el Príncipe de la Luz* (última década del XVI).

325. FOULCHE-DELBOSC, Raymond [with Adolphe COSTER]. "Observations sur LC." *Revue Hispanique* 78 (1930), 545-99.

Takes up the thread of previous studies with the same title [RH 7 (1900), 28-80 and RH 9 (1902), 171-99]. Describes five '1502' editions of the TCM, three from Seville, and one each from Salamanca and Toledo. The comparison and comments are still valid but the filiations of these five must be adjusted to conform with Norton's discoveries (1966). Also considers a 'lost' pre-1499 CCM and the 1500 TCM (Salamanca).

326. FRADEJAS, José. "LC," in *Literatura en España*, I, ed. F. Ynduráin and M. Alvar (Madrid: Ed. Nacional, 1972), 345-425.

A student anthology. The LC section has a brief prologue that touches on many relevant LC problems and tells the basic story through excerpts from Acts 1, 3-7, 10 and 12-21. The omitted acts are represented only by their 'argumentos'.

327. FRAKER, Charles F. "The Importance of Pleberio's Soliloquy." RF 78 (1966), 515-29.

He argues against Bataillon (1961) and Green (1965), in affirming that the summation Pleberio's speech gives to the themes presented throughout LC (love as a destructive force and Fortune's arbitrary role in human endeavor) was designed expressly as Rojas' final commentary on them.

328. _____. "Rhetoric in the *Celestina*: Another Look," in *Aureum Saeculum Hispanum. Beiträge zu Texten des Siglo de Oro* (Festschrift für Hans Flasche zum 70. Geburtstag), ed. K.-H. Körner and D. Briesemeister (Weisbaden: F. Steiner, 1983), 81-90.

Discusses the possibility that Rojas may have known of Terence through the writings of Donatus. This would allow us to see the *local* sense (direct or immediate use) of the rhetorical figures in the development of Rojas' art, a sense that distinguishes LC from all other humanistic comedies.

329. _____. "Argument in the *Celestina* and in its Predecessors," in *Homenage a Stephen Gilman. Revista de estudios hispánicos* (Puerto Rico) (1982), 81-86.(*)

330. _____. "Declamation and the *Celestina*." *Cel* 9, ii (Fall 1985).(*)

331. FRANK, Rachel. "Four Paradoxes in *The Celestina*." RR 38 (1947), 53-68.

Seen in the light of the norm of the sentimental novel (*Fiammetta, De duobus amantibus, Deifira, Cárcel de amor*), LC's apparent paradoxes are all solved. Rojas wanted to merge the two worlds he portrays in his work.

332. FREIRE. Tabaré J. *La Celestina*. Montevideo: La Casa del Estudiante, 1977. 123p. (Cuadernos de literatura)

A reading of LC in four parts. The first deals with external-to-text matters: editions, authorship, genre, sources, etc. The second defends the idea that LC was intended as a dramatic work, although with no goal of stage presentation. The third section is given over to characterization and the fourth to the superiority of the CCM over the TCM.

333. FUENTES DE AYNAT, José María. "La botica de la Celestina." *Medicamenta* 5, no. 44 (1951), 267-68.

Discussion of Pármeno's Act 1 description of Celestina and her house, concluding that such a realistic portrayal must have had an actual model.

G

334. GALLARDO, José Luis. "Hacia una interpretación 'otra' de LC." *Boletín Millares Carlo* 1, no. 1 (June 1980), 167-78.

A declaration that LC would respond well to a semiotic analysis.

335. GALLO, Ivana and Emma SCOLES. "Edizioni antiche della *Celestina* sconosciute o non localizzate dalla tradizione bibliografica." *Cultura neolatina* 43 (1983), 1-17.

A full description and register of locations for seven editions of LC before 1635 not known to Penney [1954] (Seville 1535; Estella 1557 and 1560; Valladolid 1561-62; Medina 1563 and 1566; and an unidentified one which N. Griffith [1980] believes to be from Valladolid), plus ten others known to Penney but for which no copies had been located (Seville 1528, 1536 and 1582; Burgos 1531 and 1536; Antwerp 1558; Cuenca 1561; Alcalá 1569, and Salamanca 1577). Additionally, for translations of the Spanish original, there are nine entries (often with multiple locations listed) of which six are Italian (Venice 1515, 1525, 1531 [2 eds.] and 1543; Milan 1519), two are French (Lyon 1529 and Rouen 1644) and one is German (Augsburg 1534).

336. GALLY, Héctor. "Filosofía de LC." *Tiempo* (Bogotá) (May 8 1977), Lecturas Dominicales, 6.

In her own way, Celestina is honest and decent. She is compared favorably to a similar character in Molière's *Tartuffe*. The real villains of LC are Sempronio and Pármeno.

337. GARAY, René. "El concepto de la máscara en LC." *Cel* 5, ii (Fall 1981), 33-38. [Read first as a paper; an abstract was printed in the *Tennessee Philological Bulletin* 18 (July 1981) 48-49.]

Celestina arranges and controls all actions in which she plays a part through deep self-awareness and discipline: she is capable of being both actress and dramaturge in her world. She fuses the roles instinctively and gains a superiority over others. Rojas' insight fashions this triumph of characterization.

338. GARCIA BACCA, J. D. "Sobre el sentido de 'conciencia' en la *Celestina*." *Revista de Guatemala* 6, no. 2 (1946), 52-66; *Humanitas* (Nuevo León, México) 14 (1973), 106-17.

Philosophical consideration of different interpretations of the concept of 'conscience' throughout history. In LC it is of a sentimental nature, similar to that which is on view in the works of Unamuno.

339. GARCIA DE ENTERRIA, M. C. "Un pliego de 1513," in her *Literaturas marginadas* (Lectura crítica de la literatura española, 22; Madrid: Playor, 1983), 53-67.

The *pliego* is the "Romance nuevamente hecho de Calisto y Melibea ...," with 780 octosyllables rhyming in -*á*. This transformation of LC is a narrative ballad, expertly adapted and condensed, frequently citing the original (eight passages are cited). Narration prevails over dialogue but the mixture proves to be aesthetically pleasing.

340. GARCIA GOMEZ, Emilio. "Celestinas en la España musulmana." *Anales Cervantinos* 1 (1940-41), 190-91.

The two Muslim forerunners of Celestina appear in the 11th-century *EL collar de la paloma* of Ben Hazm and in a 12th-century poem of Ben Said.

341. GARCIA RODRIGUEZ, J. M. "LC: época, autor e influencias." *La Torre* 20, nos. 75-76 (1972), 180-90.

Not very detailed. The Marqués de Santillana appears as a forerunner of Rojas in the use of refrains, but the other sources mentioned are familiar.

342. GARCI-GOMEZ, Miguel. "'Amor impervio' o 'amor improuo' (LC I, 94)." *Cel* 4, ii (Fall 1980), 3-8.

The reading "Y no le juzgues a él [Calisto] flaco, que el amor *impervio* todas las cosas vence" is clarified. The adjective is given the meaning of 'compelling, audacious' by virtue of a long list of such usages in literary texts before Rojas. Criado de Val's reading (entries 205, 206) of 'difficult, unattainable' is rejected.

343. _____. "'Huevos asados': afrodisíaco para el marido de Celestina." *Cel* 5, i (May 1981), 23-34.

Follows the long history of eggs as an aphrodisiac as a preliminary to suggesting a clarification of the phrase: "¡O que comedor de huevos asados era su marido!" (Act 1), meaning Celestina's husband. Examples are given from the Greco-Roman world and from medieval Europe as well as Araby.

344. _____. "'Eras e Crato medicos': Identificación e interpretación." *Cel* 6, i (May 1982), 9-14.

Evidence is presented for the rejection of all later emendations of

Act 1's 'Eras e Crato ... O piedad de silencio ...', and for retention of this reading from the early *Comedias*.

345. _____. "Sobre el 'plebérico corazón' de Calisto y la razón de Pleberio." *Hispania* 66 (1983), 202-08.

By equating 'plebérico' with *pleberio* (a documented variant of *plebeo* and *plebeyo*), the meaning of the Act 1 reference would not be to either Melibea or Pleberio but, rather, to Calisto. This new reading would fit his state of dejection perfectly, his feelings of low worth and of being 'indigno'.

346. _____. "El sueño de Calisto." *Cel* 9, i (May 1985), 11-22.

Studies the role played by dreaming (or day-dreaming) in the TCM, and concludes that for the author of Act 1, Calisto was in his bedroom day-dreaming about Melibea (this "vision" is the substance of scene 1). Rojas later (Act 2) invents another explanation that converts the dream sequence into a real encounter but continues to keep the 'dreamer' aspect as part of Calisto's personality.

347. GARIANO, Carmelo. "Amor y humor en LC." ACTAS: 51-66.

Love in LC is presented with humor quite often: the sentimental hyperbole, comic degradation, trite language, obscene gesture, satire, the grotesque and erotic irony. Many examples from the text show this treatment of worldly love.

348. _____. "El erotismo grotesco en LC." *Vórtice* 1, no. 3 (1975), 2-16.

The grotesque flourishes when the old have not relinquished control and the young have not yet grasped it. There is much ground for development of an erotic view here and it is explored in the physical deformations, the dehumanizations of personality, the profanation of the divine and in the intrusion of the infernal and the exaltation of vice.

349. GARRIDO PALLARDO, Fernando. *Los problemas de Calisto y Melibea y el conflicto de su autor*. Figueras: Ed. Canigó, 1957. 109p.

The fifteen (all listed) contradictions and impossibilities of the text of LC all disappear as the author, assuming that Pleberio, Alisa and Melibea are a family of 'conversos', explicates their hidden meanings.

a. *Destino* (April 18 1958), 39-40, A. Llopis
b. *Indice* 11, no. 109 (1959), 23, E. García Luengo
c. TLS (June 19 1959), 368, J. M. Cohen
d. TLS (July 3 1959), 399, E. M. Wilson; there is a reply from the author of the June 19 article at the end of this article
e. TLS (July 10 1959), 411, P. E. Russell, T. E. May, and yet another reply from the author of the June 19th article
f. TLS (July 17 1959), 423, A. D. Deyermond

350. _____. "Un secreto muy mal guardado." *Canigó* 74 (April 1960). (*)

351. GARRO, J. Eugenio. "Ensayo psicológico sobre la Celestina." *Anales de la Universidad de Chile*, no. 92 [= Third Series, no. 13] (1934), 5-16.

Goya's painting 'Consejos galantes' is a point of departure for some thoughts on the character of Celestina: she is instinct itself and is a superior practitioner of all her arts. She is a symbol for an age which mastered the commercialization of love.

352. GASCON VERA, Elena. "Celestina, Dama Filosofía." *Cel* 7, ii (Fall 1983), 3-10.

A study showing how the vertical structures of the dialogic situation that prevail in Boethius' *De consolatione philosophiae* are parodied when utilized in LC, especially in the Celestina-Pármeno exchanges in Act 1, analyzed here, and in the Celestina-Pármeno and Celestina-Areúsa dialogues of Act 7.

353. GELLA ITURRIAGA, José. "444 refranes de LC." ACTAS: 245-68.

Rojas and Cervantes are masters of stringing together proverbs. The 444 are listed in order of appearance by act but are neither commented upon nor analyzed. There is an index of their key words.

354. GENSKE, Sylvia S. "LC in Translation Before 1530." Diss. New York Univ., 1978. 338p. DAI 39/06, 3562-63A. No. 78-24221. J. B. Hughes.

Studies the Italian translation of Hordognez (1506), the Hebrew of c. 1520, the English printing of Rastell (c. 1525) and the French of 1527.

355. GERDAY, Jacqueline. "Le caractère des *rameras* dans LC. De la *Comédie* à la *Tragicomédie*. A propos d'une hypothèse de M. R. Lida de Malkiel." *Revue des Langues Vivantes* 33 (1967), 185-204.

Lida de Malkiel (1962) maintains that there is inconsistency in the roles and characterization of Elicia and Areúsa (in the interpolations). This this article sets out to disprove that assertion.

356. _____. "Le remaniement formel des actes primitifs dans LC de 1502." AION-SR 10 (1968), 175-82.

The theory is that Rojas, in expanding the CCM, was intent on removing words and phrases that were either superfluous or not very expressive.

357. GERITZ, Albert J. "Recent Studies in John Rastell." *English Literary Renaissance* 8 (1978), 341-50.

Some items deal with the attributed interlude, *Calisto and Melebea* (c. 1525), the first English adaptation of LC.

358. _____. "*Calisto & Melebea* [John Rastell?]: A Bibliography." *Cel* 3, ii (Fall 1979), 45-50.

Biographical studies; general and detailed interpretative studies; and studies on the authorship question of the *Interlude*.

359. _____. "*Calisto & Melebea* (c. 1530)." *Cel* 4, i (May 1980), 17-29.

Presents some points of contact between Rojas and Rastell. Notes similarities and differences, but nicely perceives the distinct moral purpose of the English version as well as its own internal unity.

360. GERLI, E. Michael. "LC, Act I, Reconsidered: Cota, Mena ... or Alfonso Martínez de Toledo?" KRQ 23 (1976), 29-46.

An accumulation of similarities between Act 1 of LC and the *Corbacho* makes it conceivable that Martínez de Toledo was its author.

361. _____. "Pleberio's Lament and Two Literary Topoi: *Expositor* and *Planctus*." RF 88 (1976), 67-74.

Rojas' Act 21 *planctus* inverts the traditional values associated with the topos. Also true of the *expositor/interpres* topos which, instead of merely summing up, breaks loose from its conventions and takes on a personal, introspective dynamic. Both ruptures of tradition confirm the negative world view of Rojas.

362. _____. "'Mira a Bernardo': Alusión sin sospecha." *Cel* 1, ii (Fall 1977), 7-10.

The Bernardo of LC, Act 1, is not the saint from Clairvaux as some critics have averred (Forcadas, entry 316) but rather the well-known Catalan poet, Bernat de Cabrera, who often wrote in an antifeminist vein.

363. _____. "Calisto's Hawk and the Image of a Medieval Tradition." *Romania* 104 (1983), 83-101.

The symbolic hunt (with falcon) as a metaphor for the pursuit of love is widespread in medieval European letters (amply documented here). Rojas utilizes it as a subversive device in LC. The assumption that Rojas and the author of Act 1 share this view is conjecture, however, as scene 1 of Act 1 contains no textual reference to the hunt.

364. GERSTINGER, Heinz. "LC," in *Lope de Vega and Spanish Drama* (New York: Ungar, 1974), 67-80. The German original, *Spanische Komödie: Lope de Vega und seine Zeitgenossen*, is Velber: Friedrich, 1968.

Situates LC in the line of development of the *comedia*, especially of the cape and sword type, with which it shares several characteristics. Some discussion of theatrical adaptations of LC to stress its eternal vitality.

365. GIANNONE, Luigi. "Pietro Aretino and Spanish Literary Influences in His Works." Diss. New York Univ., 1979. 188p. DAI 40/03, 1452A. No. 79-18962. R. J. Clements.

Chapter Four compares LC with Aretino's *La Talanta* and *La Cortigiana*.

366. GIFFORD, D. J. "El mundo de Trotaconventos," in *Congreso Internacional Sobre el Arcipreste de Hita*, ed. M. Criado de Val (Barcelona: SERESA, 1973), 129-38.

The figure of the go-between changes from Juan Ruiz' time to Rojas', along with the social order. Gifford asks questions and makes suggestions about this trajectory while citing documents as illustration. See especially pp. 135-38 for LC.

367. _____. "Magical Patter: The Place of Verbal Fascination in LC," in *Medieval and Renaissance Studies on Spain and Portugal in Honour of P. E. Russell*, ed. F. W. Hodcroft et al (Oxford: SSMLL, 1981), 30-37.

A brief excursus into incantatory techniques employed by Rojas for the psychological purpose of, first, lulling a person into lowering his or her resistance to something the enchanter desires, and, then, releasing the real message, which is often contained in a name. Alliterative sounds, rhythms and rhymes are some of the ingredients in charm-weaving, exploited by Celestina (with Melibea as victim) in acts 4 and 10.

368. GILLET, Joseph E. "'Comedor de huevos'(?): LC, Aucto I." HR 24 (1956), 144-47.

Two meanings are possible: infidelity on the part of the wife or amorous excess on the part of the husband. Positing a modified reading of "encomendador de huevos," Gillet believes it may have been an allusion to the conferring of supernatural powers, a meaning the context will support.

369. _____, ed. *"Propalladia" and Other Works of Bartolomé de Torres Naharro*, vol. 4 (1961). Bryn Mawr, Pennsylvania [Menasha, Wisconsin: Banta Publishing Co.], 1943-[1961].

Insightful comments on LC in the larger context of Renaissance drama. See the book's Index, under 'Celestina'.

370. GILLIBERT, Jean. "La chute des masques." *Rencontres* (Chateauvallon), no. 9 (January-February 1971), p. 2. (*)

371. _____. "LC." *Association Technique par l'Action Culturelle-Informations* (Paris), no. 42 (1972), 8-9.

LC reveals a strong eternal mythology, elemental and sensual, in which all is subordinated to the character of Celestina. Gillibert has constructed an adaptation along these general lines, with modifications, cuts, and reductions in the number of Rojas' characters. He staged this adaptation at Le Centre de Rencontres at Chateauvallon, July 20-27 1972, with María Casares as Celestina (see entries 1050.1 and 1050.2).

372. GILMAN, Stephen. "El tiempo y el género literario en LC." RFH 7 (1945), 147-59.

Time in LC plays a psychological role and is used for characterization in Rojas' hands: it is not truly chronological. This material also appears in Chapter 7 of Gilman's *The Art* (1956).

373. _____. "Diálogo y estilo en LC." NRFH 7 (1953), 461-69.

The word 'style' itself comes under Gilman's scrutiny. Rojas, in his search for exact words and expressions, cultivated change in language which affected the artistic process in LC. His dialogue is a ground for encounter of the *tú* and the *yo* and the setting for his stylistic innovations. This material is reprised in Chapter 2 of his *The Art* (1956).

374. _____. "A propos of 'El tiempo en LC' by Manuel J. Asensio." HR 21 (1953), 42-45.

Asensio's claim (entry 40) that there is a temporal gap between the first scene and the rest of Act 1 is not supported by the text. Previous literary tradition allows as how many lovers fall in love at first sight; therefore, no time gap is required.

375. _____. "The Argumentos to LC." *RPh* 8 (1954-55), 71-78.

The 'argumentos' to CCM compared to those of TCM. In his interpolations, Rojas(?) was intent on showing better the motivation of the action, while the author of the 'argumentos' was more concerned with a simple scheme of events in chronological order.

a. RJ 6 (1953-54), 330, n. 31a, M. Kruse

376. _____. "Fortune and Space in LC." RF 66 (1955), 342-60.

Deals with the artistic function of the way space is used in LC and the way it dovetails with Fortune's intervention throughout.

377. _____. *The Art of "LC"*. Madison: Univ. of Wisconsin Press, 1956. 262p. Rpt. Westport, Connecticut: Greenwood Press, 1976.

Almost an existentialist line is taken: the characters are allowed to 'create' themselves as they freely involve each other in dialogue (or speak to themselves). In so doing, they also create time and space in the work. This stylized *tú* and *yo* are the central nervous system and the dynamic center of Rojas' art (see entry 389).

a. *RPh* 10 (1956-57), 302-04, E. S. Morby
b. RFE 41 (1957), 434-38, M. Seco
c. NRFH 11 (1957), 215-24, M. Bataillon
d. HR 25 (1957), 1-25, L. Spitzer. Gilman replies in a rejoinder to Spitzer in HR 25 (1957), 112-21, and another reply comes from J. R. Andrews and J. H. Silverman ("On Destructive Criticism: A Rejoinder to Mr. Leo Spitzer") in *Modern Language Forum* 42 (1957), 3-24.
e. MLR 52 (1957), 122-23, A. I. Watson
f. *Hispania* 40 (1957), P. G. Earle
g. BHS 34 (1957), 160-67, P. E. Russell
h. RF 69 (1957), 171-76, H. Baader
i. BICC 13 (1958), 278-79, F. Suárez Pineda
j. RHM 25 (1959), 117, A. Porqueras-Mayo
k. *Vox Romanica* 18 (1959), 151-57, F. Monge

378. _____. "The Fall of Fortune: From Allegory to Fiction." *Filologia Romanza* 4 (1957), 337-54.

The juxtaposition of space and fortune must be understood clearly if Rojas' art is to be appreciated. It helps LC to straddle two worlds in transition.

379. _____. "The Spanish Writer, Fernando de Rojas."

Yearbook of the American Philosophical Society (1961), 503-05.

Report on Gilman's research on biographical documents in Spain.

380. _____, and Michael J. RUGGERIO. "Rodrigo de Reinosa and LC." RF 73 (1961), 255-84.

Reinosa's work, and the *Coplas de las comadres* in particular, may have provided many of the expressions used in LC.

381. _____. "Rebirth of a Classic," in *Varieties of Literary Expression*, ed. S. Burnshaw (New York: New York Univ. Press, 1962), 283-305.

New translations into English, French, German and Russian prove the continuing popularity of LC. Gilman takes the opportunity to assess the permanent qualities of Rojas' masterwork.

382. _____. "The Case of Alvaro de Montalbán." MLN 78 (1963), 113-25.

On the Inquisition's investigation of A. de M., Rojas' father-in-law.

383. _____. "Fernando de Rojas as Author." RF 76 (1964), 255-90.

Gilman does not accept that LC corresponds to intentions or criteria principally didactic in nature. For him LC is revolutionary (he gives interesting analyses of Rojas' understanding of concepts/words like 'solo' and 'gozo') in its use of irony. It is an irony that accords well with a man who must dwell in a society in which he feels uncomfortable.

a. RFE 50 (1967), 363-64, A. Llorente Maldonado

384. _____. "The 'conversos' and the Fall of Fortune." *Collected Studies in Honour of Américo Castro's 80th Year* (Oxford: Lincombe Lodge Research Library, 1965), 127-36.

The most important representative of the first generation of 'conversos' is Rojas. As a group, they showed a predilection for the works of Petrarch and particularly for a neo-Stoic interpretation of Fortune.

385. _____, and Ramón GONZALVEZ. "The Family of Fernando de Rojas." RF 78 (1966), 1-26.

Documents are discussed which support the contention that Rojas felt alienated in his world and society. It is further suggested that he may have been born in Toledo instead of La Puebla de Montalbán.

a. RFE 51 (1968), 298, A. Llorente Maldonado

386. _____. "Mollejas el hortelano." *Estudios Dedicados a James Homer Herriott* (Madison: Univ. of Wisconsin Press, 1966), 103-07.

The LC reference to this person (Act 12) is explained in the light of its continued use in Feliciano de Silva's *Segunda Celestina*.

a. *RPh* 24 (1970-71), 148, A. D. Deyermond

387. _____. "Matthew 5.10 in Castilian Jest and Earnest." *Studia Hispanica in honorem R. Lapesa*, 1 (Madrid: Cátedra-Seminario Menéndez Pidal, 1972), 257-65.

A perverted use of a Biblical phrase which promises salvation to the persecuted occurs in LC (Act 7). Its use there may well account for its appearance later in the *Lazarillo*.

388. _____. *The Spain of Fernando de Rojas: The Intellectual and Social Landscape of LC*. Princeton: Princeton Univ. Press, 1972. xv + 559p.

A study in depth of the period through its documents, its atmosphere and its realities, in order to recreate for the modern reader a sense of the circumstances in which the 'converso' Rojas succeeded in creating LC. (See also entry 578.)

a. *Library Journal* 97 (December 1 1972), 3913, R. Neiswender
b. *Choice* 10 (April 1973), 295, Anon.
c. MLN 88 (1973), 410-14, R. L. Kagan
d. *Speculum* 49 (1974), 730-34, B. Dutton
e. *Hispania* 57 (1974), 180, W. D. Truesdell
f. *RenQ* 27 (1974), 353-55, J. Casalduero
g. BH 76 (1974), 192-202, J. Rodríguez-Puértolas
h. TLS (April 5 1974), 373, A. D. Deyermond
i. *Sin Nombre* 5, no. 2 (1974-75), 104-07, L. López Baralt
j. BHS 52 (1975), 158-61, K. Whinnom
k. CL 27 (1975), 59-74, P. E. Russell; rpt. in his *Temas de LC y otros estudios* (entry 800), 343-75. (See also entry 390.)
l. RR 66 (1975), 156-58, M. Durán
m. MLR 70 (1975), 659-61, N. G. Round
n. HR 45 (1977), 80-83, A. G. Reichenberger
o. REH 11 (1977), 158-59, A. E. Wiltrout
p. RF 90 (1978), 548-50, T. Heydenreich

389. _____. *LC: Arte y estructura* (Spanish version by Margit Frenk Alatorre). Madrid: Taurus, 1974. 408p. Paper (Col. Persiles, 71).

Gilman has amplified aspects of the final two chapters for this version of his earlier book (see entry 377).

a. *Est Lit*, no. 546 (1974), 1819, J. M. Diez Borque
b. *La vanguardia española* (Barcelona), no. 33,763 (December 27 1974), 53, L. Bonet
c. BH 77 (1975), 234-35, P. Heugas

390. _____. "Sobre la identidad histórica de Fernando de Rojas." NRFH 26 (1977), 154-58.

A response in article form to Russell's CL review of *The Spain* (see above, entry 388.k). Clarification of the way in which he wants to see Rojas as a member of a class, a 'morada vital' in his own place and time. To understand this is a preliminary to appreciating the genius of LC.

391. _____. *La España de Fernando de Rojas. Panorama intelectual y social de LC*. Madrid: Taurus, 1978. 534p. (Col. Persiles, 107)

The Spanish translation of his 1972 volume (see entry 388).

a. *El País* (February 11 1979), 'Revistas', 2, J. M. Diez Borque
b. *Reseña*, no. 119 (April-May 1979), 18, Anon.
c. *Insula*, no. 390 (May 1979), 1, 14, L. Cañizal de la Fuente
d. BHS 57 (1980), 88, R. Wright

392. _____. "A Generation of Conversos." *RPh* 33 (1979-80), 87-101.

The Act 3 speech by Sempronio ("Ganada es granada...") is the point of departure for the discussion of an ahistoric sense that must have been typical of that first generation of 'conversos'. The negativism in it is so strong that Gilman is led to wonder not that Rojas wrote just a single book, but that he succeeded in writing anything at all.

393. GIRALDO JARAMILLO, Gabriel. "Don Juan Rodríguez Freyle y LC." *Boletín de Historia y Antigüedades* (Bogotá) 27 (1940), 582-86; rpt. in his *Estudios históricos* (Bogotá: Ed. Santafé, 1954), 213-23.

On the influence of LC in Freyle's *El carnero*, a 16th-century Mexican work.

394. GIUSTI, Roberto F. "Fernando de Rojas: su obra de humanidad española y de arte renacentista." BAAL 12 (1943), 121-42.

Divided into two discussions. The first is about Rojas, his family, his house, his library, etc. The second is an appreciation of LC as a Renaissance masterpiece.

395. GODDARD, V. C. "Sancho de Muñón: A Background Study and a Critical Edition of his *Tragicomedia de Lysandro y Roselia*". Diss. Birkbeck College of London Univ., 1978. (*)

396. GOLDMAN, Peter B. "A New Interpretation of 'comedor de huevos asados' (LC, Aucto I)." RF 77 (1965), 363-67.

Jews traditionally eat eggs when one of their own dies. Goldman reads the LC text figuratively to mean that Celestina's husband is declaring her to be 'dead' as far as he is concerned, this being the implication of the allusion.

a. RFE 50 (1967), 375-76, A. Llorente Maldonado

397. GOMULICKI, Juliusz W. "*Celestyna*, Lingen i Leon Schiller." *Pamietnik Teatralny* (Warsaw) 23 (1979), 343-61 [In Polish].

Reminiscences of the author's meeting in Lingen with Leon Schiller, a meeting that would lead the author to translate and Schiller to produce in Polish a stage version of *Celestina* based on Achard's 1942 French version. The staged version took place in Lodz in 1947.

398. GONZALEZ BOIXO, J. C. "La ambigüedad en LC." *Archivum* 29-30 (1979-80), 5-26.

Offers a discussion of ambiguities, contradictions, incongruencies and incidents lacking in verisimilitud in LC. Areas explored are: 1) the easy access to Melibea's garden; 2) the passing of time; 3)the change in Melibea; 4) the failure to seek marriage; 5) Alisa's behavior; 6) Pármeno's treasure; and 7) the summary execution of Sempronio and Pármeno. Both the author of Act 1 and Rojas seem less interested in anecdotal realism as they are in properly motivating—from the point of view of psychology—characters and actions.

399. GONZALEZ OLLE, Fernando. "El problema de la autoría de LC. Nuevos datos y revisión del mismo." RFE 43 (1960), 439-45.

On the basis of the use of the diminutive, a clear difference between the first act and the rest of the work has important implications for the authorship controversy.

400. _____. *Los sufijos diminutivos en castellano medieval*. Madrid: CSIC, 1962.

Pages 87-95 are the relevant ones. The bulk of the usages in LC are assigned to the members of the lower class and this has implications for valuations of Rojas' aesthetics.

401. GONZALEZ ROLDAN, Tomás. "Rasgos de la alcahuetería en la literatura latina." ACTAS: 275-89.

Studies traits of the figure in four Plautine plays (*Asinaria, Cistellaria, Curculio, Mostellaria*), an elegy by Tibullus (Engl.), and sections of a *Metamorphoses* by Apuleius. They are all perfected in LC.

402. GOYTISOLO, Juan. "La España de Fernando de Rojas." *Triunfo* (August 30 1975); rpt. in his *Disidencias* (Barcelona: Seix Barral, 1977), 13-35.

Agrees with Gilman (1972) in believing that a full understanding of Rojas' status as 'converso' is fundamental to appreciating LC and its world of lost values. The ruling ego of the characters is a sign of Rojas' rejection of his society. There is some modern counterpart in De Sade.

403. _____. "Notas sobre *La lozana andaluza*." *Triunfo* (March 1976); rpt. in his *Disidencias* (Barcelona: Seix Barral, 1977), 37-61.

Delicado, exiled in Italy, was an admirer of LC, and this article is devoted to providing textual examples to prove it, comparing and contrasting LC and *Lozana*.

404. GRAU, Mariano. "Las sendas de LC." *Estudios Segovianos* 5, no. 15 (1953), 371-72.

The practices of go-betweens have Semitic origins, according to Grau. He reviews a document from 1501 which details practices quite similar to those portrayed in LC and which were associated with the Jewry.

405. GREEN, Otis H. "On Rojas' Description of Melibea." HR 14 (1946), 254-56.

Rojas followed the medieval tradition of *amplificatio* in Calisto's Act 1 description of Melibea.

406. _____. "The *Celestina* and the Inquisition." HR 15 (1947), 211-16.

Registers some details of parts of LC censured in 1640, as well as some inconsistencies in censors' practices.

407. _____. "Fernando de Rojas, 'converso' and 'hidalgo'." HR 15 (1947), 384-87.

Rojas was not a covert judaizer, but a practicing Christian. He was a 'converso' only in the broadest sense of the term.

408. _____. "Additional Note on the *Celestina* and the Inquisition." HR 16 (1948), 70-71.

Some complaints were lodged in 1609 but produced no censoring of LC; LC was censored later, in 1640, for the first time.

409. _____. "La furia de Melibea." *Clavileño* 4 (March-April 1953), 1-3.

Melibea's anger is a response to the uncourtliness of Calisto.

410. _____. "LC aucto I: 'Minerva con el can'." NRFH 7 (1953), 470-74.

Proposes the alternate reading: "Minerva con Vulcán."

411. _____. "'Lo de tu abuela con el ximio' (LC, Auto I)." HR 24 (1956), 1-12.

Sempronio's insinuation is part of a pan-European tradition reaching from the Bible to Locke and Voltaire.

412. _____ *Spain and the Western Tradition*, vol. 1 (Madison: Univ. of Wisconsin Press, 1963), 111-22. The Spanish translation is *España y la tradición occidental* (Madrid: Gredos, 1969), 139-51.

It is the contravention of the courtly code which leads to all the tragedies in LC, a work entirely within the literary continuum. There is also a comparison of LC to Torres Naharro's *Comedia Himenea*.

a. RL 27 (1965), 199-204 (at 203), C. Morón Arroyo
b. *RPh* 19 (1965-66), 646, P. E. Russell
c. *Hispania* 50 (1967), 1012, M. Durán

413. _____. "Did the 'World' 'Create' Pleberio?" RF 77 (1965), 108-10.

The significance of Pleberio's lament is that it asks questions about the relationships of man to his world and explores them.

a. RFE 50 (1967), 376-77, A. Llorente Maldonado
b. *Hispanófila*, no. 30 (1967), 71, R. Bosch

414. GRIFFIN, Clive. "Four Rare Editions of LC." MLR 75 (1980), 561-74.

Bibliographical commentary on exemplars either considered nonexistent or unknown before now: one is in Leningrad (Valladolid: N. Thierry, between 1526 and 1540) and three are in Cracow (Estella: A. de Anvers, 1560; Cuenca: J. de Cánova, 1561; and Medina del Campo: F. del Canto, 1563).

415. GRIFFIN, Julia Ortiz. "Class Struggle in LC." Homenaje a Humberto Piñera (Madrid: Playor, 1979), 187-95.

LC presents anarchy in the social order through its portrayal of class struggle in late 15th-century Spain. With liberal text citations, Griffin advances the theory that the upper and lower classes represent equally evil forces.

416. GRISMER, Raymond L. "The Celestina and Its Continuations," in his The Influence of Plautus in Spain Before Lope de Vega (New York: The Hispanic Institute in the United States, 1944), 101-19.

Points up ideas, situations and textual similarities between a variety of Plautus' plays and works of the celestinesque genre.

417. GROULT, Pierre. "Une actualité d'autrefois et d'aujourd'hui: LC." LR 18 (1964), 329-41. A Spanish translation is in his Los místicos de los países bajos y la literatura espiritual española del siglo XVI (Madrid: Fundación Universitaria Española, 1976), II, 17-29.

Surveys recent LC studies such as Bataillon (1961), Lida de Malkiel (1962), Brault's ed. of the first French translation (entry 1049) and the new French translation of Heugas (entry 1048).

418. _____. "Une source méconnue de LC." LR 22 (1968), 202-27. For a Spanish translation, see previous entry citation, Los místicos II, 31-48.

The 13th tale of Pero Alfonso's Disciplina clericalis.

419. _____. "Sánchez de Vercial y su Libro de los exenplos por A.B.C." Cuadernos del Sur 10, no. 10 (1968-69), 1-30.

Discusses similarites of this work with the TCM on pp. 28-30.

420. GUARDIA MASSO, P. "Estudio del The Spanish Bawd de James Mabbe, con una referencia a la historia literaria de LC en Inglaterra hasta 1631." Thesis (Tesina). Barcelona, 1962. (*)

421. _____. "James Mabbe, eminente hispanista oxoniense del siglo XVII. Su personalidad literaria. Estudios de varios MSS inéditos y del The Spanish Bawd, London 1631." Diss. Barcelona, 1971. (*)

422. GUAZZELLI, Francesco. Una lettura della Celestina. Pisa: Univ. of Pisa, 1971. 105p. (Pubbl. del Istituto di Letteratura Spagnola e Ispanoamericana, 22)

Theorizes on the structure and the genre of LC in the light of new developments in literary theory, and illustrates with an analysis of the final four acts of the CCM and, in a separate section, the "Tratado de Centurio."

423. GULSTAD, Daniel E. "La lingüística y el texto de LC," in Actas del Quinto Congreso Internacional de Hispanistas (1974) (Bordeaux: Instituto de Estudios Ibéricos e Iberoamericanos-Univ. of Bordeaux III, 1977), 459-65.

Argues for re-opening the whole question of authorship of Act 1, Acts 2-16, and the interpolations of the TCM. Many people are swayed by the study of Criado de Val (1955) and Gulstad thinks the study presents a weak case for the rejection of Rojas as author of Act 1 (even though more solid linguistic evidence might bear out such a conclusion).

424. _____. "Melibea's Demise: The Death of Courtly Love." LaC 7 (1978-79), 71-80.

The idea is that the spark for the CCM may have first come from the classical tales of heroines' suicides (Hero, Thisbe, Dido) after the loss of their respective lovers. Melibea's fall may have in turn given rise to the plan for the 'falling' of Pármeno, Sempronio and Calisto. Melibea's fall from the tower is the fall of idealized woman from her pedestal; hence, the death of courtly love.

425. GURZA, Esperanza. "Una lectura existencialista de LC." Diss. Univ. of California-Riverside, 1974. 354p. DAI 35/09, 6137-38A. No. 755118. C. Ayllón. (See the following entry.)

426. _____. Lectura existencialista de LC. Madrid: Gredos, 1977. 351p. (Biblioteca Románica Hispánica, Estudios y Ensayos, 257)

An innovative study which draws much material for consideration from the parallels and emphases on the common individual that exist between the work and thought of Rojas and that of many modern authors. Authors with whom Rojas is shown to have some affinities are Unamuno, Sartre, Camus, Kierkegaard, Bernanos and Jaspers. There are others as well.

a. Diario Hablado Cultural de Radio Nacional Española (May 1977), L. Blánquez B.
b. Crítica, no. 647 (July-August 1977), 24, E. Asis
c. Diario Las Américas (August 14 1977), 6, R. Campa
d. Arbor, nos. 381-82 (1977), 150-52, J. A. Míguez
e. Boletín de la Academia Colombiana 27 (1977), 143-44, Anon.
f. Ciudad de Dios 190 (1977), 675-76, L. Pérez Blanco
g. Est Lit, nos. 618-19 (1977), 2918-19, L. Landero Durán
h. Hispania 61 (1978), 999, G. P. Andrachuk
i. Cel 2, no. ii (November 1978), 39-47, C. Morón Arroyo
j. QIA, nos. 51-52 (1978-79), 212-14, J. R. Stamm
k. ETL 7 (1978-79), 214-15, T. Fonte
l. HR 47 (1979), 258-61, E. Berndt-Kelley
m. Speculum 54 (1979), 572-74, J. F. Burke
n. Rassegna Iberistica, no. 9 (1980), 34-36, D. Ferro
o. RPh 35 (1981-82), 557-59, F. Márquez

427. _____. "Celestina en el Círculo de Bellas Artes (Madrid)." Cel 9, i (May 1985), 56-62.

Report of the Mesa Redonda, the public exposition of LC-related materials, the actual performance of the play, and two concerts (one featuring sections of Felipe Pedrell's 1903 opera based on LC), all organized to inaugurate the opening of the Circulo's Sala Fernando de Rojas. Opinions reviewed include those of Elena GASCON VERA, Antonio MARAVALL, Fernando SAVATER, Agustín GARCIA CALVO, and the director and adapter of this *Celestina*, Angel FACIO.

428. GUTIERREZ, Violeta. "LC en las comedias de Lope de Vega." ETL 4 (1975-76), 161-68.

There is mostly information from Lope's *El caballero de Olmedo* in this analysis, although bits and pieces of others are also brought to bear on LC's echoes in Lope.

429. GUTIERREZ DE LA SOLANA, Alberto. "Literatura y criminalidad: Yago y Celestina." *Círculo* 7 (1978), 81-95.

Among literary villains, Celestina is seen as more sympathetic and humane than Iago, much less innately perverse. The discussion here is intended to refute the contrary opinion, sustained by Menéndez y Pelayo.

430. GUTIERREZ MORA, José Manuel. "Lo romántico en LC." *Etcaetera* (Guadalajara, Mexico) 1 (1950), 152-57.

Posits ten typical characteristics of 'lo romántico' and then proceeds to produce a list of textual citations (unidentified by act or edition) from LC to show that indeed this is the classification Rojas' work merits. No discussion, just lists.

H

431. HALLIBURTON, Lloyd. "Symbolic Implications of the *cadenilla* in LC: Unity, Disunity and Death." *RomN* 22 (1981-82), 94-97.

The gold chain, indivisible as object, provokes much conflict and division. This leads, symbolically, to the unchaining of passions and ends in the multiple tragedies of LC.

432. HANDY, Otis. "The Rhetorical and Psychological Defloration of Melibea." *Cel* 7, i (May 1983), 17-27.

A detailed account of the role of rhetorical style in Act 10, especially in the cat-and-mouse game played out by Celestina and her willing victim, Melibea.

433. HANRAHAN, Thomas, S. J. "Sin, LC and Iñigo López de Loyola." *RomN* 11 (1969-70), 385-91.

LC was a probable source of some ideas in Loyola's *Ejercicios espirituales* of 1548.

434. HARPER, G. Diane. "Style and Authorship in LC: A Linguistic Approach." Thesis. Univ of Georgia, 1969. B. Dutton.

435. HATHAWAY, Robert L. *Love in the Early Spanish Theatre*. Madrid: Playor, 1975. 308p.

As a source of dramatic material for theatre to 1585 (pre-Lope), LC is cited *passim*, with particular regard to its amorous entanglements and attitudes toward love.

436. _____. "*La egloga de Calisto y Melibea* de Ximénez de Urrea." NRFH 27 (1978), 314-30.

A new edition of this verse imitation of part of the TCM, from a copy in the British Library. The relevant sections of the TCM are also included to facilitate comparative study.

437. HATZFELD, Helmut. "Fernando de Rojas. LC: Acto XII, el primer encuentro de Calixto y Melibea," in his *Explicación de textos literarios* (Sacramento: California State Univ. Press, 1973), 22-32.

Analyzes a dialogue between the lovers to show how Rojas uses rhetoric and language in characterization. Rojas is a master of such techniques.

438. HAWKING, Jane. "Madre Celestina." AION-SR 9 (1967), 177-90.

A discussion centered on the multiple roles Celestina plays in the TCM.

439. HAYS, Peter L., and Robert REDFIELD. "Pynchon's Spanish Source for 'Entropy'." *Studies in Short Fiction* 16 (1979), 327-34.

Pynchon's tale from 1960 is thought to have been inspired in part by LC.

440. HELLER, J. H., and R. L. GRISMER. "Seneca in the Celestinesque Novel." HR 12 (1944), 29-48.

Senecan thought is found in LC and in *Penitencia de amor, Seraphina, Thebayda, La lozana andaluza* and *Lisandro y Roselia*. For LC, the conclusions would support the theory of a separate author for Act 1.

441. HELMAN, Albert [pseudonym for Lou LICHTVELD]. *De eeuwige koppelarster* (The Eternal Go-Betweeen). Amsterdam: G. A. Van Oorschot, 1949. 74p. (De vrije Bladen, 20) [In Dutch.]

Brief chapters cover editions, identity of the author of LC, the social reality it reflects, as well as ideological, psychological and literary aspects of the work.

442. HERNANDEZ ORTIZ, José A. "El paso de LC a *La lozana andaluza*," in his *La génesis artística de "La lozana andaluza": el realismo literario de Francisco Delicado* (Madrid: Ed. Aguilera, 1974), 128-37.

Delicado learned from LC and its influence is clear in *Lozana*. But he also developed some aspects more fully than did Rojas and took fiction another step closer to the full-blown picaresque.

443. HERNANDEZ PARDOS, José María. "'El silencio

escuda y suele encubrir'." *Hojas del lunes* (Barcelona, May 6 1974). (*)

444. HERRERO, Javier. "Celestina: The Aging Prostitute as Witch," in *Aging in Literature*, L. and L. M. Porter, eds. (Troy, Michigan: International Book Publishers, 1984), 31-47.

A characterization of Celestina as essentially diabolic. Her actions accompanied by her mastery of others through language acquire new dimensions in this light: presiding over her evil empire, she not only perverts all things but—ironically—brings about her own downfall.

445. _____. "Celestina's Craft: The Devil in the Skein." *BHS* 61 (1984), 343-351.

A textual commentary of a series of images and their potentially erotic readings (Celestina as *labrandera, cirujano, remendadora de vírgenes*, and the lexical items *serpiente, hilado, agujas, puntos, etc.*), an analysis of which can elucidate the complex organization and texture of LC. The author's exploration concentrates of Celestina's initial seduction of Melibea's will, preparatory to the eventual seduction of her body.

446. HERRERO-GARCIA, M. "LC," in his *Estimaciones literarias del siglo XVII* (Madrid: Ed. Voluntad, 1930), 9-60.

The influence and knowledge of LC in the 17th century was acute, especially with regard to the figure of Celestina, whose pandering, magical dealings, religious hypocrisy, wisdom, tippling and deceitful turn of language were used to flesh out the character of her literary offspring. Calisto, Melibea and others were known, too, but seem to have had lesser appeal.

447. HERRIOTT, James Homer. "The Authorship of Act 1 of LC." *HR* 31 (1963), 153-59.

In reviewing Deyermond (see entry 237), Herriott provides an interesting defense of his own view that Rojas could have been author of Act 1.

448. _____. *Towards a Critical Edition of LC. A Filiation of Early Editions* Madison: Univ. of Wisconsin Press, 1964. vii + 293p.

A study of significant variants results in the presentation of four 'families' of grouped texts. A series of charts and graphs sets this information before the expert. Meant to be a step towards the reconstruction of an *editio princeps* of the TCM.

    a. *Anuario de Letras* 5 (1965), 47-76, M. Ferreccio Podestá
    b. *Modern Language Journal* 49 (1965), 387-88, M. E. Barrick
    c. BHS 43 (1966), 61-62, G. D. Trotter
    d. *Hispania* 49 (1966), 346-47, C. F. Fraker, Jr.
    e. *Neophilologus* 50 (1966),166-67, H. Th. Oostendorp
    f. *RenN* 19 (1966), 268-75, A. D. Deyermond
    g. *Speculum* 41 (1966), 145-46, A. Rey
    h. ZRP 82 (1966), 22-40, K. Whinnom
    i. *RPh* 20 (1966-67), 254-56, M. J. Ruggerio
    j. *Symposium* 21 (1967), 358-60, E. J. Webber
    k. MLN 84 (1969), 343-48, D. W. McPheeters

449. _____. "The 'Lost' Zaragoza 1507 edition of LC." *Homenaje a Antonio Rodríguez-Moñino* 1 (Madrid: Castalia, 1966), 253-60.

A valuation of the importance of the recently accessible printing of Zaragoza 1507 in the reconstruction of an *editio princeps* of the TCM. It would be well to keep his theories in mind (see preceding entry) when assessing these points.

450. _____. "Notes on Selectivity of Language in LC." HR 37 (1969), 77-101.

A look at locutions, particularly those from popular speech. Also archaisms.

451. _____. "Fernando de Rojas as Author of Act 1 of LC." *Studia Hispanica in Honorem R. Lapesa* 1 (Madrid: Cátedra-Seminario Menéndez Pidal, 1972), 295-311.

Rojas wrote Act 1 when young and fearful of the Inquisition and the rest when mature and resigned to his lot in life. Herriott presents a series of unifying images, structures and ideas to support this claim and believes the language differences are consistent with the time lapsed between the author's two periods of writing.

452. HESSE, Everett W. "La función simbólica de la Celestina." BBMP 42 (1966), 87-95.

Celestina plays many roles: the Great Mother, Mother Nature, the Healer, the Hypocrite and the Wise Old Dame.

453. HEUGAS, Pierre. "Variation sur un portrait: de Mélibée à Dulcinée." BH 71 (1969), 5-30.

There is a parodic process of demythification of Love and the Lady in the post-troubadour era and it is in this line of demythification that Rojas and Cervantes create, respectively, Melibea and Dulcinea.

454. _____. "LC et sa descendance directe." Diss. (Lettres), Univ. of Bordeaux III, 1972. 613p. (See following entry.)

455. _____. *LC et sa descendance directe*. Bordeaux: Inst. d'Etudes Ibériques et Ibéro-Américaines de l'Université, 1973. 612p.

A detailed accounting of the many ways in which LC affected the literature which followed it. A history of the creation of the sub-genre of 'la celestinesca'.

    a. YWMLS 36 (1974), 271-72, A. K. G. Paterson
    b. CHA, no. 296 (1975), 452-56, J. Savoye
    c. BHS 53 (1976), 139-41, K. Whinnom
    d. HR 44 (1976), 284-86, K. Kish
    e. NRFH 25 (1976), 407-12, D. E. Eisenberg
    f. CHA, nos. 322-23 (1977), 285-305, A. Castro Díaz

456. _____. "Sur une scène censurée: Encina et LC." *Les cultures ibériques en devenir: Essais ... Marcel Bataillon* (Paris, 1979), 397-403.

The shape of a scene—and the language—in *Egloga de Plácida y*

Vitoriano, which takes place between Flugencia and Eritea, has its model in LC.

457. _____. "'¿LC, novela dialogada?," in *Seis lecciones sobre la España de los siglos de Oro* (Homenaje a M. Bataillon), ed. P. M. Piñero Ramírez y R. Reyes Cano (Sevilla: Univ.-Facultad de Filosofía y Letras, 54, 1981), pp. 161-77.

Exposition of what the author understands by 'dramatic' in term of the text of LC. While some practices do anticipate the later *comedia*, others (notably *descriptio*, the use of recurrence and of memory) are all reminiscent of well-known narrative techniques of the 16th century.

458. HICKS, Margaret R. "Love in LC." Thesis. Emory Univ., 1966. 85p. L. Alpera.

459. HILLARD, Ernest H. Kilgore. "Spanish Imitations of LC." Diss. Univ. of Illinois, 1957. 479p. DA 18/02, 588-89. No. 00-25229.

Coverage is from 1499 to 1650. Twenty-five works are analyzed in three categories: continuations, close imitations and free imitations.

460. HIMELBLAU, Jack. "A Further Contribution to the Ironic Vision in the *Tragicomedia*." *RomN* 9 (1967-68), 310-13.

The three categories of irony dealt with are of character, perspective and foreshadowing.

461. HODCROFT, Fred W. "LC: errores de interpretación en el estudio de su sintaxis." *Filología Moderna* 4, no. 14 (1964), 154-56.

Finds fault with the method and conclusions of Criado de Val's 1955 *Indice verbal*. (See also Hodcroft's review of that volume, 191.d.)

462. HOOK, David. "'¿Para quién edifiqué torres?': A Footnote to Pleberio's Lament." *Forum for Modern Language Studies* 14 (1978), 25-31.

This section of the lament is important and not only for the Petrarchan echoes it boasts. It reflects back on the previous developments and continues them in the present with new and fuller implications. Thus, the tower he built is the one Melibea leaps from, the trees he planted are the witnesses to her illicit lovemaking, and so forth.

463. _____. "The Genesis of the *Auto de Traso*." JHP 3 (1978-79), 107-20.

The textual history of the *Auto*, its stylistic and structural links to the main LC text, possible motives for its insertion in Toledo 1526, and much more.

464. _____. "'Fons curarum, fluvius lachrymarum': Three Variations Upon a Petrarchan Theme (Christine de Pisan, Fernando de Rojas and Fray Luis de Granada)." *Cel* 6, i (May 1982), 1-7.

In adapting part of Petrarch's letter in *De rebus familiaribus*, Rojas shows himself, in contrast to two of his contemporaries (who also know and use it), to be both more conservative—respecting the source—and more sensitive—in preserving better the affective nature of the 'fons curarum' theme.

465. _____. "'Andar a caça de perdizes con bueyes.'" *Cel* 8, i (May 1984), 47-48.

In order to show that this manner of hunting (alluded to by Pármeno in Act 11) was known in Rojas' Spain, texts of Pedro Carrillo de Huete (h. 1420) are cited.

466. _____. "Pármeno's 'Falso Boezuelo' Again." *Cel* 9, i (May 1985), 39-42.

A follow-up to the preceding entry, expanding the geographic areas in which hunting with a pantomime ox was known (bans forbidding the practice are cited). Analysis strengthens the notion that the remark, fully negative, would have been enjoyed by readers of Act 11.

467. HORN-MONVAL, M. "Fernando Rojas [sic] (1475?-1541)," in his *Répertoire bibliographique des traductions et adaptations françaises du théâtre étranger du XVe siècle à nos jours*, vol. 4 (Paris: Centre National de Recherches Scientifiques, 1961), 65-67.

Thirty-eight entries for the period 1524-1960.

468. HORRENT, Jules. "Cavilaciones bibliográficas sobre las primeras ediciones de LC." AION-SR 5 (1963), 301-09.

Posits a manuscript of the CCM (without the 'argumentos') before the printing of Burgos 1499(?) and provides a chronology for the early editions of both the CCM and the TCM.

469. HORS, E., and A. VALBUENA. "La biblioteca de Fernando de Rojas." RFE 17 (1930), 183.

An addition to the previous identification of books and editions mentioned in Rojas' testament (RFE 16 [1929], 384-88).

470. HORSTMEYER, Gabriele. "Die Kupplerin [Go-Between]. Studien zur Typologie im dramatischen Schrifttum Europas von den Griechen bis zur Französischen Revolution." Diss., Univ. of Cologne, 1972. (*)

LC is one of the works analyzed.

471. HORTON, James Frank. "A Syntactical Analysis of LC." Diss. Univ. of Oklahoma, 1970. 453p. DAI 31/06, 2881A. No. 70-22989. L. S. Poston, Jr.

Based on the CCM of Burgos 1499(?). A systematic study of grammar and constructions used as follows: in Act 1; in Acts 2-16; and in the 'argumentos'. The latter show a different hand, but there is insufficient evidence for declaring separate authors for Acts 1 and 2-16.

472. HOUCK, Helen P. "Mabbe's Paganization of the *Celestina*." PMLA 54 (1939), 422-31.

Mabbe's substitution of pagan references in his version results in some loss of the original's feel of mixed idealism and realism. Many examples are provided.

473. HUGHES, John B. "Orígenes de la novela picaresca: LC y *La lozana andaluza*," in *La picaresca*, ed. M. Criado de Val (Madrid: Fundación Universitaria Española, 1979), 327-34.

In its view of human weakness, *Lozana* takes a more charitable view than LC; as works by *conversos*, the former is more open and explicit in its criticisms than the latter, but retains a more elegiac vision because of its more charitable resolution.

474. HURTADO, Juan. "Una nota acerca de LC." *Revista de la Universidad de Madrid*, fasc. 1 (1943), 134-39.

Etymologies of the names of all of LC's characters, including Traso.

I

475. IVENTOSCH, Herman. "Renaissance *contaminatio*; The Technique of an Imitation of LC, *La Seraphina* (1517?)." *Symposium* 16 (1962), 17-27.

Menéndez y Pelayo to the contrary, the author thinks there are substantial traces of LC in *Seraphina*. Celestina's characteristics are divided between two characters, Artemia and Pinardo. The Crito scene is used with modifications. Differences are also profiled.

J

476. JOHNSON, Carroll B. "Cervantes as a Reader of LC." *Far Western Forum* 1 (1974), 233-47.

On Don Quijote's defense of the go-between and condemnation of the 'hechicero' from Part 1, chapter 22. It clearly portrays Cervantes' attitude toward Celestina.

477. _____. "'Libro, en mi opinión divi- /si encubriera más lo huma- .'" *Vórtice* 1, no. 2 (1974), 62-65.

Comparative study of LC and *Don Quijote*. Lucrecia/Maritornes is the flesh-and-blood woman; Melibea/Dulcinea is the idealized woman. Cervantes suppresses the 'humano' (heeding his own statement about LC) and goes on to develop the theme of the power of Art over Life, even to the extreme of converting life into a work of art.

478. JOHNSON, Julie G. "Three Celestinesque Figures of Colonial Spanish American Literature." *Cel* 5, i (May 1981), 41-46.

The three are from Bernal Díaz de Castillo's *Historia verdadera*, 'Coloquio XVI' of Fernán González de Eslava's *Coloquios espirituales y sacramentales* and Juan Rodríguez Freile's *El carnero*.

479. JONES, J. R. "Isidore and the Theatre." *Comparative Drama* 16 (1982), 26-48.

Pages 43-44 and note 26 (47-48) observe that an Isidorian view of classical theatre is still current in the 16th century as evidenced in two of Proaza's concluding stanzas in the CCM (Sevilla 1501). A person should read aloud a text, changing the voice to reflect the personalities of the different characters.

480. JOSET, Jacques. "De Fernando de Rojas a Agustín de Rojas: Presencia de LC en *El viaje entretenido*." ACTAS: 347-57.

To the similarities noted by G. CIROT [BH 25 (1923), 198-211, at 208-09] several more are adduced which tend to show that Augustín de Rojas must have had a text of LC at hand. Posits that the later Rojas believed in a historical Celestina.

481. _____. "Una *Celestina* romana y francesa." *Cel* 5, ii (Fall 1981), 54.

Reflections on a staging of the Pierre Laville LC in Provence (1981) which seemed to betray the spirit of the original.

482. _____. "De Pármeno a Lazarillo." *Cel* 8, ii (Fall 1984), 17-24.

In comparing these two works, both show the common motif: "buscar amos." The author equates Sempronio and Lazarillo as seekers of remuneration for services, and Pármeno with the *escudero* because they share an additional ethical preoccupation lacking in the first pair.

483. JULIA MARTINEZ, Eduardo. "LC," in *Historia general de las literaturas hispánicas*, II, ed. G. Díaz-Plaja (Barcelona: Ed. Barná, 1951), pp. 275-302.

Summaries devoted to author, action and characterization in LC and to its impact on later literature.

K

484. KASPRZYK, Krystyna. "Nouvelles notes sur le vocabulaire de Nicolas de Troyes." *Bibliothèque d'Humanisme et Renaissance* 20 (1958), 402-04.

Concludes from lexical data that LC was known to Nicolas de Troyes.

485. KASSIER, Theodore L. "'Cancionero' Poetry and the

Celestina: From Metaphor to Reality." *Hispanófila*, no. 56 (1976), 1-28.

Just as *Don Quijote* relates to the chivalric literature which preceded it, so must LC relate to the 'cancionero' poetry of the 15th century. Rojas literalizes the metaphors of this poetry: his negative views of it contribute to our better understanding of the didactic intentions, the structure and significance of LC.

486. KASTEN, Lloyd, and Jean ANDERSON. *Concordance to the "Celestina"*. Madison: Hispanic Seminary of Medieval Studies/New York: The Hispanic Society of America, 1976.

A complete concordance to the HSA copy of the CCM, Burgos 1499(?).

487. KISH, Kathleen Vera. "An Edition of the First Italian Translation of LC." Diss. Univ. of Wisconsin, 1971. 426p. DAI 32/02, 970A. No 71-16085. M. H. Singleton. (See also entry 1072.)

488. _____. "The Wages of Sin is Life—for a Sixteenth-Century Best Seller, or, The Anatomy of a Classic." *Theoria* 47 (October 1976), 23-33.

Concise summary of the action of LC, together with a panoramic view of its continuing impact as seen in translations and stage adaptations, a long life earned by the deep human values embedded in Rojas' work.

489. _____. "Christof Wirsung's Two German Translations of LC (1520, 1534)." *American Philosophical Society Year Book 1982* (Philadelphia: APS, 1983), 383-384.

A report on a plan of study which culminated in the publication of facsimiles of the two editions with an introductory study (entry 493).

490. _____. "Celestina Speaks Dutch—in the Sixteenth-Century Spanish Netherlands," in *Hispanic Studies in Honor of Alan D. Deyermond: A North American Tribute,* ed. John S. Miletich (Madison, Wisconsin: Hispanic Seminary of Medieval Studies, 1986).

A background to the printing history of the anonymous Dutch translation of LC (1550-1616), with some comparisons to its likely Spanish source (Zaragoza 1545) and to influences from earlier foreign translations (Wirsung's: Augsburg 1520, 1534; Paris 1527 [Anon.])

491. _____, and Ursula RITZENHOFF. "The *Celestina* Phenomenon in Sixteenth-Century Germany: Christof Wirsung's Translations of 1520 and 1534." *Cel* 4, ii (Fall 1980), 9-18.

A study of the social and historical circumstances in Wirsung's Germany which allows us to see how and why the two translations are as different as the authors show them to be.

492. _____, and Ursula RITZENHOFF. "On Translating

'huevos asados': Clues From Christof Wirsung." *Cel* 5, ii (Fall 1981), 19-31.

Early translations of LC seem not to recognize 'huevos asados' as an aphrodisiac and they omit it from the passage. Wirsung was a professional pharmacist and understood the intent of the passage, for he inserts a reference to beaver testicles in order to emphasize Celestina's expertise in dealing with sexual dysfunction. This makes plausible Garci-Gómez' proposal (entry 343) that 'huevos asados' refers to an aphrodisiac Celestina prepared for her husband.

493. _____, and Ursula RITZENHOFF. *Die Celestina-Übersetzungen von Christof Wirsung. 'Ain Hipsche Tragedia' (Augsburg 1520), 'Ainn recht liepliches Buechlin' (Augsburg 1534).* Hildesheim/Zurich/New York: Georg Olms, 1984. xi, 123p. One color plate and the two facsimile editions (unpaginated) with the original woodcuts. Forward by Walter Mettmann.

A facsimile reprinting of both translations of Wirsung, illustrated by Hans Weidetz. The authors' introd. explores 1) the life and work of Wirsung (1500-1571); 2) the activity of the illustrator, and, in the most substantive section 3) the evolution and significance of the translator's changes from the earlier to the later effort.

494. KOTZMANIDOU, Maria. "The Spanish and Arabic Characterization of the Go-Between in the Light of Popular Performance." HR 48 (1980), 91-109.

There seems to be a great typological similarity in the go-between figure in Arabic shadow-plays and Celestina, doubtless the result of a cumulative process in the Mediterranean area. In Celestina, there is both a portrayal of a real-life personage and of a traditional literary figure of rich significance.

495. KRAUSE, Anna. "Deciphering the Epistle-Preface to the CCM." RR 44 (1953), 89-101.

Behind the text, Krause detects clear signs of its author's university training. LC's medieval component is rooted in its ability to dramatize the theme of a profane hyperbole; its Renaissance component is most clearly perceived in the work's dialogic structure.

496. KRUSE, Margot. "Stand und Aufgaben der *Celestina*-Forschung." RJ 6 (1953-54), 324-41.

LC studies since the time of Menéndez y Pelayo (i.e., 1899-1910). Much remains to be done in the preparation of a critical edition and in clarification of historical and linguistic features of LC.

497. KUCHLER, Walther. "Die erste bekannte Ausgabe der CCM." RJ 6 (1953-54), 315-23.

Celestina is important to the work, but Calisto and Melibea are its real center of meaning. The charm of LC is in the handling of the interplay between the world of the lovers and the world of the servants. The CCM is more unified than the TCM; the latter destroys the admirably tight construction of the 16-act version.

498. KULIN, Katalin. "A *Celestina* es az átment kor."

Filológiai Közlöny 13 (1967), 23-40 [In Hungarian]. The French translation, "LC et la période de transition," is in *Acta Litteraria Academiae Scientiarum Hungaricae* 9 (1967), 63-85 [translation by the author].

LC projects the pessimism and the crisis of its times as it chronicles the social and philosophical values then in the ascendant.

499. _____. "Leyendo LC." *Cel* 4, i (May 1980), 9-15.

A translation from the Hungarian of an "Afterword" the author contributed to a translation of LC (see entry 1067). A general overview of LC and its fascination for audiences over the centuries.

L

500. L., R. "Lo demoníaco en la *Celestina.*" *Boletín del Colegio de Graduados de la Facultad de Filosofía y Letras* (Buenos Aires), no. 18 (September 1936), 1-4.

A series of reflections on the all-consuming nature of Love in LC as a source of demonism. It is a power which affects and possesses, and ultimately destroys, the humans fascinated by Love. It makes companion reading to F. Rauhut (entry 739).

501. LAGRONE, Gregory G. "Salas Barbadillo and the *Celestina.*" HR 9 (1941), 440-58.

Herrero-García's assertion to the contrary, the author presents a sampling of citations to show that Salas Barbadillo *was* well-acquainted with LC and influenced by it.

502. LAPESA, Rafael. "LC en la obra de Américo Castro," in *Estudios sobre la obra de Américo Castro*, ed. P. Laín Entralgo (Madrid: Taurus, 1971), 247-61; rpt. in Lapesa's *Poetas y prosistas de ayer y de hoy* (Madrid: Gredos, 1977), 60-72.

Personal reminiscences of Castro's classes in Madrid and in the United States, together with an appreciation of his contributions to *Celestina* studies, 1926-63.

503. _____. "En torno a un monólogo de Calisto," in *Homenaje a Aranguren* (Madrid: Revista de Occidente, 1972), 213-28; also in *Comentario de textos* (Madrid: Castalia, 1973), 30-51; see also Lapesa's *Poetas y prosistas de ayer y de hoy* (Madrid: Gredos, 1977), 73-91.

An analysis of Calisto's Act 14 soliloquy; "O mezquino yo... ."

504. LAURENTI, J. L., and A. PORQUERAS-MAYO. "La colección hispánica de las ediciones venecianas (siglo XVI) en la biblioteca de la Universidad de Illinois," in *Aureum Saeculum Hispanum* (Festschrift für Hans Flasche zum 70. Geburtstag), ed. K.-H. Körner and D. Briesemeister (Weisbaden: Steiner, 1983), 141-170.

See page 166, entries 39-41, where are registered these three LC editions from Venice: P. N. da Sabio, 1535; G. de Gregorii, 1525; and G. A. and P. N. da Sabio, 1541.

505. LAVILLE, Pierre. "Le théâtre de Célestine." *Comédie Française*, no. 35 (1975), 9-11.

The prologue to his adaptation of LC (see entry 1052.1.) of 1975. He has introduced many modifications, explained here as the result of his view of the Celestina as a mythical projection. There are five photographs of the cast in rehearsal.

506. LAW, J. R. "Calisto as the Antithesis of Fifteenth-Century Nobility," in *La Chispa '83: Selected Proceedings. The Fourth Louisiana Conference on Hispanic Languages and Literatures* (New Orleans: Tulane University, 1983), 153-58.

Calisto is far from genuinely noble for his behavior betrays the expressed opinions of others. This is attributable to Rojas' ironic presentation. A contrasting true view, used by the author for contrast, can be found in writings of Rojas' contemporaries, Diego de Valera and Rodrigo Sánchez de Arévalo, both authors of treatises that feature old and new views on what constitutes nobility.

507. LAZA PALACIOS, Modesto. "El laboratorio de Celestina." *Farmacia Nueva* 20 (1955), 529-34.

A first sketch—a list and definition of some medicinal objects found at Celestina's house—of what will later be a full study (see following entry).

508. _____. *El laboratorio de Celestina.* Málaga: Instituto de Cultura, Diputación Provincial de Málaga, 1958. Presentación de Ernesto Salcedo Vilchéz. 221p. 4 illustrations.

Opens with sections devoted to Rojas, the work, imitations and stagings, early editions, and echoes of Trotaconventos in Celestina. The following section is an annotated dictionary listing of the items in Celestina's laboratory. A twelve-page bibliography completes this unusual study.

a. *RPh* 16 (1962-63), 372-73, M. R. Lida de Malkiel

509. LECERTUA, Jean-Paul. "Le jardin de Mélibée: Métaphores sexuelles et connotations symboliques dans quelques épisodes de LC." TRAMES (Limoges) 2 (March 1978), 105-38.

The study goes from the general to the specific (from 'lugar' to 'huerta' to 'huerto') and from the vague to the explicitly erotic metephors central to the progress of the love affair of Calisto and Melibea. The voyeuristic participation of the servants (seen often as comic) and the inversions (perversions) of both the courtly and the divine "gardens" suggest that Melibea's garden may well be the central symbol of the work's structure. Acts 1, 2, 12, 14 and 19 are commented upon.

510. _____. "Familia y anti-familia en LC." (in press) (*)

511. _____. "Oralidad en LC: la dipsomanía de la vieja." (In press) (*)

512. LeMARTINEL, Jean. "Quelques remarques sur le texte de la _Célestine._" _Mélanges à la mémoire d'André Joucla-Ruau_ (Aix-en-Provence: Univ. of Provence, 1978), II, 865-69. (Etudes littéraires, 2)

Four notes: 1) metrical observations on verses from Act 19; 2) the allusion to Nembrot in Sempronio's Act 1 speech is not to the tower of Babel but to an Arabic conqueror of heaven; 3) the "mira a Bernardo" reference is to a Catalan troubadour of antifeminist fame and not to St. Bernard; and 4) the meaning of 'renegar' in the same speech of Sempronio from Act 1 means—in context—'to blaspheme' or 'to lead astray, into error'.

513. _____. "Sobre el supuesto judaísmo de LC." _Hommage des hispanistes français à N. Salomon_ (Barcelona: Ed. Laia, 1979), 509-16.

Rojas' status as a 'converso' is superfluous to an interpretation and understanding of LC. Garrido Pallardó (1957) and Forcadas (1973) are two critics he attempts to refute. LC is perfectly understandable within the Western development of the _reprobatio amoris_ tradition.

514. LEO, Ulrich. "Die Literarische Gattung der _Celestina,_" RF 75 (1963), 54-80.

LC does not belong to a specific genre, although Leo treats it as a psychological novel here. Rojas' message fits no established mold. The concept of dialogue of both Gilman (1956) and Lida de Malkiel (1962) is treated in the discussion.

515. LEUBE, Eberhard. _Fortuna in Karthago. Die Aeneas-Dido-Mythe Virgils in den romantischen Lit. vom 14 bis zum 16 Jh._ Heidelberg: C. Winter, 1969.

The presence of this theme in LC is noted _passim_ but especially in Part C of the book.

a. RF 83 (1971), 349-54, at 353, M. Lentzen

516. LEUBE, Wilhelm. _Die "Celestina"._ Munich: W. Fink, 1971. 62p. (Literatur im Dialog, 5)

An introd. to LC as literary anomaly and as artistic masterpiece. There are nice analyses of Celestina, Calisto and Melibea, and an appreciation of the TCM and its impact on other works.

a. _RPh_ 27 (1973-74), 443, D. S. Severin

517. LIDA DE MALKIEL, María Rosa. "La originalidad de LC." _La Nación_ (Buenos Aires) (January 16 1949), Section 2 ("Artes-Letras"), 3-4. (See also entry 570.)

A preliminary study of Calisto.

518. _____. "Para la fecha de la _Comedia Thebayda_." _RPh_ 6 (1952-53), 45-48.

It is this work which fixes the basic traits of celestinesque imitations. It is a bridge between LC and its other imitations and continuations. See also McPheeters (entry 552).

519. _____. "El fanfarrón en el teatro del Renacimiento." _RPh_ 11 (1957-58), 268-91; rpt. in her _Estudios de literatura española y comparada_ (Buenos Aires: EUDEBA, 1966), 173-202.

Centurio seen in the light of tradition and originality.

520. _____. "De Centurio al Mariscal de Turena: fortuna de una frase en LC." HR 27 (1959), 150-66.

Not all of Rojas' imitators have clearly interpreted the figure of Centurio.

521. _____. _Two Spanish Masterpieces: The "Book of Good Love" and LC._ Champaign-Urbana: Univ. of Illinois Press, 1961. vii + 106p. (Illinois Studies in Language and Literature, 49)

The treatment of LC leads to greater comprehension of the ways in which the plot, dramatic techniques and characterization join to form an artistic whole of considerable originality. Time, space and irony are three points that are treated extensively.

a. _RomN_ 15 (1962), 219-21, J. B. Avalle Arce
b. BA 26 (1962), 318, T. R. Hart
c. _Speculum_ 37 (1962), 632-34, J. E. Keller
d. _Neophilologus_ 46 (1962), 238-39, J. A. van Praag
e. TLS (September 7 1962), 674, Anon.
f. _Modern Language Journal_ 46 (1962), 330, R. R. LaDu
g. _RPh_ 16 (1962-63), 127-32, O. H. Green
h. _Modern Language Quarterly_ 24 (1963), 118-120, C. Ayllón
i. MAe 32 (1963), 60-64. L. Jenaro MacLennan
j. _Notes & Queries_, N.S. 10 (March 1963), 117-18, K. S. Reid
k. _Insula_, no. 195 (February 1963), 3, 12, F. Rico
l. MLR 58 (1963), 274-75, G. D. Trotter
m. RR 55 (1964), 47-48, A. Tudisco
n. HR 32 (1964), 360-61, J. H. Herriott
o. BHS 41 (1964), 230-37, P. E. Russell; rpt. in his _Temas de LC y otros estudios_ (entry 800), 279-91
p. _Modern Philology_ 62 (1964-65), 64-66, G. W. Ayer
q. QIA 4 (1960-65), 291-95, E. Caldera
r. RJ 17 (1966), 351-55, H. Bihler
s. _Le Moyen Age_ 72 (1966), 545-67, J. Joset
t. _Erasmus_ 18 (1966), cols. 357-58, H. Rheinfelder

522. _____. _La originalidad artística de LC._ Buenos Aires: EUDEBA, 1962, 755p; 2nd ed., 1970, 784p. [including a complete bibliography of the author's works up to that time].

This is the _vademecum_ of recent LC studies, touching as it does on most all aspects of the work and its literary excellences in significant ways. Especially strong on characterization and in the positioning of LC on a literary continuum to include its forerunners and later imitations, continuations, stage adaptations, etc. It is blessed with a valuable Index.

a. RLR 75 (1962-63), 272-75, H. Guiter
b. CHA, no. 167 (1963), 428-38, I. M. Gil
c. _Razón_ (March 2 1963), n. p., Anon.
d. _Boletín de Literatura Hispánica_ (Rosario, Argentina), no. 5 (1963), 103-07, R. Boldori (*)
e. _La Nación_ (March 17 1963), Section 4, p. 4, F. L. Bernárdez
f. _Philologica Pragensia_ 6 (1963), 438-40, P. Hodousek

g. *Filología* 9 (1963), 223-29, P. R. Olson

h. *Forum der Letteren* 4 (November 1963), 215-27, J. A. van Praag

i. *Marcha* (Montevideo) (October 11 1963), 29, A. Rama (*)

j. *Clarín* (Buenos Aires) (May 9 1963), 16, O. Rodríguez-Maure (*)

k. *Approdo* (Rome) 9 (1963), 137-44, C. Segre

l. *País* (Montevideo) (November 27 1963), n. p., E. Rodríguez Monegal (*)

m. *Destino* (Barcelona) (June 19 1963), 49, A. Vilano

n. *Sur*, no. 284 (Sept.-Oct. 1963), 82-88, F. Weber de Kurlat

o. *El Territorio* (Posadas) (November 19 1963), n. p., Anon. (*)

p. *Pregón* (Jujuy) (June 9 1964), n. p., Anon. (*)

q. *La Nación* (February 9 1964), Section 4, 1, G. Díaz-Plaja

r. *Archivum* 13 (1963[1964]), 354-65, J. García García

s. BH 66 (1964), 405-18, P. Heugas

t. *RPh* 17 (1963-64), 55-74, R. Lapesa; rpt. in his *Poetas y prosistas de ayer y de hoy* (Madrid: Gredos, 1977), 25-59

u. CL 16 (1964), 269-74, E. S. Morby

v. *Neophilologus* 48 (1964), 85-87, J. A. van Praag

w. *La Prensa* (May 1 1964), 2nd section, Sunday Illustrated, E. F. Rubens

x. BHS 41 (1964) 230-37, P. E. Russell; rpt. in his *Temas de LC y otros estudios* (entry 800), 279-91

y. YWMLS 25 (1963-64), 170-71, N. D. Shergold

z. BCB 7 (1964), 276-77, E. Camacho Guisado

aa. BA 38 (1964), 172, T. R. Hart

bb. RLC 39 (1965), 109-23, M. Bataillon

cc. HR 33 (1965), 15-31, O. H. Green

dd. *Acta Litteraria Academiae Scientiarum Hungaricae* 7 (1965), 473-79, K. Kulin

ee. *Revista de Literaturas Modernas* 4 (1965), 168-71, H. Pauliello de Chocholous

ff. RJ 17 (1966), 258-73, H. Bihler

gg. NRFH 17 (1963-64 [1966]), 264-90, M. Bataillon

hh. *Revue Belge de Philologie et d'Histoire* 44 (1966), 738-48, E. Dehennin

ii. *Erasmus* 18 (1966), cols. 354-57, H. Rheinfelder

jj. *Hispania* 50 (1967), 174-81, C. F. Fraker, Jr.

523. _____. "El ambiente concreto en LC: fragmentos de un capítulo no aprovechado para *La originalidad artística de LC*," in *Estudios Dedicados a James Homer Herriott* (Madison: Univ. of Wisconsin Press, 1966), 145-65.

Accumulation of textual citations that help make the ambience of LC more concrete. These show us that Rojas could visualize a scene through insinuation, allusion, and speech indications without recourse to prolix description: it is an advance on all previous work.

a. *RPh* 24 (1970-71), 147-48, A. D. Deyermond

524. _____. *Dos obras maestras de la literatura española. El LBA y LC.* Versión española del texto, prefacio y notas por Raimundo Lida. Buenos Aires: EUDEBA, 1966. 4th printing, 1977. 118p. (Serie Teoría e Investigación)

The Spanish translation of the 1961 volume (see entry 521).

a. *La Prensa* (August 20 1967), R. Donghi Halperín (*)

b. *La Nación* (Santiago de Chile) (February 4 1968), Sunday Supplement, 5, M. Ferreccio Podestá

525. _____. "Elementos técnicos del teatro romano desechados en LC." *RPh* 27 (1973-74), 1-12.

LC departs from the Latin tradition of dialogue and this—plus other innovative features—allows for a consideration of LC as original. Many of LC's imitations and continuations adopt the Latin manner.

526. _____. "La dama como obra maestra de Dios." *RPh* 28 (1974-75), 267-324.

A wide-ranging study which establishes and illustrates the literary continuity of the title theme (along with several sub-groupings) in the West. For LC and its celestinesque progeny, pages 278-79, 295-97, 300 and 311-12 are important.

527. _____. "La técnica dramática de LC," in *Homenaje a Ana María Barrenechea*, ed. L. Schwartz Lerner and I. Lerner (Madrid: Castalia, 1984), 281-292.

The text of a previously unedited public lecture (Univ. de La Plata, 1961) in which Lida de Malkiel briefly sums up her arguments for the essentially dramatic nature (non-theatrical) of LC: 1) the implied stage directions; 2) the handling of time and space; 3) the use of symmetry and gemination in plot construction; and 4) the linking of plot situations. Examples are cited.

528. LIHANI, John. *Bartolomé de Torres Naharro.* Boston: G. K. Hall, 1979. (TWAS, 522)

Contains several references to the TCM as an influence on the work of Torres Naharro (consult his Index). Most expansive are the discussion of the *Comedia Himenea* (110-13) and the *Comedia Aquilana* (141-44).

529. _____. "The Intrinsic and Dramatic Values of Celestina's Gold Chain," in *Studies in Honor of Gerald E. Wade*, ed. S. Bowman et al (Madrid: Porrúa, 1979), 151-65.

The article praises Rojas' technique of recapitulation, which is exemplified (in part) in the role of the 'cadenilla de oro' as it becomes part of an intricate net of envy, greed and covetousness. In its way, it leads also to the series of deaths that occur. There is an interesting section which attempts to calculate the value of such a chain in Rojas' day.

530. _____. "La técnica de recapitulación auténtica en el teatro del siglo XVI," in *Lope de Vega y los orígenes del teatro español*, ed. M. Criado de Val (Madrid: Edi-6, 1981), 303-09.

Rojas did not invent recapitulation as a theatrical technique (in fact, he seems to have come by it intuitively), but he and Torres Naharro perfected it and passed it on.

531. LISTERMAN, R. W. "*La hija de Celestina*: Tradition and Morality." *The Univ. of South Florida Language Quarterly* 22 (1983-1984), 52-53, 56.

Elena, the "hija" is daughter to a Celestina-type, María, and there seems to be some similarity between them. The bulk of the article narrates some episodes of the life of Elena, with few parallels to be found in LC.

532. LIVACIC G., Ernesto. "Pervivencias medievales en LC." ACTAS: 307-12.

While LC has Renaissance characteristics, this author feels strongly that Rojas' values are more specifically medieval. He defends LC as a work which warns against worldly love and panderers, exactly as Rojas himself affirms: this is LC's first and foremost intent.

533. _____. "Nota sobre la soledad en la vida y en la obra de Fernando de Rojas." *Taller de Letras*, no. 8 (1980), 81-84.

Psychobiographical essay which posits for Rojas a genuine Christian conversion which removed him from the public eye. This solitude is reflected in LC's frequent soliloquies and asides, and in the lack of genuine love and affection portrayed.

534. LOEHLIN, Marian R. "Celestina of the Twenty Hands." *Hispania* 42 (1959), 309-16.

Celestina's hands symbolize her relationships to various clients.

535. LOPES DIAS, José. "Duas cartas de Ricardo Jorge a Menéndez Pelayo sobre LC." *Imprensa Médica* 15, no. 13 (December 25 1951), 213-17.

Vague references to the influence of LC in some Portuguese works.

536. LOPEZ BARBADILLO, J., ed. *Sancho de Muñón. La tercera Celestina: Tragicomedia de Lisandro y Roselia*. Madrid: Akal, 1977.

Rpt. of a partial ed. of this LC continuation. The "Nota preliminar" compares this text to LC, making frequent references to the studies of Menéndez y Pelayo.

537. _____, ed. *A. G. de Salas Barbadillo. La hija de Celestina*. Madrid: Akal, 1978.

Rpt. of the 1907 impression based on the Milan original (1616). Makes available this late imitation of LC.

538. LOPEZ MOLINA, Luis. "La *Comedia Thebaida* y *La Celestina*," in *Actas del IV Congreso Internacional de Hispanistas (Salamanca 1971)*, II (Salamanca: Univ. de Salamanca, 1982), 169-183.

Lists similarities and differences of the two works in terms of their structure, moral purposes, characterization, dramatic nature, etc. In part, a response to K. Whinnom's assertion (entry 909) that there is limited impact of LC in the *Thebaida*.

539. LOPEZ MORALES, Humberto. "Celestina y Eritrea [sic]: la huella de la *Tragicomedia* en el teatro de Enzina." ACTAS: 315-23.

Eritea is not really celestinesque. This character from the *Egloga de Plácida y Vitoriano* is, however, popular with later writers.

540. _____. "LC," in *Historia de la literatura española* I, ed. J. M. Diez Borque (Madrid: Guadiana, 1974), pp. 114-23.

A good general introd. to the text which adheres rather closely to Lida de Malkiel (1962) in its views. Believes that Rojas took the plan of the original author in quite another direction.

541. LORENZO-RIVERO, Luis. "La celestinesca como creación de Castilla la Nueva." *Duquesne Hispanic Review* 7, ii (1968), 1-14.

Using Criado's meaning for "la celestinesca" (1960, 1965), the author sees LC as reflecting the social fusion in New Castile that was current in Rojas' day.

542. _____. "El bien y el mal en LC." *Estudios Iberoamericanos* 2 (1976), 31-37.

Rojas criticizes passion but not love. Virtue is emphasized through the presentation of vice, a view common in the Middle Ages.

M

543. MACAYA LAHMANN, E. "La evocación local española en LC." *Repertorio Americano* 30, no. 9 (March 2 1935), 136-142; rpt. in his *Estudios hispánicos* (San José, Costa Rica: Soley & Valverde, 1938), II, 31-40.

The lack of geographical signposts which have led to various cities being proposed as the locale of LC's action (Sevilla, Salamanca, La Puebla de Montalbán, Toledo) corresponds to the Renaissance propensity for universalizing.

544. _____. "La evocación local española en el grupo de las Celestinas," in his *Estudios hispánicos* (see preceding entry), II, 43-58.

Lack of local color in LC is a trait also of some imitations: *Serafina, Thebayda, Segunda Celestina, Lisandro y Roselia* and *La lozana andaluza*.

545. McCORMICK, Robert. "New Approaches to Literary Criticism. Maeztu's *Don Quijote, Don Juan y la Celestina* and Psycho-History." *Basque Artistic Expression* 2 (1981), 61-67.

Maeztu, although he did not know the term 'psycho-history', put forth some ideas in line with Freud's theories on it. Some of these are explored with the conclusion that Rojas lived as a 'cristiano nuevo' in an alien world. The bitterness of his existence produced the text of LC.

546. McCRARY, William C. "*Alcahuetería* and *Brujería*," ch. 3 in his *The Goldfinch and the Hawk: A Study of Lope de Vega's Tragedy, "El caballero de Olmedo"* (Chapel Hill:

Univ. of North Carolina Press, 1966), 51-82. (UNCSRLL, 62)

Lope, aided by the often-hysterical reactions to witchcraft practices of his day, took this element of Celestina's character and expanded it as he was creating Fabia. He modifies Rojas by de-emphasizing the flesh-merchant role of his go-between.

547. McCREADY, Warren T. *Bibliografía temática de estudios sobre el teatro español antiguo.* Toronto: Univ. of Toronto Press, 1966.

For LC, see pp. 54-60. Coverage is approximately 1850-1950.

a. *RPh* 28 (1975-76), 135-37, C. Stern

548. MacDONALD, Inez. "Some Observations on LC." HR 22 (1954), 264-81.

In trying to answer the questions of why Melibea rejects Calisto in Act 1 and why the lovers need a go-between, she suggests looking back to works in the same literary tradition: the LBA, *Corbacho, Amadís* and *De duobus amantibus.*

549. MACIAS DE CARTAYA, Graziella. "La infrahistoria de LC." *Horizontes* 11, no. 21 (1967), 5-33.

LC can be seen as a "costumbrista" document, as in this study of the world in which the characters of LC move.

550. McPHEETERS, D[ean] W[illiam]. "Alonso de Proaza. Representative Figure of the Spanish Renaissance." Diss. Columbia Univ., 1952. 305p. DA 12, p. 631. No. 00-04217. (See below, entry 555.)

551. _____. "The Element of Fatality in the TCM." *Symposium* 8 (1954), 331-35.

The TCM interpolations do not alter the original sense of fatality.

552. _____. "Comments on the Dating of the *Comedia Thebayda.*" *RPh* 9 (1955-56), 19-23.

Takes issue with Lida de Malkiel (entry 518) about the priority of the *Thebayda* as the first of the LC imitations.

553. _____. "The Corrector Alonso de Proaza and LC." HR 24 (1956), 13-25; included in ch. 7 of his book on Proaza (entry 555).

Proaza must have participated in the preparation of Rojas' *Prólogo* but not in its composition. There is no evidence of his hand anywhere else in the text, not even in the acrostic verses.

554. _____. "The Present Status of Celestina Studies." *Symposium* 12 (1958), 196-205.

Menéndez Pidal's 1950 article ushers in a new period in *Celestina* studies. The scholarly contributions from the 1950s are reviewed.

555. _____. *El humanista español Alonso de Proaza.* Valencia: Castalia, 1961.

Chapter 7 for LC commentary. Reaffirms his already-stated beliefs that documentation shows that Proaza did not compose any part of LC.

a. *Insula*, no. 187 (June 1962), 8, J. Ares Montes
b. *Neophilologus* 46 (1962), 246-47, B. Rekers
c. MLN 77 (1962), 193-95, E. L. Rivers
d. RJ 13 (1962), 375-80, B. König
e. *RenN* 15 (1962), 221-22 V. R. B. Oelschläger
f. *RPh* 19 (1962-63), 384, M. R. Lida de Malkiel
g. *Burgense* 4 (1963), 511-13, N. López Martínez (*)
h. BHS 40 (1963), 54-56, R. B. Tate
i. HR 31 (1963), 264-65, E. von Richthofen

556. _____. "Cervantes' Verses on LC." *RomN* 3 (1962-63), 136-38.

An attempt to further pinpoint what Cervantes meant by 'divino' and 'humano'.

557. _____. "Newly Discovered Correspondence of Alonso de Proaza, Editor of LC." *Symposium* 17 (1963), 225-29.

These new letters only tend to confirm further that Proaza did not author any part of LC.

558. _____. "Una traducción hebrea de LC en el siglo XVI," in *Homenaje a Antonio Rodríguez-Moñino* 1 (Madrid: Castalia, 1966), 399-411.

Notes on the Hebrew version of LC by Joseph ben Samuel Zarfati.

559. _____ "Melibea and the New Learning," in *Historical and Literary Perspectives. Essays and Studies in Honor of Albert Douglas Menut,* ed. S. Sticca (Lawrence, Kansas: Coronado Press, 1973), 65-81.

The Renaissance attitude that allowed greater learning for women is portrayed in Melibea, where it is an integral part of her character. She is a well-read woman, it appears, and definitely rejects medieval female models so that she can exert more independent control over the private aspects of her life.

560. _____. "LC en Portugal en el siglo XVI." ACTAS: 367-76.

There are echoes of LC in the works of all of the following: Gil Vicente, Sá de Miranda, Jorge Pinto, Jorge Ferreira de Vasconcellos, Camões and Antonio de Ferreira.

561. _____. "La 'dulce ymaginacion' de Calisto." *Actas del Sexto Congreso Internacional de Hispanistas (1977)* (Toronto: Univ. of Toronto, Dept. of Spanish and Portuguese, 1980), 499-501.

An analysis of Calisto's Act 14 soliloquy, with the key concept being 'ymaginacion'.

562. _____."Alegorismo, epicureísmo y estoicismo en LC," in *Actas del IV Congreso International de*

Hispanistas (Salamanca 1971), II (Salamanca: Univ. de Salamanca, 1982), 251-262.

Traces of Bruni, Petrarca, Valla, el Tostado, Nebrija and others in LC show that Rojas was in touch with Epicurean and Stoic trends, although none seems to offer any permanent solutions to the vital problems of any of LC's characters.

563. MADARIAGA, Salvador de. "Discurso sobre Melibea." *Sur* 10 (1941), 38-69; rpt. in his *Mujeres españolas* (Madrid: Espasa-Calpe, 1972), 51-90.

Analysis of Melibea from start to finish. She is not seduced, but enters into her affair with her eyes wide open. There is very interesting material on the personality of Calisto and Celestina as well.

564. _____. "Libros que han hecho a Europa." *Cuadernos del Congreso de la Libertad de la Cultura*, no. 73 (1963), 17-22.

Places LC alongside the writings of Vives and Cervantes as important in helping to forge a new image of woman as neither sinner nor saint, but as a human being.

565. MADRIGAL, J. A. "Entrevista a José Blanco Gil, Director de LC en Portugués." *Cel* 9, ii (Fall 1985).

A director looks at the value of staging LC for modern audiences, and addresses some of the technical problems involved.

566. MAEZTU, Ramiro de. "LC, o el saber," in his *Don Quijote, Don Juan and La Celestina: ensayos de simpatía* (Madrid: Ed. Calpe, 1926), 189-289. Later included in Colección Austral, no. 31, in 1938, and rpt. many times since: this essay appears on pp. 107-60.

Calisto the mystic and Melibea the sensuous woman are contrasted with Romeo and Juliet. Passion is always fatal for such lovers. The great wisdom which characterizes Celestina is seen as owing to Rojas' Jewish heritage. The pessimism of the world seen in LC is a reflection of Rojas' loss of faith.

567. MAILLARD, Lucien. "L'histoire de Calixte et Mélibée." *Comédie Française*, no. 35 (1975), 6-9.

Combines an interview with Marcel Maréchal (who directed the Laville French adaptation of LC: see entry 1052.2) with personal observations on the strength of Celestina's character, the nature of LC and the significance for the theatre world of LC.

568. MALDONADO de GUEVARA, Francisco. "La casa de Celestina." *Anales Cervantinos* 7 (1958), 287-89.

Subjective essay which places the action of LC in Salamanca.

569. MALKIEL, Yakov. "A Brief History of M. R. Lida's *Celestina* Studies." *Cel* 6, ii (Fall 1982), 3-13.

An unusual 'memoria' in which Lida's interest in and work on *Celestina* is chronicled, from an initial schoolgirl encounter with the text to the long period of absorption (involving various stages

and reworkings) ending in the publication of *La originalidad artística* (1962).

570. _____. "M. R. Lida de Malkiel's Ur-*Celestina* (1949)." *Cel* 8, i (May 1984), 15-28.

A précis really of some of the sections of what would evolve into her book on LC, particularly important for her early thinking on characterization. Yakov Malkiel, in a preface and postscript, comments on the genesis of this public lecture (read in Buenos Aires in 1949; see also entry 517).

571. MALLO, Jerónimo "¿Hay un problema racial en el fondo de LC?" *Cuadernos del Congreso de la Libertad de la Cultura*, no. 37 (1959), 51-57.

The lovers do not marry because they listen to the impulses of passion. There is no justification for creating a racial problem for them.

572. MALO, Martha. "El diálogo de los amantes en LC de Fernando de Rojas y en la *Segunda Celestina* de Feliciano de Silva." *El Guacamayo y la Serpiente* (Cuenca, Ecuador), no. 8 (1973), 45-63.

Comparative study of themes, style and length of speeches. Discovers deep differences in the presentation of themes dealing with love.

573. MANCING, Howard. "Fernando de Rojas, LC y *Lazarillo de Tormes*." KRQ 23 (1976), 47-61.

A study of the many similarities of the two works leads to a theory that Rojas may be the author of *Lazarillo*.

574. MANDEL, Adrienne Schizzano. "A Thematic Survey of LC Studies (1824-1968)." Diss., Univ. of California-Los Angeles, 1970. 336p. DAI 31/06, 2927A. No. 70-24358. E. J. Dudley. (See the following entry.)

575. _____. *LC Studies: A Thematic Survey and Bibliography, 1824-1970*. Metuchen, NJ: Scarecrow Press, 1971. 261p.

Studies seven thematic groups: author and date; editions; sources and literary tradition; influence of LC; LC as a work of art; ethical values; and its historical moment.

a. *Choice* 9 (July 1972), 626, Anon.
b. *Symposium* 27 (1973) 182-85, D. Testa
c. ZRP 89 (1973), 691-93, E. Leube
d. BHS 51 (1974), 170-72, P. E. Russell
e. BH 76 (1974), 226, P. Heugas
f. RF 87 (1975), 171-75, G. Siebenmann
g. NRFH 25 (1976), 407-12, D. E. Eisenberg
h. *RPh* 30 (1976-77), 314-17, K. V. Kish

576. _____. "Nuevas perspectivas en la crítica celestinesca." ACTAS: 523-28.

Focus on the past 15 years, especially the flood of articles and studies on the Jewishness of Rojas and how this plays (or does not play) a role in the interpretation of LC, as well as the ancillary theme of the moral posture of the work. The author's personal feeling is that excessive claims have been made on behalf of the religious status attributed to Rojas that simply do not explain adequately many features of the text.

577. MARAVALL, José Antonio. *El mundo social de LC.* Madrid: Gredos, 1964; 2nd ed. 1968; 3rd ed. 1972 (rpt. in 1976). (Biblioteca Románica Hispánica, Estudios y ensayos, 80).

Maravall sets out to fill in the background of the times in which LC was composed, with a reflection of special importance of the socio-economic realities. His portrayal of the different social classes gets at the heart of some of the more important conflicts registered in LC.

   a. RL 26 (1964), 208-09, L. Romero
   b. *Anales de la Universidad de Murcia* 23 (1964-65), 291-96, L. Rubio García
   c. CHA, no. 190 (1965), 159-66, J. J. Trías Vejarano
   d. *Est Lit*, no. 318 (1965), 15, E. Miró
   e. *Insula*, no. 221 (April 1965), 8. J. Ares Montes
   f. *Revista de Estudios Políticos*, nos. 141-42 (1965), 249-53, L. González Seara
   g. RO, no. 31 (1965), 115-27, J. A. Gómez Martín
   h. BA 40 (1966), 68, J. Angeles
   i. BHS 43 (1966), 125-28, P. E. Russell
   j. *Indice*, no. 207 (1966), 45-46, R. García
   k. BH 69 (1967), 495-502, P. Heugas
   l. *Hispania* 50 (1967), 181-82, C. Ayllón
   m. *Recensiones*, no. 6 (1967), 143-48, J. B. Buxó (*)
   n. *Deutsche Literaturzeitung für Kritik der Internationalen Wissenschaft* (Berlin) 89 (1968), 602-03, W. Krauss
   o. *RenQ* 21 (1968), 118-24, A. A. Parker

578. MARCIALES, Miguel. *Carta al Profesor Stephen Gilman.* 2nd ed., Mérida, Venezuela: Univ. of the Andes, Fac. de Humanidades y Educación, 1973. Multigraph; with a 2nd ed. in 1975. viii + 89p. A new printing, with a new title, *Sobre problemas rojanos y celestinescos [Carta al Dr. Stephen Gilman a propósito del libro "The Spain of Fernando de Rojas"]*, is Mérida: Univ. of The Andes, 1983. 169p. Paper.

The 1975 ed. is here re-issued. A detailed response to Gilman's book and some issues with which Marciales is in disagreement. In part, an *esbozo* of Marciales' 1985 critical study in that it anticipates some of its more important conclusions: Cota was the author of Act 1; the Centurio episodes—originally of a piece with the *Auto de Traso*—were not written by Rojas; Rojas was the translator of the *Historia de los dos amantes* de Piccolomini, etc. Some of Gilman's documentation and assertions regarding Rojas' family also come under sharp scrutiny.

579. _____. *LC. Estudio crítico. Edición crítica.* Urbana, Illinois: Univ. of Illinois Press, 1985. 2 vols. (Illinois Medieval Monographs, 1-2.)

The critical study presents the most complete assessment of the character, problems and relationships among the early printed editions of LC yet available, as well as the most complete statement to date of the case for Rodrigo de Cota being the author of Act 1 of LC. The *Tratado de Centurio* section is

distinguished from Rojas' genuine interpolations (as seen by Marciales) and attributed to a third author, probably Sanabria. Unusual readings are treated extensively in the critical text, which is divided into verses (like the Bible), scenes, and its parts (according to Marciales theories on authorship). The text is accompanied by a full set of variants. The study is interspersed with comments on language, pronunciation, Rojas' literary relationships, and a wealth of erudition backing up the editor's choices for his readings. There are many interesting remarks, too, on the illustration schemes of the early editions. In short, there is truly something here for scholars and students of practically all aspects of *Celestina* studies.

580. MARIN CAMPOS, Manuel. "La mujer al través de LC." *Arte y Letras* 2 (1958), 5.

Celestina's 'oficio' as a purveyor of perfumes may be a consequence of the importation from Portugal in the 15th century of the custom by Juana when she married Enrique IV. It is another leaving behind of a medieval trait ("la hembra de escasa higiene") and the adoption of a Renaissance one ("la mujer enriquecida por las pinturas").

581. MARION, Denis. "La première pièce moderne (LC)." *Cahiers de la Compagnie Madeleine Renaud/Jean-Louis Barrault*, no. 14 (1955), 18-21.

LC as a piece to read, dramatically, aloud. It does not offer spectacle; in its place is a rich analysis of people in dynamic conflict.

582. MARISCAL DE RHETT, Beatriz. "Los fantasmas de la libertad en LC." PSA 84, no. 251 (1977), 109-24.

Liberty is a factor in the density of characterization and there is comment here on Sempronio, Pármeno, Celestina, Calisto and Melibea. The so-called trend to liberty called into play by the incipient capitalist system of the period has also its illusory aspects. Rojas weds personal and social kinds of liberty together in his masterpiece.

583. MARQUEZ, Antonio. "LC y la Inquisición," in his *Literatura e inquisición en España: 1478-1834* (Madrid: Taurus, 1980), 201-16. (Col. Persiles, 124)

Challenges certain suppositions of Castro and Gilman that, for Rojas the 'converso', the Inquisition was a creative force, responsible for the particular character of LC.

584. MARQUEZ VILLANUEVA, Francisco. "Ecos de las 'Celestinas'," in his *Fuentes literarias cervantinas* (Madrid: Gredos, 1973), 55-63.

LC and its literary offspring are often remembered and recorded in Cervantes' writings.

   a. BH 77 (1975), 240-41, G. Araya

585. MARTI-IBANEZ, Félix. "El arte médico de la Celestina." *El Siglo Médico* 96 (1935), 133.

Celestina is an archetypal figure as a practitioner of the medical arts in the pre-history of scientific medicine. [Abstract of a conference paper]

586. _____. "The Medico-Pharmaceutical Arts of la Celestina: A Study of a Fifteenth-Century Spanish Sorceress and Dealer in Love." *International Record of Medicine and General Practice Clinics* (New York) 169 (1956), 233-49; rpt. in *Centaur: Essays in the History of Medical Ideas* (New York: MD Publications, 1958), 149-66.

A fair amount of detail in this study of Celestina as witch and healer.

587. _____. "The Magical Arts of la Celestina." *M. D.* (October 1967), 11-16.

Impressionist evocation of Celestina's magical arts based on the contents of her laboratory. There is appreciation, too, of her mastery of human psychology.

588. MARTIN, John W. "Some Uses of Old Spanish Past Subjunctive With Reference to the Authorship of LC." *RPh* 12 (1958-59), 52-67.

Linguistic evidence adduced so far is insufficient for making definitive statements about the authorship of Act 1 as opposed to Acts 2-16.

589. MARTIN, June Hall. "The Problem of Parody and Three Courtly Lovers: Aucassin, Troilus, and Calisto." Diss. Emory Univ., 1967. 223p. DA 28/10, 4136-37A. No. 68-04483. J. M. Smith. (See following entry.)

590. _____. "Calisto," in *Love's Fools: Aucassin, Troilus, Calisto and the Parody of the Courtly Lover* (London: Támesis, 1972), 71-134. (Serie A - Monografías, 21)

Rojas does not so much parody the courtly lover as he does the false lover he sees in his Calisto. This seems to be a logical extension of both the didactic and the pessimistic view Rojas displays in LC.

a. CL 25 (1973), 171-75, S. G. Nichols, Jr.
b. *Cahiers de Civilisation Médiévale* 17 (1974), 295, A. T. Harrison
c. ZRP 90 (1974), 547-48, U. Mölk
d. *Speculum* 49 (1974), 362-64, S. Barney
e. BHS 52 (1975), 94-96, J. M. Aguirre
f. *RPh* 29 (1975-76), 344-46, K. V. Kish

591. MARTIN-ARAGON ADRADA, Félix Julián. "La medicina en LC." *Boletín de la Sociedad Española de Historia y de la Medicina* (Madrid) 2, no. 2 (1962), n. p.

An attempt to deduce from the text of LC what Rojas knew of illness, cures and human psychology.

592. _____. *Los saberes médicos en LC*. La Puebla de Montalbán, 1974. 65p. The original is 1961 but it was newly printed for the Primer Congreso Internacional Sobre LC (Madrid 1974). It was also presented as a doctoral thesis (Toledo 1962).

On the display of medical wisdom shown by Rojas, divided into three sections: anthropology, pathology and therapeutics. It involves considerable textual interpretation. Lists of terms are supplied.

593. _____. "Vocabulario popular de La Puebla de Montalbán." ACTAS: 267-71.

Short listing of words and expressions in actual use in La Puebla: a few appear in the text of LC.

594. MARTIN MORENO, José Gregorio. "Celestina, madre de pícaros." *Santa Cruz* (Valladolid) 16 (1956), 10-11.

Celestina's real role is to bridge socially-disparate worlds in LC. The members of the lower classes do not survive for they live in a world where heroic values prevail still. The *pícaro* is the product of a mean spirit, that of Rojas, the 'converso'.

595. MARTINEZ-LACALLE, Guadalupe. "A Manuscript Version of Mabbe's LC." RLC 39 (1965), 78-91.

The Alnwick Castle manuscript differs in certain aspects from Mabbe's printed translation of 1631. Marginal notes help to convince the author that Mabbe actually wrote a more precise translation than the version prepared for printing.

596. _____. "La traducción de LC de James Mabbe: estudio de un manuscrito del siglo XVII." Diss. Univ. of Madrid, 1970. E. Pujols. (*)

597. _____. "La traducción de LC de James Mabbe: Estudio de un manuscrito del siglo XVII." *Revista de la Universidad de Madrid* 19, no. 76 (1970), 44-47.

Notice of her dissertation (preceding and following entries) and its contents.

598. _____. *La traducción de LC de James Mabbe: Estudio de un manuscrito del siglo XVI*. Madrid, 1970. 61p.

Extract of the doctoral thesis and an advance of her study and edition published in London (see entry 1024).

599. MARTINEZ MARIN, Juan. "Coordinación y subordinación oracional en LC. Contribución al estudio de la sintáxis histórica española." Diss. Univ. of Granada, 1975. A. Llorente Maldonado. (See following entry.)

600. _____. *Sintáxis de LC. I: La oración completa*. Granada: Univ. of Granada-Secretario de Publicaciones, 1978). 333p. (Col. Filológica, 27)

A detailed classification scheme of compound sentences in LC. Three approaches to them are offered in all sub-classifications: formal, functional and semantic. A 2nd volume is promised.

a. *Via Domita* (Toulouse), no. 24 (1980), 65-66, A. Leal

601. _____. "Uso y frecuencia de los relativos en LC." *RFE* 63 (1983), 123-140.

Basing this study on Criado de Val-Trotter's edition, the author evaluates the linguistic factors important in the choice of relatives in LC. Diachronically, LC shows a modern trend in its marked tendency towards the abandonment of the less differentiated type which prevailed in the pre-1500 period.

602. MARTINEZ-MILLER, Orlando. "La ética judía y LC como alegoría." Diss. Univ. of Southern California, 1973. 448p. DAI 33/09, 5189-90A. No. 73-7259. J. D. Smith. (See following entry.)

603. _____. *La ética judía y LC como alegoría*. Miami: Ed. Universal, 1978. 280p. (Col. Polymita)

A study of ethical influences on Rojas which considers certain Jewish works he may well have read and known—especially I. Aboab's *Almenara de la Luz*. What Rojas does not say can be as meaningful as what he does say in LC. We are treated to analyses of the character, the moral, the ideas, themes and allegorical overtones in LC.

a. *Cel* 3, ii (Fall 1979), 25-26, K. Whinnom

604. MARTINEZ RUIZ, José (= Azorín). "Las nubes," in *Castilla*, ed. and notes by J. M. Rozas (Barcelona: Labor, 1973), 133-38. (Textos hispánicos modernos, 21). The original is from ABC, August 27 1912.

Azorin's famed lyric invention of a new ending for LC's lovers.

605. _____. "LC," "La Celestina, la pelegrina," and "Dejemos al diablo...," in *Obras completas*, 2 (Madrid: Aguilar, 1947), 990-1011. The original versions appeared in ABC (1913) and were rpt. in *Los valores literarios* (Madrid/Buenos Aires: Renacimiento, 1913), 87-116.

Really a series of reflections occasioned by the publication of Cejador's LC edition (1913). Two points are important: he argues that the CCM is a superior version of the work, a product of Rojas' youth, and he challenges Menéndez y Pelayo's, and Cejador's, views that Celestina is evil incarnate by showing that she is as subject to fate and her own circumstances as are all the other characters.

These attacks did not go long unanswered. Cejador defended his (and Menéndez y Pelayo's) stance in a 3-part series titled "Cuestiones celestinescas," which appeared in *Los Lunes de El Imparcial* (Madrid) on September 15 and 22, and October 20 1913, p. 3 of each issue.

606. _____. "Comentarios a un suceso," in *El oasis de los clásicos* (Madrid: Biblioteca Nueva, 1952), 38-43, and in *Obras Completas*, 9 (Madrid: Aguilar, 1954), 926-30. The original is ABC, May 12 1925.

Takes up Melibea's suicide. The crucial scene for understanding this act is not—as many assert—the garden scene of Act 19 but, rather, Melibea's overhearing Pleberio and Alisa in Act 16 (of the TCM). It is then that real conflict enters her life.

607. _____. "Tragedia en Toledo," in *Dicho y hecho* (Barcelona: Destino, 1957), 23-36. A collection of articles from ABC, August 9, 16, and 23 of 1934.

Everything about LC seems to identify its locale as Toledo.

608. _____, and others. "¿Dónde colocamos la acción de la CCM?: Debate sensacional," in "Páginas literarias" of *Arriba*, (March 9 1958), 21-22; (March 16 1958), 25-26; (March 23 1958), 32; (August 10 1958), 31-32.

Azorín asks Pedro de Lorenzo, editor, this question. Lorenzo opines Cuenca and opens a dialogue, with the following results: Salamanca (A. Valbuena Prat, F. García Sanchíz, F. Maldonado de Guevara, E. Montes), Toledo (G. Marañon, J. de Entrambasaguas, J. M. Pemán, J. Calvo Sotelo), Sevilla (V. Aleixandre), Puerto de Santa María (M. Halcón), Talavera de la Reina (R. Morales), and unwilling to choose (J. M. de Cossío, F. de Valle Lersundi, and M. Criado de Val). This 'debate' is commented upon in Romero y Sarráchaga [entry 768: pp. 39-45].

609. MARTINEZ RUIZ, Juan, and Joaquina ALBARRACIN NAVARRO. "Farmacopea en LC y en un manuscrito árabe de Ocaña." ACTAS: 409-25.

The authors present a lexical comparison of the manuscript and LC. The similarities seem to situate Celestina in a Judeo-Arabic medieval tradition and to indicate that Rojas knew both Arabic and Hebrew.

610. MAXWELL DIAL, Eleanor M. "Sobre el tema del amor en LC." Thesis (Tesina). Mexico City College, 1955. 89p. (*)

611. _____. "Spanish Classical Theatre in Mexico in the 1950s." LATR 4, ii (1970-71), 29-38, especially 30-31 and 37.

Notes on the presentation and critical reception of Alvaro Custodio's 1953 and 1957 stagings of LC.

612. _____. "Alvaro Custodio and his Continuing Dream: The 'Teatro Clásico de México' in the 1960s." LATR 7, ii (1973-74), 45-57.

Offers observations on Custodio's work, with LC highlighted on pp. 50-52 and 55-57 (stagings of 1953, 1957, 1960, 1963 and 1968).

613. _____. "Notes on Adapting and Interpreting LC: The Art of Alvaro Custodio and Amparo Villegas." *Cel* 1, i (May 1977), 23-45.

Notes and observations of the collaboration of director and actress. There is biography, Mexican theatre history and also review excerpts of LC productions in which Villegas interpreted Celestina.

614. MAZZONI, Guido. "Qualche accenno italiano alla *Celestina*." *Rendiconti della Accademia Nazionale dei Lincei*, 6th Series, 7 (1931), 249-52.

Collects mentions of and allusions to LC from 16th and 17th-century Italian works (theatre, prose, poetry).

a. M.'s note inspired Francesco Torraca to write a reflective piece, "Il libro divino," in *La Tribuna* (Rome) (April 1, 1932), p.

3. Long before Green (entry 410), T. proposes the reading, "Minerva con Vulcán" (LC, act 1). Several Italian authors report them as man and wife, and this may account for it being Rojas' intended reading.

615. MELE, Eugenio. "Un 'villancico' della *Celestina* popolare in Italia nel Cinquecento." *Giornale Storico della Letteratura Italiana* (Turin) 106 (1935), 288-91.

Attributes the appearance of the *villancico* ("la medianoche es pasada/e no viene:/sabedme si hay otra amada/que lo detiene" [LC, act 19]) in a presentation in Siena in 1537 to LC's great popularity in Italy.

615bis. MELLIZO, Carlos. "LC como 'diálogo'." *Ensayistas*, nos. 14-15 (March 1983), 135-144.

The main proposal is that Rojas' use of dialogue may have had as a model the *Diálogos de amor* of Judás Abravanel.

616. MENDELOFF, Henry. "Protasis and Apodasis in LC." *Hispania* 42 (1959), 376-81.

The study of this aspect of LC's language shows a lack of syntactical stability as well as the presence of much verbal ambiguity.

617. _____. "The Passive Voice in Old Spanish." RJ 15 (1964), 269-87.

LC is one of a dozen texts utilized. See pp. 285-86 for the results of passive voice configurations in LC.

618. _____. "The Passive Voice in LC (with a Partial Reappraisal of Criado de Val's *Indice verbal*." RPh 18 (1964-65), 41-46.

An independent study carried out by the author shows that the use of the passive voice in Act 1 shows a difference from either the CCM taken as a whole, or Acts 2-16 considered separately.

619. _____. "On Translating LC into French and Italian." *Hispania* 51 (1968), 111-15.

The first French translation of 1527 (ed. G. Brault, entry 1049) still is a superior version to either the recent French translation (René Doyon, entry 1043) or an Italian one (Corrado Alvaro, entry 1068).

620. _____. "The Epithet in LC (1499)." *Studi di filologia romanza offerti a Silvio Pellegrini* (Padua, 1971), 355-62.

The epithet in LC fulfills specific tasks related to theme, plot and characterization.

621. _____. "Pleberio in Contemporary LC Criticism." *RomN* 13 (1971-72), 369-73.

Reprises the Pleberio polemic between the literalists and the transcendentalists: both factions are guilty of extremism and exclusivism.

622. _____. "Sharing in LC." BICC 32 (1977), 173-77.

On the artistic application of the aphorism that "goods are not goods if not shared." Celestina perverts its Christian intentions as do Sempronio and Pármeno. An irony is that the latter murders the former when she does practice what she has preached.

623. MENDOZA NEGRILLO, Juan de Dios, S. J. "Fernando de Rojas," in his *Fortuna y providencia en la literatura castellana del siglo XV* (Madrid: Real Academia Española, 1973), 270-75. (BRAE, Anejo 17)

For Rojas the world is absurd. He is alone, without his Jewish customs in a Christian world. His views of Fortune are formed in this kind of a crucible and are reflected in the external form of LC as well as in its interior conflicts.

624. MENENDEZ PIDAL, Ramón. "La lengua en tiempo de los Reyes Católicos: del retoricismo al humanismo." CHA, no. 11 (1950), 9-24.

For LC, this look at language confirms that the differences between Act 1 and the rest of the work suggest two distinct authors.

625. MENENDEZ Y PELAYO, Marcelino. "LC," in *Estudios y discursos de crítica histórica y literaria*, 2 [= vol 7 of the Edicion Nacional of the *Obras completas*], ed. E. Sánchez Reyes (Santander: CSIC, 1941), 237-58.

First appeared as an article (1895) and later modified as the introd. to the Krapf ed. of the TCM (Vigo, 1899-1900). Rojas is the sole author of the TCM. Additional comments cover the sources (in particular, the Latin *Pamphilus*), the literary excellences of the work, its genre and its literary descendants. Incorporated into his more ample study in *Orígenes de la novela* (1910). (See following entry.)

626. _____. *La Celestina*. Madrid: Espasa Calpe, 1947. 229p. Paper (Col. Austral, 691). A 5th printing is 1979.

(See preceding entry for history of this study.) An expansion of earlier discussions of LC, adding to his comments on the topics of authorship, locale, the humanistic comedy of the 15th century, sources, style, characterizations, and impact outside of Spain.

627. MEREGALLI, Franco. "LC," in his *La presenza della letteratura spagnola in Italia* (Florence: G. Sansone, 1974), 12-22.

LC as part of the diffusion of Spanish books during the reigns of Ferdinand and Isabella and Carlos V.

a. *Modern Language Journal* 59 (1975), 465-66, J. G. Fucilla

628. METTMANN, Walter. "Melibeas Ende Servius als Quelle der *Celestina*." RF 86 (1974), 445-46.

Beginning with names, the author treats LC and Servius' Latin commentaries on the *Aeneas*. There are many similarities.

629. _____. "Anmerkungen zum ersten Akt der *Celestina*." HR 44 (1976), 257-64.

A high number of Biblical citations makes Mettmann wonder whether the author of Act 1 may not have been a cleric. Other notes treat difficult lexical items from Act 1 ('petreras,' 'impervio,' 'guija marina,' 'mantilla de niño,' and 'tela de caballo'.

630. MIGUEL MARTINEZ, Emilio de. "A propósito de los apelativos dirigidos a Celestina." *Studia Philologica Salmanticensia* 3 (1979), 193-209.

A study of hypocrisy as practiced by Sempronio, Pármeno, Calisto, and Melibea and turned toward Celestina throughout the TCM, seen through the medium of the positive and negative apellations used to refer to her at any given moment.

631. MILLARES CARLO, Agustín. *Literatura española hasta fines del siglo XV*. Mexico: Antigua Librería Robredo, 1950.

Introd. to the work (pp. 300-10) touching on locale, authorship, early editions, etc. Bibliography (pp. 321-24).

632. MIRANDA, Edelmira E. "Safo en LC y en la *Imitación de diversos* de Fray Luis de León." BAAL 7 (1939), 577-84.

The inclusion of Sappho in Pleberio's Act 21 lament is probably owing to Rojas's having read Ovid's *Heroidas* in a Latin version.

633. MIYAME, Kiyoshi. "A Study of Existential Structures in Five Major Novels of Spain's Golden Age." Diss. Univ. of Indiana, 1977. 341p. DAI 38/05, 2833-34A. No. 77-22666.

LC plus *Lazarillo, El Buscón, Don Quijote* and *Guzmán de Alfarache*. Coordinates treated are space, time and the 'yo'.

634. MONGE, Félix. "*La Dorotea* de Lope de Vega." *Vox Romanica* 16 (1957), 60-145.

The section titled "LC y *La Dorotea*"(pp. 133-45) postulates that Lope's work would have been different without the antecedent of LC, even though many similarities are superficial. Monge believes that LC is deeply serious while the later work is a literalization of a love conceit which, far from evoking tragedy, manages to be rather gentle. Lope's irony is benevolent; Rojas' is black and ominous.

635. _____. "Celestina: la seducción y el lenguaje," in *Orbis Medievalis: Mélanges ... offerts à Reto Raduolf Bezzola*, ed. G. Güntert et al (Bern: Francke Verlag, 1978), 269-80.

Lope's Gerarda (from *La Dorotea*) employs language which is more flexible than Celestina's, an observation supported by internal attitudes towards language in Lope's work. Gerarda inherits some of her ability to seduce through language skills from Celestina, but her characterization is consonant with the times and tastes of a post-LC world.

636. MONK, I. A. "The *Segunda Celestina* of Feliciano de

Silva: A Study and an Edition." Diss. Exeter Univ., 1973. 2 vols. 155, 361p. K. Whinnom. (*)

637. MONTAÑES FONTENLA, Luis. "El incunable toledano de la CCM (LC)." *Anales Toledanos* 8 (1973), 130-79. An offprint circulated separately as a monograph (Toledo: Dip. Provincial de Toledo, 1973. 51p.).

A thorough and complete presentation of arguments supporting the priority of the Toledo 1500 copy as the *editio princeps* of the CCM. The author marshalls data showing his doubts about the surviving Hispanic Society of America copy being either printed in Burgos or being printed as early as 1499.

638. _____. "Sobre la manipulación de una octava del exordio de LC en las ediciones de la tragicomedia." *Cuadernos de Bibliofilia*, no. 3 (January 1980), 5-15.

An attempt to determine the fortune of the final octave of the acrostic which appeared in Toledo 1500 and Seville 1501, and was then transferred to the TCM as the first octave of the section, "Concluye el autor". The author thinks it shows that Rojas was the sole author of all of LC as well as a practicing Christian.

639. _____. "Un análisis bibliográfico de las modernas ediciones de LC." *El Libro Español*, no. 270 (June 1980), 327-36; no. 271 (July 1980), 384-93. [The introd. is rpt.in *Cuadernos de Bibliofilia*, no. 6 (October 1980), 3-14.]

States what all ought to know about the early editions of LC and then goes on to comment on 28 modern editions of the work, calling attention to the lapses, inexactitudes and errors in the accompanying studies and editorial notes. Coverage runs from 1912 to 1977.

640. MONTERDE, Francisco. "LC y las obras de Sor Juana." *El Nacional* (Mexico) (February 7 1960), Supplement, 7.

Formulates two questions: could Sor Juana have read LC and is there any trace of LC in her work? (See following entry.)

641. _____. "Fernando de Rojas y Sor Juana." *El Nacional* (Mexico) (May 1 1960), Supplement, 4.

A reference to a Celestina in the second *sainete* of Sor Juana's *Los empeños de una casa* seems not to allude to Rojas' protagonist. (See following entry.)

642. _____. "Sor Juana y las Celestinas." *El Nacional* (Mexico) (May 15 1960), Supplement, 2.

The Celestina alluded to in Sor Juana's sainete (see preceding entry) is modeled on the one in Salazar y Torres' *El encanto es la hermosura y el hechizo sin hechizo*.

643. MONTESER, Frederick. *The Picaresque Element in Western Literature*. Tuscaloosa, Alabama: Univ. of Alabama Press, 1975. 152p. (Studies in the Humanities, 5)

States, but does not explore with detail, the belief that LC is an early manifestation of the picaresque.

a. *Studia Neophilologica* 48 (1976), 167-68, G. Hoffmeister

b. *Nineteenth Century Fiction* 81 (1976-77), 453-55, A. A. Parker

644. MONTESINO SAMPERIO, José V. "Sobre la cuantificación del estilo literario: una contribución al estudio de la unidad de autor en LC de Fernando de Rojas." *Revista Nacional de Cultura* (Caracas), no. 55 (March-April 1946), 94-115; no. 56 (May-June 1946), 63-88. Published together as a pamphlet (Caracas, 1946). 57p.

Lots of math and statistics, and the conclusion is that Act 1 was not written by the same hand that wrote Acts 2-16 (CCM). However, data does not indicate a third person for the interpolations, but points to the same hand at work as in Acts 2-16.

a. *Genus* 9 (1950-52), 270-75, at 273-74, E. Caranti

645. MONTESINOS, José F. "Dos reminiscencias de LC en comedias de Lope de Vega," in his *Estudios sobre Lope* (Mexico: El Colegio de México, 1951), 112-14 [later published in Salamanca: Anaya, 1969]. It originally appeared as a note in RFE 13 (1926), 60-62.

The author detects Areúsa (of Act 9) as a presence in *El galán escarmentado*, and Celestina's tricking of the French ambassador (Act 1) is echoed in *Por la puente, Juana*.

646. MOORE, John A. "Ambivalence of Will in LC." *Hispania* 47 (1964), 251-55.

Free will and destiny in a fight over the individual who acts impudently. LC lies somewhere between outright didacticism and advocacy of immorality.

647. MORALES, José Ricardo. [Interview with Antonio Joven.] *Primer Acto*, no. 192 (Jan. Feb. 1982), 108-110.

Part of a homage tribute to Margarita Xirgu in which Morales recalls moments of meeting with the famed actress for whom he adapted his version of LC. The premiere, with Xirgu playing Celestina, was held in Montevideo in 1949 (later seen in Buenos Aires; see entries 976.2 and 976.4).

648. _____. "¿Tres Celestinas en el Museo del Prado?" *Cel* 9, i (May 1985), 3-9.

The enormous impact of LC was not only on the reading public but on painters as well. Examination of Rojas' text alongside descriptions of Quentin Metsys' 'Vieja mesándose los cabellos,' Ribera's 'Vieja usurera,' and Goya's 'Dos mujeres y un hombre' demonstrates this broad appeal to the visual that LC exerted.

649. MORALES, Rafael. "Otro escenario más para LC." *Cuadernos de Literatura* (Madrid) 7 (1950), 221-31.

His candidate is Talavera de la Reina.

650. MORENO BAEZ, Enrique. "Meditación sobre LC." *Archivum* 8 (1958), 206-14.

Meditates on themes, magic, intention and the interpolations, all in the light of biographical data.

651. _____. "La obra y el autor," in his *Nosotros y nuestros clásicos* (Madrid: Gredos, 1961), 140-50.

Discusses the issues forced on the critic by the peculiar process of text formation of LC. Rojas, being a 'converso', seems to invest the work with deep and true pessimism and there is not—this author finds—the moral lesson in LC so often ascribed to it.

652. MORGAN, Erica C. "Rhetoric and Irony in LC." B. A. Diss. Portsmouth Polytechnic (England), 1977. ii + 78p. (*)

653. _____. "Rhetorical Technique in the Persuasion of Melibea." *Cel* 3, ii (Fall 1979), 7-18.

The rhetorical primers (Quintilian's is a good example) speak of the "colores rhetorici" in the mouths of the highborn. However, such recommendations, in the hands of Rojas, are easily adapted to ignoble beings, as Morgan shows in her detailed analysis of Celestina's Act 4 encounter with Melibea.

654. MORO, Donatella. "*El Buscón* de Quevedo a la luz de LC y del *Lazarillo*," in *La picaresca*, ed M. Criado de Val (Madrid: Fundación Universitaria Española, 1979), 689-704.

Shows that the plays on the word 'justicia' (LC, act 7) are clearly the basis of similar ones in the *Lazarillo* and, later, in *El Buscón*. Not just the word-play but also the context from LC is recalled in the other texts, establishing a trajectory for such word-play originating in Rojas' work.

655. MORON ARROYO, Ciriaco. *Sentido y forma de LC*. Madrid: Ed. Cátedra, 1974. 126p.

Sets out to clarify the philosophical posture of LC in the context of its times. Rejecting the extreme positions of the existential, moralistic, psychological and moral-literary approaches, this is in essence a synthesis of positive aspects of all of them.

a. *Segismundo*, nos. 19-20 (1974), 368-71, Antonio Rey
b. *Est Lit*, no. 547 (September 1974), 1830-31, G. Torres Nebrera
c. YWMLS 36 (1974), 271, A. K. G. Paterson
d. BHS 53 (1976), 344, K. Whinnom
e. *RPh* 34 (1980-81), 376-79, D. S. Severin

656. _____. *Sentido y forma de LC*. Madrid: Cátedra, 1984. 134p. Paper (Crítica y estudios literarios).

This is an expanded and corrected edition of the preceding entry.

a. *Cel* 9, i (May 1985), 47-48, I. A. Corfis

657. MÖRTINGER-GROHMANN, Gertrud. "*Tragedia Policiana* von Sebastián Fernández. Untersuchung einer spanischen Imitation der *Celestina*." Diss. Univ. of Salzburg, 1979. (*)

658. MUNOZ GARRIGOS, José. "Contribución al estudio del léxico de LC." Diss. Univ. of Murcia, 1972. M. Muñoz Cortés. (See following entry.)

659. _____. *Contribución al estudio del léxico de LC* [extract of his diss., Univ. of Murcia, 1972]. Murcia: Univ. of Murcia, 1974. 128p.

A theoretical study which delimits and gives coherence to various semantic groupings. An appendix contains a vocabulary and a list of proverbial expressions.

660. _____. "'Andar a pares los diez mandamientos': un pasaje oscuro de LC," in *Homenaje al Prof. Muñoz Cortés* (Murcia; Univ.-Facultad de Filosofía y Letras, 1976), 437-46.

An attempt to explain Elicia's remark about Melibea. Believes that Elicia feels that Melibea either does not comply with the Ten Commandments or with some strict code of beauty and, for that reason, does not deserve to be thought of as 'gentil'.

661. _____. "Tibulo y el vocabulario amoroso de los elegíacos en LC," in *Simposio Tibuliano* (Murcia: Univ. de Murcia—Sección de Filología Clásica, 1985), 347-361.

Probably not a direct source, Tíbulo shares many common traits with Rojas, one of which is the use of common lexical fields in the expression of passionate love, especially where a certain inexpressable quality is desired. Much of this descends to Rojas through the Latin elegaic poets and, closer to home, through Petrarch.

662. MUNOZ-MARINO, Enrique. "Metodología crítica e interpretativa de/y para la TCM de Fernando de Rojas." ACTAS: 111-23.

LC as a counterexample; that is, an example of the opposite of what is greatly to be admired and imitated. LC is the work of an orthodox thinker and the theological sense is well-grounded throughout. The author presents new readings for two of the verses in the acrostics to support his reasoning.

663. MURPHY, Allen F. "Irony in LC." *The Bulletin of the Pennsylvania State MLA* 62 (Spring 1984), 29-37.

Brief mentions—with some examples—of thirteen types of irony, all in the service of pessimism in the TCM.

N

664. NAGY, Edward. *Lope de Vega y LC: perspectiva pseudo-celestinesca en comedias de Lope.* Xalapa: Univ. Veracruzana, 1968. 189p. (Cuadernos de la Fac. de Filosofía, Letras y Ciencias, 39)

Chronicles Lope's liking for the less serious aspects of LC and shows where LC is incorporated into various of Lope's own works.

a. RJ 22 (1971), 383-84, G. Schüler

665. NEPAULSINGH, Colbert. "The Rhetorical Structures of the Prologues of the LBA and LC." BHS 51 (1974), 325-34.

The tri-partite structure of both prologues corresponds to the sermonizing attitude present in both authors. Studies the possible influence of the *accessus* and of rhetorical models.

666. NEWTON. Jeremy. "Two Eighteenth-Century English Adaptations of the *Celestina. Celestina: or, the Spanish Bawd. A Tragicomedy*, and *The Bawd of Madrid*." Diss. Westfield College-London Univ., 1974. 259p. + a supplement with photocopies of the texts. A. D. Deyermond. (*)

667. NIETO, Lídia. "De Doña Endrina a Melibea (dos amores y una alcahueta)." ACTAS: 169-83.

A comparative study of the heroines of the two works, their physical and their moral being. Juan Ruiz—in terms of the recommendations of the *artes poeticae*—is more independent than is Rojas. The latter develops enormously the character of Trotaconventos to create a real archetype.

668. NIVEIRO, Emilio. "LC y Talavera." ABC (June 25 1974), n. p.

Believes that LC may well have been written in Talavera.

669. NORTON, Frederick John. *Printing in Spain, 1501-1520, with a Note on the Early Editions of LC.* Cambridge: The Univ. Press, 1966.

The "Note" is on pp. 141-56. Shows that the editions bearing the imprint 'Sevilla 1502' are in reality all post-1511.

a. *The Library*, Series 5, 22 (1967), 364-65, H. M. Adams
b. BHS 44 (1967), 291-93, E. M. Wilson
c. BH 70 (1968), 537-46, P. Heugas
d. MLN 84 (1969), 343-48, D. W. McPheeters
e. HR 37 (1969), 524-29, C. L. Penney
f. *Filología* 14 (1970), 192-96, F. Weber de Kurlat

670. _____. *A Descriptive Catalogue of Printing in Spain and Portugal, 1501-1520.* London/New York/Melbourne: Cambridge Univ. Press, 1978.

A careful description of nine exemplars of LC (one CCM, seven TCMs and a "romance"). See the book's Index, under 'Calisto'.

a. RFE 59 (1977 [1979]), 315-16, F. López Estrada
b. TLS, no. 4019 (April 1980), 398, P. Needham
c. MLR 75 (1980), 214-16, D. W. Cruikshank
d. *Hispania* 63 (1980), 428-29, D. W. McPheeters
e. *RenQ* 33 (1980), 82-84, R. Mortimer

O

671. O'CONNOR, Thomas A. "On the Authorship of *El encanto es la hermosura*: A Curious Case of Dramatic

Composition." *Bulletin of the Comediantes* 26 (1974), 31-34.

This work by Agustín de Salazar y Torres (*El hechizo sin hechizo*) was probably completed by J. de Vera Tassis and then known as *El encanto de la hermosura*. It inspired a second ending in the 18th century by another collaborator who circulated it under the name of *La segunda Celestina*, thus paying homage to Rojas' immortal go-between.

672. _____. "La desmitificación de Celestina en *El encanto es la hermosura* de Salazar y Torres." ACTAS: 339-45.

Vera Tassis' ending for the play Salazar y Torres left incomplete at the time of his death seems to continue the intent of exaggerating the celestinesque figure in order to then 'demythify' her, to strip her of her magical trappings, and to reveal that her power was really her reputation, i. e., what others believed of her.

673. O'KANE, Eleanor. "The Proverb: Rabelais and Cervantes." CL 2 (1950), 360-69.

Sheds some light on the proverb used by Tristán in Act 14: "Biviendo con el conde que no matasse al hombre" (pp. 365-66).

674. _____. *Refranes y frases proverbiales españolas de la Edad Media*. Madrid: Real Academia Española, 1959. 267p. (BRAE, Anejo 2)

A dictionary listing by key word of proverbs and proverbial expressions from several medieval works, LC among them.

675. OKONSKA, Anna. "La TCM y la *Tragedia Policiana* de Sebastián Fernández." Thesis (Tesina). Rome. E. Scoles. (*)

676. OLIVA MARTIN, Anastasio. *Sentencias, pensamientos y refranes en LC*. Toledo: [Impta. de Gómez-Menor], 1970. 55p. (Biblioteca Toledo, 20)

He extracts from LC almost 400 proverbial items and lists them by acts with separate sections for the preliminary materials and the *Auto de Traso*. Some analysis of the totals is given at the end. There is no commentary; no conclusion.

677. OLSON, Paul R. "An Ovidian Conceit in Petrarch and Rojas." MLN 81 (1966), 217-21.

Rojas in Act 4 expounds on the idea that a disease and its cure may come from the same source. It is an idea akin to one featured in a sonnet by Petrarch.

678. ONIEVA, Antonio. *Agudezas, sentencias y refranes en la novela picaresca española*. Madrid: Paraninfo, 1974. 136p.

On pages 21-32 there appears a listing, by acts, of *sententiae*, proverbs and the like from LC. No commentary.

679. OOSTENDORP, H. Th. *El conflicto entre el honor y el amor en la literatura española hasta el siglo XVII*. The Hague: Van Goor Zonen, 1962. 215p.

Rojas is a conservative moralist of a medieval coloration and his LC is highly ethical and anti-individualistic (107-52). Already LC is pointing the way towards a perfect order: its imitations achieve this order to a more complete degree.

a. *Boletín de Filología Eespañola* 4 (1963), 39-40, V. Ruiz Ortiz
b. HR 31 (1963), 164-66, G. Correa

680. _____. "De invloed van de Spaanse tragikomodie LC op enige Nederlandse toneelschrijvers" (The Influence of the Spanish Tragicomedy LC in Some Dutch Dramatists). *De Nieuwe Tallgids* 57 (1964), 353-64. [In Dutch]

LC has helped Dutch dramatists develop a path to realist theatre.

681. ORDUNA, Germán. "Algunas calas para la caracterización del español medieval." *Revista Universitaria de Letras* (Mar del Plata) 1 (1979), 24-40.

Includes LC, for its phraseological structures, as a work influenced by new humanist currents abroad in late 15th-century Spain.

682. OROL PERNAS, Antonio. "Las monedas en la época de LC." ACTAS: 427-32.

Fascinating commentary on the currency alluded to in LC, and the rough values of the gold chain Calisto gives to Celestina. It adds to our understanding of the greed that motivates the characters.

683. OROZCO DIAZ, Emilio. "El huerto de Melibea. Para el estudio del tema del jardín en la poesía del siglo XV." *Arbor* 19, no. 65 (1951), 47-60; rpt. in his *Paisaje y sentimiento de la naturaleza en la poesía española* (Madrid: Prensa Española, 1968), 83-103.

The garden is the only place in LC described in any detail and it is unforgettable. With love and death being enacted there in close union with nature, the author believes it to be the first dramatization of Nature in Spanish literature.

684. _____. "LC: Hipótesis para una interpretación." *Insula*, no. 124 (1957), 1, 10.

Just who and what are Melibea and Calisto? She is a 'conversa' and he a 'cristiano viejo'. This is why Celestina is necessary to their union. This article and Garrido Pallardó's book (1957) began the rush to atttribute religious status to the characters of LC.

685. ORTEGA, Teófilo. "El amor y el dolor en la TCM," in his *Hervor de tragedia* (Madrid: Biblioteca Nueva, 1932), 23-112. It appeared first with the subtitle, "Notas al margen de LC," in Valladolid: [Impta. Castellana], 1927.

Basically a textual commentary of impressionistic coloration. One of the more unusual discussions involves the 'suicide' of Calisto. There is actually another explicated reading of LC offered in a long epilogue by Rosa ARCINIEGA (233-89). She offers her own views on Sempronio, Celestina, Calisto and Melibea as well as her reactions "as a woman" to the central plot and its resolution. (See also entry 30.)

686. ORTIZ DE PINEDO, S. "Melibea." *ABC* (May 28 1957), n. p.

Affirms that Melibea is the central figure of Rojas' work.

687. OSMANOVA, A. G. "Osobennosti avtorski positsii v *Tragikomedii o Kalisto i Melibee*" (Peculiar Features of the Author's Position in the TCM by Fernando de Rojas). *Filologicheskie Nauki*, no. 122 (1981) 44-50. [In Russian]

Presents Rojas as a man in a dialectic and philosophical encounter with his text. A world freeing itself of the straitjacketed didacticism of the Middle Ages is made, in part, the subject of the LC text. Rojas' attitude is critical rather than pious and what emerges in LC is an individualistic expression that is the keystone of the complex and even contradictory nature of the characters.

688. OYOLA, Eliezer. "LC," in his *Los pecados capitales en la literatura medieval española* (Barcelona: Puvill, 1979), 163-255.

Ch. 4 is a somewhat facile narration of the story of LC in which the author is at pains to point out instances of the Deadly Sins in the text. Mostly, though, we get Anger, Lust and Avarice.

a. *ZRP* 95 (1979), 533-35, A. Gier
b. *Nueva Estafeta*, no. 16 (May 1980), 71-73, C. H. Mamonde
c. *RPh* 36 (1982-83), 98-102, C. Stern

P

689. PABST, Walter. "'¿Ay tal muger nascida en el mundo?': Zur göttlichen Abkunft der Celestina." *Studia philologica. Homenaje a Dámaso Alonso* 2 (Madrid: Gredos, 1961), 557-76.

The cosmovision of woman as portrayed in *Celestina* is infernal.

690. PAGANO, Angela. "La funzione espressiva dei proverbi nella *Celestina*." Thesis (Tesina). Rome. E. Scoles.(*)

691. PALAU Y DULCET, Antonio. *Manual del librero hispanoamericano*, 2nd ed., vol. 3 (Barcelona: Author, 1950), 363-69.

Descriptions of select editions of the CCM and the TCM (to 1920). Some additions to this listing can be found in vol. 17 of the series (1965), under 'Rojas'.

692. PALMER, Margaret Eva. "An Interpretation of LC." Diss. Univ. of Washington, 1955. 242p. DA 15/12, 2528-29. No. 00-14258.

On the clash in LC between the heresies of the code of courtly love and the realities of the Spanish code of honor.

693. PANE, Remigio. *English Translations from the Spanish (1484-1943)*. New Brunswick, NJ: Rutgers Univ. Press, 1944.

Lists five translations from the period c. 1526 to 1739 (p. 174).

694. PANORAMA DEL TEATRO EN ESPANA. Madrid: Ed. Nacional, 1973.

Brief reports and photographs detailing some adaptations of LC in the 20th century.

695. PARKER, A. A. "Recent Scholarship in Spanish Literature." *RenQ* 21 (1968), 118-24.

The LC section takes up the theme of social conflict in recent studies on LC, which Parker does not consider essential to comprehension of the work.

696. PARKER, Margaret A. "The Transmission and Treatment of Mythological Material in some Medieval Spanish Texts." Diss. Westfield College-London Univ., 1978. 320p. A. D. Deyermond.

Mythological material in LC is treated on pp. 226-44 and 252-53.

697. PARR, James A. "LC: *Ut pictura poesis*." *LaC* 3, ii (1975), 22.

Abstract of a paper presented at the MLA (New York 1974) meeting, in which Parr presented a view of LC as a series of triangular configurations reflecting some of the precepts common in visual theories of Rojas' times.

698. _____. "Correspondencias formales entre LC y la pintura contemporánea," in *Estudios sobre el Siglo de Oro en homenaje a Raymond R. MacCurdy* (Albuquerque: Univ. of New Mexico/Madrid: Cátedra, 1983), 313-26. Illustrated.

Defines some formal and structural correspondences between techniques used in LC and those preeminent in contemporary painting: perspectivism, symbolism, accumulation of details, and triangulation of elements.

699. PAVIA, Mario N. "The Celestinas," in his *Drama of the Siglo de Oro: A Study of Magic* (New York: Hispanic Institute in the United States, 1959), 30-46.

On the role magic plays in LC and in its imitations.

a. *Archivum* 10 (1960), 432-35, J. M. Santano Cilleros
b. *LR* 16 (1962), 401, P. Groult

700. PEDRAZA, Felipe B., and Milagros RODRIGUEZ. "LC y el género celestinesco," in their *Manual de literatura española* (Tafalla: Cenlit, 1981), II, 61-116.

The authors underline the dramatic character of LC and highlight the coherence of its dramatic movement. They also analyze the *dramatis personae*, the meaning of the work and its influences on later works (especially *La lozana andaluza*). Ironies of situation and language are touched upon.

701. PEETERS-FONTAINAS, J. F. "Une édition perdue de LC: Anvers, 1558." *Papyrus* 1 (1936), 28-30.

An unknown edition cited by Amarita in 1835 seems to be the same one found cited in a London book catalogue from 1674.

702. PEIXOTO DA FONSECA, F. "Considerações sobre o estilo de LC." *Labor: Revista de Ensino Liceal* (Aveiro) 19, no. 143 (1954), n. p. (*)

703. PELICARIC, Iván M. "Turbación en el amante a través de LC." *Letras* (Buenos Aires), no. 5 (1982), 103-108.

Using as a point of departure these words of Sempronio from Act 1: "¡O soberano Dios (...)! ¡Quánta *premia* pusiste en el amor, que es necesaria turbación en el amante!," the author studies the impact of haste in the structure of LC and in the denouement of the lives of the individual characters, especially Calisto and Melibea.

704. PEÑA PRADO, M. "LC," in his *Cuatro ensayos de literatura castellana* (Lima: Ed. Altura, 1937), 53-74.

A superficial run-through of LC, marred by factual error in many places (e. g., the CCM with 17 acts, Calisto [text says Centurio] dies when a ladder is pulled out from under him, and so on).

705. PENNEY, Clara Louisa. *The Book Called "Celestina" in the Library of The Hispanic Society of America*. New York: Hispanic Society of America, 1954. viii + 157p.

Catalogue of the Society's editions with a list of editions and translations prior to 1635. Much useful information on early eds. is given in the early pages.

   a. *Bulletin des Etudes Portugaises et de l'Institut Français au Portugal* 17 (1953 [1954]), 271, I. S. Révah
   b. *Arbor* 28, no. 101 (1954), 207-08, M. Dolç
   c. NRFH 8 (1954), 196-200, H. Serís
   d. *Symposium* 8 (1954), 191-96, D. W. McPheeters
   e. BHS 32 (1955), 116-17, G. D. Trotter
   f. HR 24 (1956), 239-40, J. E. Gillet
   g. *Atenea* (Concepción, Chile) 127 (1957), 169-71, J. Loveluck
   h. RHM 23 (1957), 59, M. S. Carrasco Urgoiti

706. PEREZ, J. Bernardo. "La alcahueta devota: una perspectiva islámica de Celestina." *Abside* 39 (1975), 456-69.

Celestina has a religious sense which none of her Western literary antecedents has. It comes—so the author thinks—from the Arabic *El collar de la paloma*, in which work the go-betweens pretend to religious piety.

707. PEREZ, Louis C. "Coplas desconocidas del tema celestinesco." *Homenaje a Antonio Rodríguez-Moñino* 2 (Madrid: Castalia, 1966), 51-57.

Notes on some 16th-century verses dealing with the fraudulent

ways of a go-between, which seem part of an entire genre of such poems inspired by the figure of Celestina.

708. PEREZ DE LA OSSA, Huberto. "La modernidad de la TCM." *La gaceta ilustrada* (June 1 1957), 23-25.

From an adapter of LC (with Luis Escobar), notes on the vivid realism in LC's language and on the era which produced such a remarkable work. There are color photos of many members of the cast. See entry 979.2.

709. PEREZ ESTRADA, Francisco. "LC en folklore nicaragüense." *Estudios Centroamericanos* (July 1954), 341-45; rpt. in his *Cuatro estudios de folklore* (Managua: Ed. Novedades, 1954), n. p., and in *Nicaragua indígena*, nos. 9-10 (January-June 1956), 60-64. It appears again in the author's *Estudios de folklore nicaragüense* (Managua: Tip. Brenes, [1968?]), 55-60.

Cites some elements of magic and medicine, superstitions, proverbs and folk wisdom linked to social types from LC that are alive and well in Nicaragua today.

710. PEREZ GOYENA, Antonio. "Sobre la TCM." *Boletín de la Comisión de Monumentos Históricos y Artísticos de Navarra*, Fourth Series, 20 (1936), 127-30.

Notes on the French-Spanish ed. of Pamplona: Carlos Labayen, 1633, and on several editions of the *Index* relevant to the history of the circulation of LC (viz., 1667, 1790, 1793 and 1805).

711. PEREZ NAVARRO, F. "El diablo en Occidente. En torno a LC, a la Cañizares, y a la madre del Buscón, don Pablos." *Indice* 13, no. 126 (1959), 19.

The magic arts as practiced by these three fictional women.

712. PEREZ SAENZ, Vicente. "Sobre lo popular y lo culto en LC." *Humanitas* (Tucumán), no. 13 (1960), 171-81.

The two worlds of LC are seen in the division of upper and lower class characters, the action seen in double points of view in recapitulations, and the double levels in language and style. LC is a meeting ground of the elegant style of humanist tradition and the popular style springing from such works as *Corbacho*.

713. PETRICONI, Hellmuth. "Die Schuldfrage," in his *Die Verführte Unschuld* (Hamburg: Cram-de-Gruyter, 1953), 34-36.

Always the didactic author, Rojas so manipulates the action that neither Calisto nor Melibea, nor both in concert, share the great responsibilities for their actions and the aftermath.

714. PHILLIPS, Katherine Kaiper. "Ironic Foreshadowing in LC." KRQ 21 (1974), 469-82.

The theme is treated here with the help of previous criticism on irony in LC.

715. POPEANGA, Eugenia. "Ecos de LC en la literatura

rumana." *Revista de Istorie și Theorie Literara* (Bucharest) 24 (1975), 81-84, and in ACTAS: 391-94.

There is a 20th-century prose work, *Craii de Curtea Vecge* (The Princes of the Old Court), by Mateiu Caragiale, which shows analogies with LC: in situations and in character portrayal, especially in the case of a go-between, Pirgu, and Celestina.

716. PORTUONDO, Aleida T. *Conflicto racial en LC*. San Juan, Puerto Rico: Ed. Bassan, 1977. 38p.

Survey of writings on the topic to about 1965, both pro and con. The author's own conclusion leans towards seeing LC as the work of a *cristiano nuevo*.

717. POSTON, JR., Lawrence S. "An Etymological Vocabulary to *The Celestina*." Diss. Univ. of Chicago, 1938. 138p. DA 15 (for 1939), 503A. H. Keniston. Also printed privately, New York: Wilson, 1938.

Within the alphabetical limits set (A-E), this is a project containing vast amounts of lexical data. What makes it hard to use is that it is keyed to Foulché-Delbosc's 1902 edition of the CCM.

718. POUSA, Patria C. "LC y el *Lazarillo de Tormes*." *Lotería*, no. 217 (1974), 10-16.

A few introductory notes to guide the new reader of LC.

719. POYAN DIAZ, Daniel. "Literatura y Pirineos: LC al gusto francés." *Filología Moderna* 8, nos. 31-32 (1968), 229-51.

The question of taste as seen through a series of translations and theatrical adaptations in French.

720. PRADO BALBOA, Evelia. "Lenguaje coloquial de LC." Thesis (Tesina). Univ. of Madrid, 1955, R. Lapesa. (*)

721. PRIETO, Adolfo. "El sentimiento de la muerte a través de la literatura española: Fernando de Rojas. LC." *Revista de Literaturas Modernas* 2 (1960), 161-70.

In conflict in LC are the opposing tendencies of affirmation and negation of the value of life. The attitude towards death is by and large a product of a life embittered by a loss of faith: this leads irrevocably to the pessimistic outlook shaping LC.

672. PUPO-WALKER, Enrique. "La historia como pretexto: formas de la invención literaria en *El carnero*," in his *La vocación literaria del pensamiento de América* (Madrid: Gredos, 1982), 123-155.

Explores the many relationships between LC and the episode, "Un negocio con Juana García," from this work by Juan Rodríguez Freyle.

723. PURCELL, H. "LC and the *Interlude of Calixto and Melibea*." BHS 44 (1967), 1-15.

Finds that the frequent assertion that French and Italian translations are the basis for the *Interlude* (ca 1530) is incorrect.

Presents instead a sampling of the parts of the Spanish LC that provide materials for the translator-adapter.

Q

724. QUANN, Joanna. "Poetic and Pragmatic Discourse in LC." Diss. The George Washington Univ., 1980. 263p. DAI 41 (1980-81), 2144A. No. 80-23866. I. Azar.

On the poetic and pragmatic levels of discourse in LC. There is a demonstration—for each main character of LC—of the interdependence of these levels. In this demonstration it is shown that Rojas was aware that the real distinction between the two levels has more to do with their contextual function than their linguistic forms.

725. QUIJANO Y TERAN, Margarita. "LC y *Otelo*: ensayo de literatura dramática comparada." Thesis (Tesina). Univ. Nacional Autónoma de México, 1955. (See following entry.)

726. _____. *LC y Otelo. Estudio de literatura dramática y comparada*. Mexico: Univ. Nacional Autónoma, 1957. 180p. (Filosofía y Letras, 15)

Otelo wins all the prizes in this showdown with LC. Characterization is better in it, its artistic structure is better drawn and, since it does not suffer from a didactic overload, it makes for better theatre.

a. *Metáfora* 3, no. 16 (1957) 44-45, J. Arellano
b. *Revista de la Universidad de Mexico* 12, no. 3 (1957-58), 29, A. Bonifaz Nuño
c. *Shakespeare Quarterly* 10 (1959), 113-14, J. L. Lievsay

R

727. R. "La Celestina; o traji-comedia de Calixto y Melibea." *Cel* 5, i (May 1981), 49-52.

The original version of these reflections of a reader of LC appeared in *Semanario pintoresco español* (Madrid), in 1836. It offers some interesting insights on reaction to LC in the 19th century.

728. R., P. C. "Inhumación definitiva de los restos de Fernando de Rojas." *El Libro Español*, no. 274 (October 1980), 521-22.

A brief notice of the commemorative festivities marking the return of Rojas' remains to his hometown, with some additional information on the past history of those remains.

729. RAMIREZ CALVENTE, A. "Jarchas, Moaxajas, Zéjeles (II)." *Al-Andalus* 41 (1976), 147-78.

The 'C' section (p. 152) adduces from Ben Quzman (zéjel 96) the idea of wine being a bed-warmer. Its parallel is found in LC, act 9.

730. RAMOS JIMENEZ, José. *'Algo más que tenerías.' Algunas notas en torno a la localización de LC.* Salamanca: Trabajos y Días, 1950. 8p. [Cited in YWMLS 14 (1952), 147.] (*)

731. RANDALL, Dale J. B. *The Golden Tapestry: A Critical Survey of Non-Chivalric Spanish Fiction in English Translation, 1537-1657.* Durham, North Carolina: Duke Univ. Press, 1963.

See the first part of ch. 7 for the presence of LC in England.

732. RANK, Jerry Rees. "An Edition of the CCM, Seville 1501, with Commentary on Variants and Filiation of Early Texts of LC." Diss. Univ. of Wisconsin, 1967. 2 vols. cclxxxi + 352p. DA 28/12, 5067A. No. 67-12466. J. H. Herriott. (See entry 1117.)

733. _____. "Awareness and Reaction: The Underlying Elements of Characterization in the Servants of LC." KRQ 19 (1972), 223-36.

The characters of LC are distinguished by the strong sense of self they all have and express, but especially those from the lower class. Illustrated with analyses of several scenes.

734. _____. "The Significance of León Amarita's 1822 Edition of LC." *The Papers of the Bibliographical Society of America* 69 (1975), 243-55.

A general treatment of the edition, its sources and its influence on later editions. Amarita's is the first modern edition of LC.

735. _____. "The Uses of 'Dios' and the Concept of God in LC." *Revista Canadiense de Estudios Hispánicos* 5 (1980-81), 75-91.

A complete panorama of the occurrences of the word 'Dios' in LC shows that it fulfills a definite rhetorical function in characterizing Celestina and Calisto especially. In LC, there exists a concept of God, and it is linked closely to an awareness of Time.

736. _____. "Fritz Holle's 1911 Edition of the *Comedia.*" Cel 5, i (May 1981), 47-48.

A review of the contents of Holle's volume and a high assessment of the value it still has for the historian of celestinesque literature.

737. _____. "Los argumentos de las primeras ediciones de LC: guías para la filiación de la *Comedia.*" [Forthcoming in AEM]

738. _____. "Narrativity and *Celestina,*" in *Hispanic Studies in Honor of Alan D. Deyermond: A North American Tribute,* ed. John S. Miletich (Madison,

Wisconsin: Hispanic Seminary of Medieval Studies, 1986).

Concentrates on three sections of LC in which the present, through memory and forms of narration, is impinged upon by the past to create for the reader a world closer to that of later, more openly narrative forms of fiction. These are: Pármeno's descriptions of Celestina in Act 1, Celestina's recounting of her days with Claudina (Acts 3 and 7), and Celestina's Act 9 banquet-table reminiscences about the good old days. In all of these, we have clear traces of the emerging autobiographical narrative.

739. RAUHUT, Franz. "Das Dämonische in der *Celestina,*" in *Festgabe zum 60. Geburtsdag Karl Vosslers*, ed. Leo Jordan et al (Munich: Max Hueber Verlag, 1932), 117-48.

A lengthy exposition of the daemonic presence in LC, and of its role(s) in the shaping of plot, character and action.

740. RAUHUT, Helmut. "Herr und Knecht in der spanischen Literatur: LC, *Lazarillo, Guzmán, Quijote.*" Diss. Univ. of Heidelberg, 1971. 259p. DAI-C 39/04, 588C. (See following entry.)

741. _____. *Herr und Knecht in der spanischen Literatur; LC, Lazarillo, Guzmán, Quijote.* Munich, 1971. 259p + xv [= Bibliography].

LC on pp. 18-117, seen in Hegelian terms (especially the contrast of master and servant). Celestina comes in for special attention, for she is master of all the characters in one way or another, as well as a servant to many. This ambiguity is one Rojas tries to resolve by having Celestina foment action on the part of the servants against the masters: his treatment of the theme is innovative in Spanish letters.

a. BH 75 (1973), R. Pageard

742. READ, Malcolm. "LC and the Renaissance Philosophy of Language." *Philological Quarterly* 55 (1976), 166-77.

Humanists advocated a natural use of language, to include a realistic level of rhetorical flavoring. Celestina's control of language is so thorough and complete that she ends up by abusing it, and thus brings about her own fall. It may be—the author feels—that Rojas distrusted the humanist approach to language and expressed this distrust dramatically in the TCM.

743. _____. "Fernando de Rojas' Vision of the Birth and Death of Language." MLN 93 (1978), 163-75.

For Rojas, language is intuitive, direct and disconcerting. It can also pervert and distort and, thus, abuse its essential function: communication. In the light of such ideas, the author re-interprets the source of the distance between Melibea and Calisto, and of the role played by Pármeno in the early part of LC. The vacuum that is left by the degradation of language is part of the catastrophe at the end of Rojas' great masterwork.

744. _____. "The Rhetoric of Social Encounter: LC and the Renaissance Philosophy of Language," in his *The Birth and Death of Language: Spanish Literature and*

Linguistics (1300-1700) (Madrid: Porrúa Turanzas, 1983), 70-96.

a. JHP 8 (1983-1984), 159-162, M. Johnston

Knits together the discussions contained in the previous two entries (see above) in which the natural and the artifical are seen, through language usage, to be at the center of a social crisis in Rojas' Spain.

745. REAL DE LA RIVA, César. "Notas a LC." *Acta Salmanticensia* 16 (1962), 383-92.

Five brief notes on: Jewish influence on LC; authorship; Melibea's songs from Act 19; the 'Salamanca 1500' TCM; and the original date of composition.

746. RECKERT, Stephen. "La textura verbal de LC." *Studies in Honour of Rita Hamilton* (London: Támesis, 1976) 161-74.

Selects seven groups of "principal ideas" (each to include its opposite) from LC and shows how the verbal context reveals the source of cosmic anarchy which gives form to Rojas' negative presentation of the world. Proposes that words and concepts be taken more literally than they have been in past interpretations of LC.

747. REDONDO, Agustín, "Fernando de Rojas et l'Inquisition." *Mélanges de la Casa de Velázquez* 1 (1965), 345-47.

New documents on Rojas that deal with fines he had to pay.

748. REYES, Antonio. "LC, el tercer mito hispano." *Boletín de la Academia Venezolana* 27, nos. 101-02 (1959), 37-50.

The other two are Don Juan and Don Quijote.

749. REYNIER, Gustave. "LC," in *Les origines du roman réaliste* (Paris, 1912; rpt. Geneva: Slatkine, 1969), 282-314.

Mostly on the character of Celestina and her actions throughout the work. Concludes with a firm statement about how strong the impact of LC was in 16th-century France.

750. REYNOLDS, John J. "'La moça que esperaua al ministro' (LC, aucto III)." *RomN* 5 (1963-64), 200-02.

This statement is a cover for Crito who is hiding upstairs. It has one meaning for Sempronio, and another for Elicia and Celestina.

751. RICARD, Robert. "Sobre la moralidad de LC." *Abside* 4 (1950), 15-18.

LC is basically an immoral work because it denies human liberty—free will—and depicts characters of no ultimate interest.

752. _____. "LC vista otra vez." CHA, no. 198 (1966), 469-80; rpt. in his *Nouvelles études religieuses. Espagne et Amérique espagnole* (Paris: Centre de Recherches Hispaniques, 1973), 83-95.

The world of LC is not Christian and there was no Christian sensibility invoked in its creation as a literary work. It is not moral.

753. RICO, Francisco. "Brujería y literatura," in *Brujología* (Madrid: Seminarios y Ediciones, 1975), 97-117.

Rojas' LC is discussed (98-103) along with other apt works. Rico takes Lida de Malkiel to task for proposing as decorative the magical elements in LC and argues, to the contrary, that they are realistic and well integrated. They would be so judged by the contemporary public. The work is ambiguous, however, in that the efficacy of the magic in Melibea's transformation is not clearly perceived. This openness to readings on multiple levels is characteristic of Rojas' art.

754. RICO-AVELLO, Carlos. "Perfil psicobiográfico de LC." ACTAS: 155-61.

A sketch: it presents lists of Celestina's traits and her former and current activities. In all of the classifications listed, she exerts firm control over both people and situations.

755. RIPOLL, Carlos. *LC a través del Decálogo y otras notas sobre la literatura de la Edad de Oro*. New York: Las Américas, 1969.

Three notes on pp. 11-87: 1) "LC a través del Decálogo" (11-52) catalogues passages which record transgressions against each of the Ten Commandments, assigning them structural importance in the work; 2) "El sí-no de Melibea" (53-65) studies the psychology of Melibea and concludes that she is finally dominated by egoism; and 3) "El planto de Pleberio" (67-87) tries to see in the rhetoric of the lament a key to an understanding of the pessimistic vision in LC.

a. *La Torre* 18, no 69 (1970), 153-56, A. I. Bagby, Jr.
b. BHS 48 (1971), 263-64, R. W. Truman
c. *Insula*, no. 292 (1971), 8-9, R. Rexach
d. *Hispanófila*, no. 43 (1971), 75-77, J. B. Avalle Arce
e. RPh 25 (1971-72), 480-81, D. S. Severin

756. RIQUER, Martín de. "Fernando de Rojas y el primer acto de LC." RFE 41 (1957), 373-95.

Rojas did not write Act 1. His job was to interpret and edit it, and he doubtless made small changes in the manuscript in his possession. When he revised it in 1501, greater changes occurred after Act 2. Riquer posits that scene i of Act 1 takes place in a church.

757. RIUS, Luis. "LC," in his *Los grandes textos de la literatura española hasta 1700* (Mexico: Ed. Pormaca, 1966), 163-73.

An account of the formation of the text of LC and some brief praise of its literary merits.

758. ROBB, James Willis. "Grata compañia: una charla erudita de María Rosa [Lida de Malkiel] con Don Alfonso [Reyes]." *Humanitas* (Nuevo León, Mexico) (October 8 1968), 235-48.

Observations on the correspondence the two scholars maintained.

In one letter Lida de Malkiel speaks of studies by Gilman (1956) and Bataillon (1961) and contrasts them with opinions of her own to be found in her *La originalidad artística de LC* (1962).

759. RODRIGUEZ, Fermín. "Las técnicas de avance y retroceso en *Diálogo entre el amor y un viejo* y LC." ETL 7 (1978-79), 151-55.

Exposition with examples of the theme announced in the title: El Viejo and Melibea surrender under the constant verbal attack of Amor and Celestina, respectively. While the techniques are similar, the artistic realizations are rather different.

760. RODRIGUEZ, Sagrario. "Hacia unos caracteres comunes en la literatura hebreo-española." ACTAS: 299-306.

Believes that more emphasis ought to be given to the traditional role of Jews as medical experts and the fact that Rojas' Jewishness gave him a special perspective on medicine. He was able to create this aspect of Celestina not only from literary models but also from within a living tradition of which he was part.

761. RODRIGUEZ-LUIS, Julio. "La pasión imposible de Calisto y Melibea: hacia una revaloración de datos contradictorios." REH 13 (1979), 339-58.

Provides a resumé at the outset of previous opinion on the topic of why the lovers do not get married. His solution is that Rojas, himself bourgeois, saw that new lines were being drawn between what once was considered the nobility and the new, emerging commercial class. This new social difference prevented the lovers from marrying.

762. RODRIGUEZ MENDEZ, José María. "LC y otras cosas." *El Noticiero Universal* (Barcelona) (October 8 1968), 31.

Thoughts on LC occasioned by the news that Casona's stage version had recently surpassed 2,000 performances.

763. RODRIGUEZ-PUERTOLAS, Julio. "El linaje de Calisto." *Duquesne Hispanic Review* 7, no. 2 (1968), 15-23; also in *Hispanófila*, no. 33 (1968), 1-6; rpt. in his *De la Edad Media a la edad conflictiva: estudios de literatura española* (Madrid: Gredos, 1972), 209-16.

The scarce references to Calisto's bloodline and lineage and the large number to Melibea's seem to reflect the social disgrace many Jewish families suffered. Calisto is 'converso' in LC, not Melibea.

764. _____. "Nueva aproximación a LC." *Estudios Filológicos* (Valdivia, Chile) 5 (1969), 71-90, and *AEM* 6 (1969), 411-32; rpt. in his *De la Edad Media* (see preceding entry), 217-42.

Rojas' vision of society is both faithful and corrosive; it is also ironic. Tragic solitude as a theme makes LC a superlative work: its realization of the isolated existence within the universe of the characters (without real ties, each to the other) makes it the first 'modern' work of Spanish literature.

765. _____. "LC, o la negación de la negación," in his *Literatura, historia, alienación* (Barcelona: Labor Universitaria, 1976), 147-71.

Rojas rejects both the past and the present, the latter characterized by a middle class caught up in its own egoism and reification of values, a class which perverts language and meaning and gets lost in the struggle between essence and existence, between a desire to be and a need to be.

    a. *Insula*, no. 365 (April 1977), A. Romero Márquez
    b. BHS 54 (1979), 56-57, A. D. Deyermond

766. RODRIGUEZ S., J. G. "LC," in his *Literatura española trascendental* (Caracas: Univ. Central de Venezuela—Dirección de Cultura, 1980), 127-139.

After the dutiful presentation of LC as a work written in an age of transition (with its problems touching on editions, authors and the like), the author takes up the central issue of love as the unifying factor in the action of the work and death as its unravelling. LC is one of the earliest Spanish representations of the dramatic qualities of everyday life.

767. ROIG, Adrien. *La comédie de Bristo ou l'entremetteur (Comedia do Fanchono ou de Bristo), d'António Ferreira (1562). Etude et analyse lexicale.* Paris: Presses Universitaires de France, 1973.

Traces the debt to LC of the Portuguese work for the assassination of its go-between (pp. 42-44). It may have been owing to an intermediary text, a Portuguese translation of LC, from 1540.

768. ROMERO Y SARRACHAGA, Federico. *Salamanca, teatro de LC, con algunos apuntamientos sobre la identidad de sus autores.* Madrid: Escelicer, 1959. 117p.

The locale of LC is Salamanca, Cota is the author of the CCM, and the work was finished by Proaza, using the name of Fernando de Rojas.

    a. RL 15 (1959), 137-38, R. Esquer Torres

769. ROSA, William. "La experiencia de Celestina: un arma de dos filos." *Tropos* (East Lansing, Michigan) 7, i (Spring 1978), 1-13.

Uses modern psychological techniques of analysis to demonstrate how the experience accumulated by Celestina helps her in every phase of her career but, at the same time, is insufficient to prevent her bringing about her own death. Her own avarice blinds her to avarice in others.

770. ROSLER, Margarete. "Beziehungen der *Celestina* zur Alexiuslegende." ZRP 58 (1938), 365-67.

Explores some verbal echoes linking LC's Act 21 lament and similar scenes from the extant texts of the legends of Saint Alexis.

771. ROSSELLI, Ferdinando. "Iterazione sinonimiche nella *Celestina*." *Miscellanea di Studi Ispanici* (Pisa) 14 (1966-67), 121-49.

A catalogue of synonymous expressions from LC, using the ed. of Criado de Val/Trotter (entry 1116).

772. ROUND, Nicholas G. "Conduct and Values in LC." *Medieval and Renaissance Studies on Spain and Portugal in Honour of P. E. Russell*, ed. F. W. Hodcroft et al (Oxford: SSMLL, 1981), 38-52.

The central conflict peculiar to LC—and whose expression allows fully incompatible interpretations of the text to co-exist—is that of *bienes ajenos vs bienes propios*. A formulation, exploration, and reformulation of the interrelationships of these values in the light of the observable conduct of the characters in LC allows us to see that factors other than Rojas' being a *converso* may weigh heavily in the negatively-charged world view etched by him in acts 2-21.

773. ROZEMOND, J. J. "'Eclipse ay mañana, la puente es llevada...': Dos notas sobre la fecha de *Celestina*." *Cel* 6, ii (Fall 1982), 15-18.

If historical, as Foulché-Delbosc claimed it was, the eclipse Sempronio refers to must be one of those that occurred in 1491 or 1485, and not the one of 1482 (as posited by F-D). Also, the bridge carried away by the waters offers interesting speculation on, perhaps, a date of composition for the CCM later than 1498 or 1499.

774. RUANO, Argimiro. "*El ingenioso hidalgo Don Quijote de la Mancha* y LC." *Atenea* (Puerto Rico) 2 (1965), 61-70.

The two works are compared in Aristotelian terms.

775. RUBENS, Erwin Félix. "Sobre los actos interpolados en LC." *Criterio* (Buenos Aires) 33 (1961), 16-18.

Why would Rojas have wanted to modify an already popular work? Rubens believes that Rojas wanted—in the TCM—to motivate the tragedies with a new purpose in mind.

776. _____. "Algunas notas sobre lengua y estilo de LC." *Cuadernos del Idioma* 3, no. 10 (1968), 125-32.

In this fully-dialogued work, dramatic values repose in the *tú-yo* and *mío-tuyo* relationships. Refrains are important, but so is the superimposition of differing levels of language, in signaling the disaster that results when ideal love meets reality head-on.

777. RUBIO, Carlos. "El juego de seducciones de LC: una estructura dramática." *Cel* 2, i (May 1978), 13-23.

A scrutiny of LC's seduction scenes, the abstract as well as the real. All the characters play roles as both seducer and seduced: in this scheme, symmetries and oppositions are interrelated to the point that the sensitive reader is provided with keys to a fuller appreciation of Rojas' art.

778. _____. "Lectura semántica de LC." Diss. Univ. of California, Berkeley, 1979. 268p. DAI 40/7 (1979-80), 4078A. No. 80-00498. C. Faulhaber.

A fresh reading of LC which uses *semas* or units of meaning as a basis for interpretation. The three major areas of meaning turn out to be love, deceit and death, the latter ruling, in the end, the others.

779. RUBIO GARCIA, Luis. "LC." *Revista de Archivos, Bibliotecas y Museos* 69 (1961), 655-749.

A substantial study which suggests that Rojas subjects medieval thought to a rigorous intellectual probe in order to delimit the conflicts he dramatizes in LC. The author perceives that Rojas effects an authentic liberation of Will from the hold of Reason, that Rojas was not a Judaizer but a Christian thinker—almost an Erasmist—who sensed the religious crisis pervading the Renaissance.

780. _____. "Más sobre LC." *Anales de la Universidad de Murcia* 28 (1969-70), 4-139.

Includes: a defense of Salamanca as LC's locale; a very useful and detailed chronology of the action of LC (with its contradictions); the presentation of Celestina as humane; Melibea's age; the concept of love in LC; the so-called Jewish element in LC; and the problem of nobility. LC reflects the Renaissance religious crisis.

781. _____. *Estudios sobre LC*. Murcia: Dept. de Filología Románica, 1970. 241p. (Biblioteca Filológica, 1)

Reprints the two preceding entries, plus his review of Maravall (entry 577.b).

782. _____. "Censuras y prohibiciones de LC." *Homenaje al Prof. Muñoz Cortés* (Murcia: Univ.-Facultad de Filosofía y Letras, 1977), 659-71.

A recapitulation of various movements to censor LC.

783. RUDDER, Robert S. *The Literature of Spain in English Translation*. New York: Ungar, 1975.

The section on LC is pp. 95-97.

784. RUEGG, August. "Rationalismus und Romantik in der *Celestina*." ZRP 82 (1966), 9-21.

LC is not only a morality and an instructive satire: it also portrays the appealing aspect of Love's power over Calisto and Melibea. The author advocates harmonizing the rational with the romantic, for LC can justify both views.

a. RFE 51 (1968), 320, A. Llorente Maldonado

785. RUGGERIO, Michael John. "The Evolution of the Go-Between: Eros and Witchcraft." Diss. Harvard Univ., 1964. 130p. CDI 29 (1973), 574. S. Gilman. (See following entry.)

786. _____. *The Evolution of the Go-Between in Spanish Literature through the Sixteenth Century*. Berkeley: Univ. of California Press, 1966. 102p. (UCPMP, 78)

The main idea is that Celestina is principally a witch who also is a go-between. Magic and witchcraft in LC are not merely adornments but rather they are basic to the characterization of

Celestina. Both earlier and later related literary types are adduced as illustration.

a. *Romanitas* 8 (1967), 404-08, A. de Jesús Santos
b. *RPh* 22 (1968-69), 111-14, D. W. McPheeters
c. RF 81 (1969), 274-78. B. Ophey
d. NRFH 21 (1972), 119-22, R. Kersten
e. BH 76 (1974), 208-11, P. Heugas

787. _____. "LC: Didacticism Once More." RF 82 (1970), 56-64.

The author cites from the anonymous mid-16th-century *Celestina comentada* to show that contemporary readers did not read LC as a strictly didactic work.

788. _____. "The Religious Message of LC." *Folio. Papers on Language and Literature* (State University of New York-Brockport), no. 10 (1977), 69-81.

This is a study that guides the reader through the complicated imagery of LC, which masks a rejection of the Christian hope for salvation. Rojas does this under an appearance of conformity and it is another sign of his artistic genius. There are several passages of the text analyzed to show how the hyperbolic excesses of language—in the hands of a master of ironic insinuation—are clear signs of the anti-Christian attitude portrayed.

789. RUIZ, Higinio, and Carmen BRAVO-VILLASANTE. "Talavera de la Reina (1479-98), ¿lugar de acción de LC?" *AEM* 3 (1966), 553-62; also in *Actas del Segundo Congreso Internacional de Hispanistas (1965)* (Nijmegen, 1967), 525-41.

Textual clues point to Talavera as the locale of LC.

790. RUIZ RAMON, Francisco. "Dos amores trágicos en la literatura española." *Atenea* (Puerto Rico) 1 (1964), 7-19.

Deals with the loves of Calisto and Melibea and those of Diego and Isabel (the "Amantes de Teruel").

791. _____. *Historia del teatro español. I: Desde sus orígenes hasta 1900*. Madrid: Alianza, 1967; 2nd ed. 1971, pp. 53-78. A third edition of the work (Madrid: Cátedra, 1979), is updated (pp. 56-75), and rpt. in 1983.

Myth in LC is of universal dimension as it presents a society in the midst of conflicting values. The characters take on life as they experience life. An appendix lists early editions.

792. _____. "Nota sobre la autoría del Acto I de LC." HR 42 (1974), 431-35.

The Act 1 phrase, "el plebérico coraçón," indicates that Rojas wrote Act 1, since he left the phrase intact; he must already have had in mind a character named Pleberio. The phrase would have been too problematic for a Rojas reading an unannotated manuscript.

793. RUMEAU, A. "L'introduction à LC: ' ... una cosa bien escusada ...'." *Les Langues Neo-Latines* 60, no. 176 (1966), 1-26.

LC should be read as it was read by its contemporaries, as Bataillon advocated (1961). Of especial importance is the correct reading of the opening scene, since it is intimately tied up with the final catastrophe.

794. RUSSELL, Peter E. "A Stuart Hispanist: James Mabbe." BHS 30 (1953), 78-84.

Mabbe was more than a translator of Spanish works; he also was the first critic of Spanish literature in England. His role as a diplomat is related to his labors as translator.

795. _____. "LC." TLS (July 10 1959), 411.

Melibea is not in love with Calisto from the outset of that famous first scene of LC.

796. _____. "La magia como tema integral de la TCM." *Studia Philologica. Homenaje a Dámaso Alonso* 3 (Madrid: Gredos, 1963), 337-54; rpt.—slightly expanded and updated—in his *Temas de LC y otros estudios* (see entry 800), 243-76.

The value of magical practice in the 15th century was real for LC's readers and Russell develops this at length here, with an eye to restoring to LC a dimension of meaning modern critics have not taken seriously enough.

a. ZRP 80 (1964), 588, H. Kröll

797. _____. "Literature in the Time of the Catholic Monarchs (1474-1516)," in *A Companion to Spanish Studies* (London: Methuen, 1973), 267-76, at 273-76.

Densely written resumé of the authorship problem in LC, the evolution of the text, the uniqueness of the work (with special emphasis on the brilliance of characterization and psychological motivation).

a. BHS 52 (1975), 79-82, F. Pierce

798. _____. "*Celestina comentada.*" *Studies in Honour of Rita Hamilton* (London: Támesis, 1976), 175-93; rpt. in his *Temas de LC y otros estudios* (see entry 800), 295-321 [in Spanish translation].

The work discussed is c. 1550 and is in manuscript at Madrid's Biblioteca Nacional. Russell describes it and gives a good idea of its contents. It is fundamental for an understanding of how LC was read in its own times. It is here that the first detailed study of LC's sources was made. The manuscript comments tend to observations on the literal meaning of the text and to juristic knowledge displayed by the author. There is less on LC as a work of art.

799. _____. "LC y los estudios jurídicos de Fernando de Rojas," in *Actas del IV Congreso International de Hispanistas (Salamanca 1971)* Salamanca: Univ. de Salamanca, 1982), II, 533-42; it also appears in his *Temas de LC y otros estudios* (see following entry), 323-40.

Passages from the text permit us to recognize the jurist mentality of the author. Two are particularly well developed: the section on the trial of Claudina (Act 7) and the behavior of the judge who sentences Pármeno and Sempronio (Act 14).

800. _____. *Temas de LC y otros estudios.* Barcelona: Ariel, 1978. 508p. Paper (Col. Letras e Ideas, Maior, 14).

LC section is pp. 241-375 and includes his reviews of Gilman (1956) and Lida de Malkiel (1962), two articles previously published in 1963 and 1976, and one published here for the first time (see preceding entry).

a. MLN 95 (1980), 480-82, P. N. Dunn
b. BHS 57 (1980), 341-42, A. D. Deyermond
c. *Cel* 4, i (May 1980), 35-44, J. R. Rank
d. *Hispania* 64 (1981), 151, R. V. Brown
e. *Letras* (Buenos Aires), no. 4 (1982), 127, L. D. Garabelli

S

801. SALCEDO, Emilio. "Notas sobre LC: Judíos y cristianos." *Boletín Informativo del Seminario de Derecho Político* (Salamanca), no. 26 (1962), 103-11.

Rojas is the sole author of LC, having reworked and elaborated an old medieval *aucto.* The mysteries and problems of LC are products of the period of great tension between Christians and Jews in which it was reworked. For Rojas, it a work of protest.

802. SALVADOR MARTINEZ, H. "Cota y Rojas: Contribución al estudio de las fuentes y la autoría de LC." HR 48 (1980), 37-55.

On the basis of 43 borrowings, similarities and shared structural ideas in works by Cota—especially his *Diálogo entre el Amor y un viejo*—and the TCM, it is suggested that Cota might be the author of the CCM and Rojas the interpolator in the TCM. [See also Severin, entry 837.]

803. SALVADOR MIGUEL, Nicasio. "Huellas de LC en la *Lozana andaluza,* in *Estudios sobre la literatura española del Siglo de Oro (Homenaje a F. Yndurain)* (Madrid: Ed. Nacional, 1984) (*)

804. SAMONA, Carmelo. *Aspetti del retoricismo nella Celestina.* Rome: Facoltà di Magisterio dell'Università di Roma, 1953. 247p. (Studi di Letteratura Spagnola, Quaderno 2)

Rojas' treatment of traditional rhetorical materials is original and he refines it in accord with his own superior sensitivity. From this perspective, the author feels that Rojas was trying—in the TCM—to be faithful to the spirit and the artistic unity of the CCM.

a. *Cultura Neolatina* 15 (1955), 170, E. Vuolo
b. RL 7 (1955), 258, J. de Entrambasaguas
c. NRFH 10 (1956), 73-80, S. Gilman

805. _____. "Una reminiscenza della *Celestina* nell'*Auto de los desposorios de Joseph,*" in *Aspetti e problemi delle letterature iberiche: Studi offerti a F. Meregalli,* ed. G. Bellini (Rome: Bulzoni, 1981), 353-58.

Finds parallels and verbal echoes of Pleberio and Alisa's conversations about Melibea.

806. SANCHEZ, Alberto. "Fernando de Rojas," in the *Enciclopedia dello spettacolo* VII (Rome: Casa Editrice Le Maschere, 1961), pp. 1086-90.

Treats of many themes as befits an encyclopedia, but concentrates most on theatrical representations. Illustrated with a photograph from the Polish production at Lodz [1947].

807. SANCHEZ, Elizabeth. "Magic in LC." HR 46 (1978), 481-94.

Magic functions to underscore the fact that rational explanations have also a limit. Celestina's magical powers permit her to overestimate her own prowess in some situations. This leads her to unleash unwittingly the concatenation of tragedies. S. comments on and evaluates other scholars' considerations of magic.

808. SANCHEZ, Roberto G. "On Staging LC Today." *Estreno,* no. 2 (Spring 1975), 4-10.

Sánchez has twice staged LC (see entries 982.9, 1012.2 and 1012.3) and here shares his views on directing. He sees in LC an essentially dramatic work.

809. SANCHEZ ALBORNOZ, Claudio. "De la honra del rey a la de la Celestina y el verdugo," in his *España: Un enigma histórico,* I (Buenos Aires: Ed. Sudamericana, 1956; 2nd ed. 1962), 636-44. An English translation is by C. J. Reed and D. S. Reher (Madrid: Fundación Universitaria Española, 1975), I, 546-53.

Even before Calderón, the preoccupation with honor had reached great proportions. With its roots in the Middle Ages and important to all social levels, honor is accurately reflected in LC in the lives of all the characters.

810. SANCHEZ-CASTANER, Francisco. "Antecedentes celestinescos en las *Cantigas de Santa Maria.*" *Mediterráneo,* 1, no. 2 (1943), 33-90.

The go-between appears in cantigas 64 and 312 as a social type depicted in realist terms. An antecedent, not a source, of LC.

811. SANCHEZ GONZALEZ, A. "La peña Celestina." *Cel* 7, ii (1983), 23-24.

The original from 1928 is illustrated. A rpt. of a journalistic essay which evokes the 'sabor' of LC from atop the geographic landmark associated with Rojas' work.

812. SANCHEZ ROMERALO, Jaime. "Alonso de Villegas: semblanza del autor de la *Selvagia.*" *Actas del Quinto Congreso Internacional de Hispanistas (1974)* II (Bordeaux, 1977), pp. 783-93.

Bio-bibliographical study of Villegas and his celestinesque imitation of 1554, both products of Toledo.

813. SANCHEZ SANCHEZ-SERRANO, Antonio, and María R. PRIETO DE LA YGLESIA. *Solución razonada para las principales incógnitas de LC*. Madrid: Authors [Gráficas Breogán], 1971. 112p.

The author of LC is Juan del Encina! Rojas reworked it with scissors and paste to change its style and original intention. The sketch of the original is in Encina's *Egloga de Plácida y Vitoriano*. The authors set out to prove all this by highlighting those text passages with interpretations that best support their view.

a. *Est Lit*, no. 503 (1972), 1129, E. Aguado

814. SANDERS, Ronald. "Interlude: In a Garden," in his *Lost Tribes and Promised Lands. The Origins of American Racism* (Boston/Toronto: Little Brown, 1978), 133-40.

Rojas is a *cristiano nuevo*. LC is a spiritual allegory of the times: Calisto, the nobility fallen on hard times, seeks redemption in Melibea and, not finding it, perishes. Melibea is a corrupting force. Celestina is a satire of the Church. The opening scenes of *Amadís* and of *Esplandián* (1508, 1510), also occurring in gardens, show the positive aspects of the vogue for Christian chivalry, as opposed to the pessimism emanating from the un-Christian garden scene which opens LC.

815. SANDOVAL MARTINEZ, Salvador. "Sintagmas no progresivos trimembres en la prosa de LC." *Estudios Literarios Dedicados al Profesor Mariano Baquero Goyanes* (Murcia, 1974), 471-86.

These sintagms are listed according to their being nominal, adjectival or verbal. They point to a Renaissance equilibrium, especially some whose members are binary.

816. SANZ PASCUAL, Julián. "LC, ¿precedente inédito?" *Est lit*, no. 373 (1967), 13.

Auberée, a French fabliau, contains narrative parallels with LC and features a go-between who may be an antecedent of Celestina.

817. SATRUSTEGUI, José María. "LC en la literatura popular vasca." RL 16, nos. 31-32 (1959), 146-58; also in *Boletín de la Sociedad Vascongada de Amigos del País* 19 (1960), 165-80.

Study of a Basque text with a celestinesque theme which seems clearly to have known LC, as seen in its narrative line and in its subtle psychological portrayals. Transmission is thought to have been by oral tradition.

818. SCHIEL, Nicholas Edward. "A Theological Interpretation of LC." Diss. St. Louis Univ., 1965. 194p. DA 26/08, 4675. No. 64-14662.

A Manichaean-resembling attitude pervades LC, since studies of the characters show that they all display thought and behavior patterns of this vital but non-Christian way of confronting life. It is a souce of internal unity in LC.

819. SCHMIDELY, Jack. "La statistique lexicale: un exemple des rapports entre mathématiques, lingüistique et littérature." *Les Langues Neo-Latines*, no. 190 (1969), 3-10.

Believes that mathematical models and methods could be applied to the authorship problem in LC.

820. SCHOECK, R. J. "The Influence of LC in England." *Boston Public Library Quarterly* 7 (1955), 224-225.

A response to Ugalde (entry 918) concerning the *Interlude of Calixto & Melebea* (c. 1525). He rejects two lines of thought: that it was prepared by a student of Vives' when the latter was at Oxford, and that it was the first English drama based on a foreign work.

821. SCHREIBER, Eva. "Zur Wortstellung in der *Celestina*". Diss. Univ. of Freiburg im Breisgau, 1972. (*)

822. SCOLES, Emma. "Note sulla prima traduzione italiana della *Celestina*." *Studi Romanzi* 33 (1961), 155-217.

A study with many finely-made points, relating the CCM and the early TCM exemplars with other, later editions. The author establishes a tentative genealogy among them all and manages to cover a lot of important ground in terms both of comparative content and of significant variants.

a. *Boletín de Filología Española* 4 (1963), 41, V. Ruiz Ortiz

823. _____. "La prima traduzione italiana della *Celestina*: repertorio bibliografico." *Studi di Letteratura Spagnola* (1964), 209-30.

A description of the editions of the translation by Hordognez from 1505(?) to 1551, as well as of their interrelationships.

824. _____."Due note di filologia quattrocentista: 2. 'Seleucal'." *Studi di Letteratura Spagnola* (1965 [1967]), 180-86.

Offers a solution to two variants from Act 1 (Herriott [1964], nos. 94 and 95) suggested by the M. Gast ed. of the TCM, Salamanca 1570. (See also Garci-Gómez, entry 344.)

825. _____. "Il testo della *Celestina* nell'edizione Salamanca 1570." *Studi Romanzi* 36 (1975), 7-124.

The best and most detailed consideration of Salamanca 1570, an ed. independent of the families established by Herriott (1964) and Whinnom (1966). The author compares it to several earlier and later eds. and establishes its importance in the future reconstruction of a critical ed. of LC. Variants in an extensive Appendix compare the 1570 text with the Seville 1518-20 TCM (the base ed. used by Criado de Val and Trotter [1958 etc.]).

a. YWMLS 36 (1974), 272, A. K. G. Paterson

826. SELIG, Karl-Ludwig. "The *Celestina* and Literary

Portraiture: Prolegomenon." *Estudios Literarios de Hispanistas Norteamericanos Dedicados a Helmut Hatzfeld con Motivo de su 80 Aniversario* (Barcelona: Hispam, 1974), 471-75.

A catalogue of 24 passages from LC which furnishes material for a study of multiple perspective on characters, from descriptions of features to behavior and gesture. One important element of Rojas' originality.

827. _____. "Identification and Information in the *Celestina*: Prolegomenon by way of a Florilegium." *Les cultures ibériques en devenir: Essais ... Marcel Bataillon* (Paris, 1979), 393-96.

Reflections on events that happened before the actual time of the action in LC (e.g. Celestina's memories of Claudina) which are key narrative elements of the whole.

828. SENDER, Ramón. "LC en los Estados Unidos." *El Universal* (Caracas) (June 18 1955), Indice Literario, 1.

A series of observations occasioned by L. B. Simpson's translation of the CCM (entry 1011). North Americans will not like LC because they are less liberated than the Europeans of Rojas' times. LC is the first novel and Sempronio is the first 'pícaro'.

829. SENELICK, Laurence. "The Bard and the Bawd." *Prologue* 30, no. 2 (November 1974), 1.

Musings about the contact Shakespeare might have had with LC (in the English versions of Rastell(?) and Mabbe (c. 1598) and how there is in *Romeo and Juliet* a certain celestinesque spirit. This spirit exists also in the characterization of Falstaff.

830. SENIFF, D. P. " 'El falso boezuelo con su blando cencerrar': or, the Pantomime Ox Revisited." *Cel* 9, i (May 1985), 43-45.

Reviews the recent literature on this Act 11 passage by Severin (entry 838), Whinnom (960) and Hook (465), and emphasizes that hunting with a pantomime ox was known outside of Spain before and after Rojas' time, although he deserves credit for deft literary application of this hunt motif to the love theme in LC.

831. SERIS, Homero. "LC," in his *Nuevo ensayo de una biblioteca española de libros raros y curiosos*, vol. 1, fasc. 1 (New York: Hispanic Society of America, 1969), 279-303.

Describes: a Sevilla 1528 ed. belonging to the Hispanic Society of America (not in Penney [1954]) and the ten eds. and eight translations of LC at the Boston Public Library. He also discusses many critical studies on LC (books, articles and review-articles).

832. _____. *Guía de nuevos temas de literatura española* (transcrita, editada y cotejada por D. W. McPheeters) (New York: The Hispanic Society of America, 1973), pp. 140-51.

A guide to new orientations concerning LC and its complex textual and literary problems. Also contains commentary on many studies on these and other aspects of 'la celestinesca'.

a. *Hispanófila*, no. 55 (1974-75), 103-04, F. DeArmas
b. *Boletín de Filología*, nos. 25-26 (1974-75), 348-49, M. Ferreccio Podestá
c. HR 44 (1976), 179-80, O. H. Green
d. *Modern Language Journal* 60 (1976), 227-28, J. T. Snow
e. NRFH 25 (1976), 438-41, B. Entenza de Solare
f. REH 9 (1977), 473-74, A. Hacthoun

833. SERRANO PONCELA, Segundo. "El secreto de Melibea." CHA, no. 100 (1958), 488-510; rpt. in his *El secreto de Melibea y otros ensayos* (Col. Persiles, 8; Madrid: Taurus, 1959), 7-36, this latter with two illustrations, woodcuts from early editions.

Melibea as a perverse Jewess and Calisto as a good Christian. Also doubtless a converso is Pármeno. [See A. Custodio's response (entry 211).

a. *Ficción* (Buenos Aires), no. 19 (1959), 163-65, T. C.
b. *Arbor* 45 (1965), 297-98, C. Bravo-Villasante
c. *Cuadernos del Congreso de la Libertad de la Cultura*, no. 41 (1960), 110-11, J. Iglesias
d. BA 27 (1961), 362, C. Ayllón

834. SEVERIN, Dorothy Sherman. "Memory in LC." Diss. Harvard Univ., 1967. 166p. CDI 29 (1973), 195. S. Gilman. (See following entry.)

835. _____. *Memory in LC.* London: Támesis, 1970. x + 73p. (Serie A, Monografías, 19)

It is in memory that we can sense the point of meeting of the internal, subjective life and the external, objective life of the characters in LC. Time's flow is not something that all perceive in the same way and Rojas uses this knowledge in the individualization of his characters. It is a technique which declares the modernity of LC and points up a literary use of memory which will flower in the *Lazarillo*.

a. RJ 22 (1971), 382-83, J. Amícola
b. ZRP 87 (1971), 661, A. Rothe
c. BHS 49 (1972), 297-98, K. Whinnom
d. *MAe* 41 (1972), 76-77, L. P. Harvey
e. CL 24 (1972), 357-59, J. H. Martin
f. *Hispania* 55 (1972), 383, P. Smyth
g. MLN 87 (1972), 353-54, H. Sieber
h. MLR 67 (1972), 672-74, G. Martínez Lacalle
i. *RPh* 27 (1973-74), 264-66, K. V. Kish
j. BH 76 (1974), 204-08, P. Heugas
k. RR 66 (1975), 243-44, M. J. Ruggerio
l. TLS (May 23 1975), 576, Anon.
m. NRFH 25 (1976), 407-12, D. E. Eisenberg

836. _____. "Humor in LC." *RPh* 32 (1978-79), 274-91.

A presentation of four different levels of humor in LC: verbal, parodic, satiric, and a fourth based on theatrical techniques. Further, these are distinguished in accord with the successive elaborations of the original *esbozo* (whose author is perceived—in terms of use of humor—to be other than Rojas).

837. _____. "Cota, His Imitator, and LC: The Evidence Re-examined." *Cel* 4, i (May 1980), 3-8.

Reviews the arguments proffered by Salvador Martínez (entry 802) in favor of Cota's authorship of Acts 1-16 (i.e., the CCM) and finds they will not support such an identification.

838. _____. "'El falso boezuelo', or the Partridge and the Pantomime Ox." *Cel* 4, i (May 1980), 31-33.

Uses an illustration to explain what might be meant by the allusion to the 'falso boezuelo' (Act 11). The visual here receives support from the interpretation of the passage to be found in the anonymous *Celestina comentada* (c. 1550).

839. _____. "Parodia y sátira en LC." *Actas del Sexto Congreso Internacional de Hispanistas (Toronto 1977)* (Toronto: Univ. of Toronto-Dept. of Spanish & Portuguese, 1980), 695-97.

Observations and illustrations from the text of the different levels of satire and parody (on both high and low levels) in LC. This humorous side of LC is often overlooked.

840. _____. "Fernando de Rojas and *Celestina*: The Author's Intention from *Comedia* to *Tragicomedia de Calisto y Melibea*." *Cel* 5, i (May 1981), 1-5.

A consideration of the successive appearances of the preliminary as well as the appended verses of LC. The conclusion is that the work underwent a gradual change in purpose in the direction of greater emphasis on moral purpose and didactic tone as it passed from CCM to TCM.

841. _____. "Aristotle's *Ethics* and LC." *LaC* 10 (1981-82), 54-58.

Rojas' often ambivalent approaches towards love's pleasures may reflect a scale of values more closely associated with Aristotelian ideas than previously conceded.

842. _____. "Is LC the First Modern Novel?" *Revista de Estudios Hispánicos* (Puerto Rico) 9 (1982), 205-209.

The answer is: yes. Like *Don Quijote*, often called the first modern novel, LC demolishes the antecedent literature that it parodies (the sentimental romance; for DQ it was the chivalric novel). In attempting to lead lives between a literary past and a realistic present, the lovers of LC are trapped between invented and living history and this is the novelistic commonality linking Rojas and Cervantes. It also gives priority to Rojas' LC as the first modern novel.

843. _____. "A Minimal Word-Pair Study of *Celestina*: More Evidence About the Authorship of Act I." *Cel* 7, ii (Fall 1983), 11-12.

Even this small statistical sampling of word-pairs tends to uphold the claim that Rojas is not the author of Act 1.

844. _____. "Calisto and Orphic Music," in *Creation and Recreation: Experiments in Literary Form in Early Modern Spain. Studies in Honor of Stephen Gilman* (Newark, Delaware: Juan de la Cuesta, 1983), 1-5.

Rojas as a creator of new uses for traditional material, with Calisto's music as an example. Music, in normal circumstances, alleviates the pains occasioned by love's agonies; for Calisto, such pain is intensified. This may be a humoristic touch, even a humanist joke that Rojas deployed for the amusement of his knowledgable contemporaries.

845. _____. "La parodia del amor cortés en LC," in *Congreso Edad de Oro* (Madrid: Univ. Autónoma, 1983), III, 275-79. (*)

846. SEVILLA, Manuel. "Fernando de Rojas y LC." *Tribuna Israelita*, no. 86 (January 1952), 18-19.

Traces the Jewish ancestry of Rojas and comments on its effect in LC when Calisto declares himself 'Melibeo'.

847. SHEPARD, Sanford. "Crypto-Jews in Spanish Literature." *Judaism* 19 (1970), 99-112, especially 106-12.

Celestina as a symbol of an inconstant Jerusalem. Notes also on the lexical references to crypto-Jews in Salas Barbadillo's *La hija de Celestina*: a description of some customs kept alive in the era of fanatical advocacy of Christianity.

848. _____. "Prostitutes and Pícaros in Inquisitional Spain." *Neohelicon* 3 (1975), 365-72.

Most works which are celestinesque (including LC) deal with females who are both prostitutes and new Christians. There are Biblical precedents for associating prostitutes with Godless people (e. g., the Jews).

849. SHIPLEY JR., George Arthur. "Functions of Imagery in LC." Diss. Harvard Univ., 1968. 274p. CDI (1973), 195. S. Gilman. (*)

850. _____. "'El natural de la raposa': un proverbio estratégico de LC." NRFH 23 (1974), 35-64.

Observations on proverbial language based on the theories of Kenneth Burke and applied to LC: the proverb as a basic unit of a poetic process. The specific one dealt with here elucidates aspects of personalities in LC and comments on special functions of articles of clothing.

851. _____. "'Non erat hic locus': The Disconcerted Reader in Melibea's Garden." *RPh* 27 (1973-74), 286-303.

The configuration of the elements of Melibea's garden plays a role in the physical and the literary worlds, evoking all manner of associations. The double function of the elements disconcerts not only the occupants of the garden but the reader as well.

852. _____. "Usos y abusos de la autoridad del refrán en LC." ACTAS: 231-44.

Analysis of 28 refrains with animal imagery (Acts 1-19) to show that they often reveal unsuspected traits of LC's characters and help explain certain crucial actions in the work. The relationship can be direct or ironic.

853. _____. "Bestiary References in Fernando de Rojas' LC (1499): The Ironic Undermining of Authority." *LaC* 3, ii (1975), 22-23.

Abstract of a paper read in Seattle, Washington, in February of 1975.

854. _____. "Concerting Through Conceit: Unconventional Uses of Conventional Sickness Images in LC." *MLR* 70 (1975), 324-32.

A look at the dialogues of Melibea and Celestina in acts 4 and 10, both of which feature several images of sickness, with a view to showing how Rojas revitalizes the often trite character they have acquired. The imagery heightens the psychological struggle of the two women in these scenes.

855. _____. "'¿Qué dolor puede ser tal…'?: A Rhetorical Strategy for Containing Pain in LC." *MLN* 90 (1975), 143-53.

An archetypal theme (*doleo ergo sum*) is scrutinized because it turns up five times in LC and, in a paradigmatic way, provides a panorama of the action of the TCM. Knowledgeable comments on language, rhetoric and re-contextualization occur throughout.

856. _____. "Reflections on the Shield: Stephen Gilman's *The Spain of Fernando de Rojas*." *JHP* 3 (1979), 197-238.

A contribution to the polemic Gilman's book of 1972 has created. The essay reviews the content and central themes while pondering its fundamental importance to *Celestina* and Rojas studies. He sees that this volume, and a previous one (1956), are formulated from the theories of Américo Castro and attempt to carry them further. The earlier book deals with the 'what' and the latter with the 'how' of LC. The work is like a shining shield which reflects its surroundings while protecting its wielder.

857. _____. "Authority and Experience in LC." *BHS* 62 (1985), 95-111.

Although Rojas, in his Prologue, seems to approve of the type of reader who respects authority, he manages to subvert the conventions of such respect—for both written and oral authority— through a complicated series of ironic positions taken in the text. Not age, not wisdom, not verbal superiority are final guides to the complex dilemmas of life (Celestina, ironically, who understands all this, is a prime victim). Three textual commentaries are made to illustrate: The Calisto-Sempronio dialogue of Act 1; Melibea's discourse of Act 20; and Pleberio's monologue from Act 21.

858. SIEBENMANN, Gustav. "Supervisión de los estudios celestinescos desde 1957." ACTAS: 529-51.

Covers 1957 to 1974 in 14 sections, each accompanied by a brief note of introduction which helps point out the more important works in the section (entries are not otherwise annotated). See also the next entry.

859. _____. "Estado presente de estudios celestinescos (1956-1974)." *Vox Romanica* 34 (1975), 168-212.

Thirteen divisions: critical text, author, language and style, difficult passages, social context, sources, themes, originality, influences, and a list of editions, translations and adaptations.

860. SIEMANS, William L. "Celestina as *Terra Nostra*." *Mester* 11, no. 1 (1982), 57-66.

The author's view is that Carlos Fuentes exploits the Earth Mother aspect of Rojas' original in this 1975 novel, thus making Celestina an archetypal figure associated with positive happenings, e. g., rebirth.

861. SIERRA, Arnaldo C. "La figura celestinesca a través de seis novelas dialogadas de los siglos XVI y XVII." M.A. Thesis, Brown Univ., 1961. 66p.

Principally a study of the character of the go-between as developed in three continuations (*La Segunda Celestina, Lisandro y Roselia, Tragedia Policiana*) and three imitations (*Selvagia, La Lena, La Dorotea*).

862. SIMON DIAZ, José. "LC," in *Bibliografía de la literatura hispánica*, III (Madrid: CSIC, 1953), 802-23; expanded list in vol. III, ii (Madrid: CSIC, 1965), 265-96.

Lists editions, translations and studies. The expanded version was updated with 123 additional entries.

863. _____. *Manual de bibliografía de la literatura española*, 3rd ed., revised and augmented (Madrid: Gredos, 1980), see *Indice de Materias*, under 'Celestina' and 'Tragicomedia'.

A selection of approximately 190 entries, usefully arranged by subject headings.

864. SIMS, Edna. *El antifeminismo en la literatura española hasta 1560*. Bogotá: Ed. Andes, 1973. 128p.

LC section is on pp. 47-52. The antifeminism centers on Rojas' portrait of the go-between, who is a classic 'madre cruel'. Juan Ruiz had emphasized the physical in Trotaconventos but Rojas features the psychological in Celestina, although it is sometimes through a mediating physical characteristic (Celestina's hands, for example).

865. SINGERMAN, Robert. *The Jews in Spain and Portugal: A Bibliography* (New York/London: Garland Publishing Co., 1975), pp. 200-01.

Lists 26 books and articles (1902-1973: nos. 2938-2963) which cover Rojas and his Jewish background. No commentaries.

866. SINGLETON, Mack H. "Morality and Tragedy in LC." *Studies in Honor of Lloyd A. Kasten* (Madison: Univ. of Wisconsin Press, 1975), 249-59.

Recent studies have tended to focus on LC's morality in one of two ways: as either a Christian consideration of vice or as a reflection of a courtly love system in decline. For Singleton, the real moral tragedy results from a submission to *cupiditas*, or sinful pride. This destroys almost all the characters.

867. SISTO, David T. "The String in the Conjurations of LC and *Doña Bárbara*." *RomN* 1 (1959-60), 50-52.

Both women believe in the magical power a 'string' can exert over the will of others.

868. SKWARCYNSKA, S. "Celestyna w Koncepcji Poetyckiej Rojasa, Acharda, i L. Schillera," in *Studia i Szkice Literackie* (Warsaw: Wydawnictwo, 1953), 183-217. ("Pax", 3)

The Polish adaptation of LC (Lodz, 1947), based on Achard's French one (1942), is studied as a poetic concept. It also reviews the basic (and much distorted) plot line of Achard's adaptation.

869. SLOMAN, Albert E. "Calderón and Falconry: A Note on Dramatic Language." *RPh* 6 (1952-53), 299-304.

In *Basta Callar*, Margarita, following a hawk, finds Ludovico, wounded, and falls in love with him. Possible LC influence.

870. SMITH, Roy Roger. "Recapitulation, Reiteration and Repetition: Techniques of Restatement in LC." Diss. Univ. of Kentucky, 1979. 204p. DAI 40/11, 5891-92A. No. 80-10521. J. Lihani.

Rojas, in his use of these three techniques, is a pivotal figure in their development. Recapitulation relates to the re-statement of facts concerning previous occurrences, reiteration deals with themes (love, madness, death, temptation, exercise of free will, and self-interest), repetition functions more on the level of metaphorical language and symbols as it contributes to structure, characterization and tone in LC.

871. SMYTH, Philip. "Two Contrasting Adaptations of LC to the Stage." *The Univ. of South Florida Language Quarterly* 17, nos. 3-4 (1978-1979), 29-30.

These are the English adaptation of Eric Bentley entry 1015,(which is mostly conscious of the text tradition of LC) and the Dutch adaptation by Hugo Claus (entry 1007.1, which tends to the experimental and the personal). Mostly descriptive notes based on a reading of the texts.

872. SNOW, Joseph T., Jane F. SCHNEIDER and Cecilia C. LEE. "Un cuarto de siglo de interés en LC, 1949-1975: documento bibliográfico." *Hispania* 59 (1976), 610-60.

For the period covered, includes theses, studies in books, articles, homage volumes and monographs, plus editions, translations and all manner of adaptations (stage, music, ballet, etc). Together with supplements to this work (see following entry), it is the core of the present volume (with many additions, much reworking and all annotations now in English).

873. SNOW, Joseph T. "La Celestina: documento bibliográfico." *Cel* 1, i (May 1977), 23-45; 1, ii (November 1977), 39-53; 2, i (May 1978), 49-64; 2, ii (November 1978), 39-47; 3, i (May 1979), 45-54; 3, ii (November 1979), 51-55; 4, i (May 1980), 51-58; 4, ii (November 1980), 51-58; 5, i (May 1981), 59-62; 5, ii (November 1981), 57-58; 6, i (May 1982), 47-48; 6, ii (November 1982) 26-29; 7, i (May 1983), 41-45; 7, ii (November 1983) 37-42; 8, i (May 1984), 61-63; 8, ii (November 1984), 49-53; and 9, i (May 1985), 71-77.

These 17 supplements to the original bibliography (see preceding entry), added approximately 450 new items to the documentation of world interest in LC in less than five years. Now part of the present volume.

874. _____. "La TCM de Juan de Sedeño: algunas observaciones a su primera escena, comparada con la original." *Cel* 2, ii (Fall 1978), 13-27.

An analytical and comparative commentary of scene 1 from LC and the verse adaptation of some 40 years later by Sedeño (of that scene) which puts on display one contemporary reading of Rojas' work. The originality of LC is underscored, but the merits of the adaptation make it worthy of further study.

875. _____. "LC of Felipe Pedrell." *Cel* 3, i (May 1979), 19-32.

Tells the tale of the composition of the opera Pedrell composed in 1903 but which never has been given a full performance in Spain. Pedrell's libretto adheres rather closely to Rojas' text.

876. _____. "The *Calisto & Melibea* of Edwin Honig." *Cel* 3, ii (Fall 1979), 32-40.

Summarizes the story line of this arrangement (a libretto for Jerome Rosen's operatic work, see entry 1098.) and notes the similarities and differences it maintains with respect to Rojas' work. (See also entry 1096.)

877. _____. "An Additional Attestation to the Popularity of Rojas' Character Creations from an Early Seventeenth-Century Manuscript." HR 48 (1980), 479-86.

The 1612 manuscript is *Rueda de la Fortuna* by Miguel Casanova and it contains some interesting parlor riddles in which, among many other literary figures, appear Celestina, Elicia, Calisto and Melibea. It offers some small insight into how Rojas' characters were perceived in the 17th century.

878. _____. "The Iconography of the Early *Celestinas*: I. The First French Translation (1527)." *Cel* 8, ii (Fall 1984), 25-39.

Takes up the specific case of Paris 1527, and the limited scope of its illustration scheme, against a background of various ways in which printers elsewhere illustrated their *Celestinas*.

879. _____. "Celestina's Claudina," in *Hispanic Studies in Honor of Alan D. Deyermond: A North American Tribute,* ed. John S. Miletich (Madison, Wisconsin: Hispanic Seminary of Medieval Studies, 1986).

Traces closely the full story of Claudina (acts 1, 3, 7 and 12) and her role in the plot complications of LC as well as her importance in Rojas' scheme of characterization for Celestina herself.

880. SOBRINO, J. A. de. "Pornografía y manipulación del Hombre." *RyF*, no. 946 (November 1976), 315-32.

Pages 326-27 offer a synopsis of a paper read by Carmen Castro on the topic of passionate love; the second part entails some discussion of Calisto and Melibea.

881. SORENSEN, Jorge E. "La escena inicial de LC: la iglesia de Martín de Riquer vs. tradición literaria." *Tropos* (East Lansing, Michigan) 6, no. 1 (1977), 47-55.

See also Riquer (1957). The language of the first scene—extended to most of the rest of LC—should be seen as a poetic reflection of 15th-century 'cancionero' conventions in love poetry. It is not necessary to posit a church for the locale of this opening scene.

882. SPECTOR, N. B. "THe Procuress and Religious Hypocrisy." *Italica* 33 (1956), 52-59.

Comparative study featuring LC and works by Aretino and M. Régnier which also feature go-betweens.

883. SPITZER, Leo. "Zur *Celestina*." ZRP 50 (1930), 237-40.

Calisto's finding a reflection of the Divine in Melibea's beauty is not as innovative as Castro (entry 161) claims; it appears as early as Chrétien de Troyes and is topical. Also, Castro's idea that Sempronio's statement about each looking to his own 'honor' being a Renaissance trait is misguided: it extends back at least to Aquinas.

884. STAMM, James R. "De 'huerta' a 'huerto': elementos lírico-bucólicos en LC." ACTAS: 81-88.

The 'huerta' of scene 1 is not described (we learn of it only in Act 2). Not so the garden of Act 19, in the interpolations of the TCM. The garden passes from mere function to a lyrical Paradise and strikes a false note in the otherwise realist 'paisaje' of LC.

885. _____. "El tesoro de Pármeno." ACTAS: 185-91.

Alberto's legacy is an invention of the author of Act 1. Rojas joins this to a second temptation (Areúsa) for Pármeno, and links the two in Act 7. Rojas' handling of this small item is a sign of a conscientious artist with mastery of the psychological manipulation of characters.

886. _____. "'Trobando está nuestro amo': LC. Act III." *LaC* 4, i (1975), 6-7.

Abstract of a paper read at the MLA meetings, December 1975. The verses in Act 3 have a structural importance. Those of Act 19, however, reveal aspects of Melibea's character. Previously, Juan de Flores and Diego de San Pedro had also used verses in their prose to heighten desired effects.

887. _____. "'El plebérico coraçon': Melibea's Heart." *Cel* 3, ii (Fall 1979), 3-6.

Stamm's reading of the phrase lends support to the theory that Rojas was not the author of Act 1.

888. _____. "Inconcinnity in the *Tragicomedia*, Act XIV." *Cel* 8, i (May 1984), 43-46.

Three cases of incongruency in the materials interpolated in Act 14 show that Rojas (or whoever was the author of these interpolations) had little concern for logic in making this graft onto an original which was more fastidiously worked out.

889. _____. "Inconcinnity Pursued: The Secret of Sosia and Related Matters." *Cel* 9, ii (Fall 1985).

Incongruencies in the plotted action and logic of Act 17.

890. SZERTICS, Joseph. "Notas sobre un caso de ironía en LC." *RomN* 11 (1969-70), 629-32.

In the deaths of Sempronio and Pármeno, the author sees a case of tragic double irony.

T

891. TAMAYO, Fermín J. "LC y el problema del monólogo." ACTAS: 203-12.

Asides and monologues are studied in a structuralist light. Two results are that ambition determines both the triumph and the fall of Celestina and the servants of Calisto, and that the concepts of 'love' and 'social norm' lead to the fall of Calisto and Melibea (the lovers possess them, but in inverse proportion, and this results in constant conflict and, in the end, tragedy).

892. TEIXIDOR, Laurent. *Observations sur LC*. Perigueux: Pierre Fanlac, 1968. 44p.

Exegetic essay which considers the racial problem central to an understanding of LC. Even the initial tensions of scene 1 are best comprehended as a function of this pervasive Jewish-Christian conflict.

893. TERRON, Carlo. "Le ragioni di un intervento." *Sipario*, no. 191 (March 1962), 4-5, 23-24.

An adapter discusses his confrontation with the original literary text. (See also entry 1070.2.)

894. THOMAS, Henry. "Antonio (Martínez) de Salamanca, Printer of LC, Rome, c. 1525." *The Library*, Fifth Series, 8 (1953), 45-48.

Describes this exemplar from the British Library.

895. THOME, J. R. "Sur des éditions illustrées de LC (du XVe au XVIIIe siècle)." *Le livre et ses amis* 2 (March 1946), 31-36; appears in Spanish translation as "Hans Weidetz (Johannes Giudictius): primer ilustrador dramático de LC." *Cuadernos de Bibliofilia* (July 1979), 41-50.

The first illustrations to LC are lifeless. When they really take on dramatic roles is with this illustrator of the 1520 German translation of Christof Wirsung. He created a frontispiece and 27 engravings.

896. THOMPSON, B. Bussell. "Misogyny and Misprint in LC, Act I." *Cel* 1, ii (Fall 1977), 21-28.

Two notes on misogynistic humor in LC. The first deals with the possibility that "Minerva con el can" is humorous and not a misprint (see Green [1953]), while the second sees the humorous element in Calisto's adding two names to Sempronio's catalogue of misogynists.

897. TITTMAN, B. "LC: The First Act Re-Examined." Thesis. Univ. of Alberta, 1962. (*)

898. TORO-GARLAND, Fernando. "Celestina, hechicera clásica y tradicional." CHA, no. 180 (December 1964), 438-45.

Celestina as a witch and a procuress. The idea of controlling the will of others through magic (or psychology, from another point of view) is classical, but Rojas' own era was alive to the type and he did not rely on the traditional formulations exclusively.

899. _____. "LC y *Las mil y una noches*." RL 29 (1966), 5-33, and in somewhat reduced form in *Actas del Segundo Congreso Internacional de Hispanistas (1965)* (Nijmegen, 1967), 627-34.

Comparative look at the two works with some speculations about possible Arabic influence on LC.

900. _____. "La versión inglesa de LC del Capitán John Stevens." ACTAS: 383-89.

On Stevens' prose version of 1707, which takes place in Madrid and has nine chapters. The exposition here is sketchy, in anticipation of an expanded study.

901. TORRES MARTINEZ, José Carlos de. "El léxico taurino en el ciclo celestinesco." ACTAS: 433-68.

Including the LBA and *Corbacho*, plus LC and many of its continuations and imitations, a list is made of references to all aspects of bullfighting. There is a nice organization to the study and it is completed with a bibliography of bullfighting on horseback to 1644.

902. TORRES MONREAL, Francisco. "El teatro español en Francia, 1935-1973: análisis de la penetración y de sus mediaciones." Diss. Univ. of Murcia, 1974. L. Rubio García. (*)

903. _____. *El teatro español en Francia (1935-1973). Análisis de la penetración y de sus mediaciones* (Madrid: Fundación Juan March, 1976), pp. 14-18.

In the light of French interest in translating the TCM and adapting it for the stage, the author briefly describes two productions, Paul Achard's (1942) and J. Gillibert's (1972). (See entries 1036.2 and 1050.1-2.)

904. _____. "LC de J. Gillibert (Adaptación teatral francesa de la obra de Rojas)." *Homenaje al Prof. Muñoz Cortés* (Murcia: Univ.-Facultad de Filosofía y Letras, 1977), 765-76.

A substantial discussion of Gillibert's version of LC (entries 1050.1-2), typified by a mythical view, sensuality, nudity, rough language, etc., all compared with Rojas' LC.

905. TRISLER, Barbara Jean. "A Comparative Study of the Character Portrayal of Celestina and Other Golden Age Celestinesque Protagonists." Diss. Univ. of Oklahoma, 1977. 104p. DAI 38/04, 2165A No. 77-21416. P. Liria.

From Trotaconventos to Celestina to the latter's many literary progeny in works both dramatic and narrative in form. The survey ends with the 17th century go-betweens.

906. TROTTER, G. D. "Sobre 'La furia de Melibea' de Otis H. Green." *Clavileño* 5 (January-February 1954), 55-56.

Thinks courtly love does not enter into the rejection of Calisto by Melibea, as suggested by Green (entry 409). The rejection is necessary, however, from a dramatic standpoint since it serves to bring Celestina's diabolical powers into play.

907. _____. "The *Coplas de las comadres* of Rodrigo de Reynosa and LC." *Studia Philologica. Homenaje a Dámaso Alonso* 3 (1963), 527-37.

Suggests many points common to the works of Rojas and Reynosa.

908. _____. "The Date of the *Comedia Thebayda*." MLR 60 (1965), 386-90.

Further clarifies the dating of this work at c. 1520 and offers some additional notes to Lida de Malkiel's (entry 518) and McPheeters' (entry 552) comments about the relationship of this work to LC.

909. _____, and Keith WHINNOM, eds. *La Comedia Thebaida*. London: Támesis, 1969. lxii + 270p. (Serie B - Textos, 8)

In the introd., the editors show that the work is more independent of LC than is often supposed.

a. BHS 48 (1971), 62-66, A. D. Deyermond

910. TRUESDELL, William David. "A New Reading of Act 1 of LC." Diss. Brown Univ., 1969. 207p. DAI 31/02, 770-71A. No. 70-08803. J. López-Morillas and A. Trueblood.

The original double thrust of Act 1 was meant to 1) parody courtly love, and 2) describe a religious allegory (the Fall). When Act 1 is studied in isolation, it presents a character markedly different from the one we normally associate with the integrated CCM or TCM.

911. _____. "The *Hortus Conclusus* Tradition, and the Implications of Its Absence in LC." KRQ 29 (1973), 257-77.

The Act 1 garden is transformed into the lush amorous trysting place of Act 19 by a conscious decision on the part of Rojas. He transforms as well his almost stereotypical lovers into more real and concrete human beings in the process.

912. _____. "Pármeno's Triple Temptation: LC, Act I." *Hispania* 58 (1975), 267-76.

Calisto's servant is seduced by the offer of carnal pleasure, financial gain and the hope of climbing the social ladder so far as rights and privileges are concerned.

913. TRUXA, Sylvia. "Rubias Melibeas y *dark ladies* en la novela contemporánea." *Arbor*, no. 432 (December 1981), 291-304.

Medieval and Renaissance descriptive *topoi* crop up in the modern novel's positive and negative portrayals of females (seen from the purely extrinsic point of view). Rojas (Melibea) and Shakespeare (the dark ladies) typify these portrayals, which are, in part, replicated in texts of Matute, Laforet, Marsé, Martín-Santos and others.

914. TYLER, Richard. "Más sobre el 'pecado nefando'." *Crítica Hispánica* 2 (1980), 125-34.

On the popularity in Spain's Golden Age of references to the sin of Sodom: the earliest work cited here is LC.

915. _____. "*Celestina* in the *Comedia*." *Cel* 5, i (May 1981), 13-22.

A survey of citatations from a wide range of Golden Age dramatists that shows their debt to LC. Arranged by theme or by character being recalled.

U

916. U., M. "LC en la literatura vasca." *Boletín de la Sociedad Vascongada de Amigos del País* 16 (1960), 484-85.

A note to the Satrústegui article (1959 and 1960) which serves to emphasize Celestina's professional standing as a reconstructive surgeon of virgins.

917. UGALDE, Louis. "LC of 1502." *Boston Public Library Quarterly* 6 (1954), 206-22.

The Boston Public Library acquired this edition and the article is a note to that effect, plus a general commentary on the particular critical problems Rojas' text engenders.

918. _____. "A Reply." *Boston Public Library Quarterly* 7 (1955), 226-27.

See Schoeck (entry 820). The author offers evidence to the effect that Sir Richard Morrison could have written the English *Interlude of Calixto & Melebea* (c. 1530), and thinks that it was probably the first work modeled on a Spanish source.

919. UNGERER, Gustav. "LC in England," in *Anglo Spanish Relations in Tudor Literature* (Schweizer Anglistiche Arbieten, vol. 38; Bern: Francke Verlag, 1956), 9-41. Rpt. New York: AMS Press, 1972.

Good exposition of LC's impact in England, not only in terms of the translations made of it, but also of its effect on other works.

920. _____. "The Printing of Spanish Books in Elizabethan England." *The Library*, Fifth Series, 20 (1965), 177-229.

Two notices concerning LC in England: p. 218, entry 44, and 223, entry 9.

921. URIARTE DE REBAUDI, Lia Noemí. "Notas para un paralelo entre Trotaconventos y Celestina." *Revista de Educación* (La Plata) 5, nos. 9-10 (1960), 67-76.

Both authors must have had, in addition to literary models, models from real life. Both bawds participate in an age-old rite, although Celestina is the better realized of the two characterizations.

922. _____. "Los estudios de Menéndez y Pelayo y María Rosa Lida sobre LC." *Letras* (Buenos Aires), no. 4 (1982), 121-124.

An appreciation of the importance of the respective contributions to LC studies of these two scholars, it points up agreements and disagreements that they had, and allows as how Lida made advances over her predecessor.

923. URQUIZA GONZALEZ, J. I. "LC: una llamada permanente." *Anuario de Estudios Filológicos* (Cáceres) 1 (1978), 283-94.

Selected passages from LC are discussed in which the master-servant relationship is dramatized; others selected deal with the erotic male-female relationships. The erotic and the social are closely intertwined in LC.

V

924. VALBUENA PRAT, Angel. "LC y los prosistas de los Reyes Católicos," in his *Historia de la literatura española*, 1 (Barcelona: Gili, 1937; 6th ed., 1960), 373-86.

Introductory in character but places LC between the medieval world and the Renaissance and outlines in what ways it had developed a new concept of life through art.

925. _____. "La acción y los personajes en LC," in his *Literatura española en sus relaciones con la universal* (Madrid: Saeta, 1965), 174-82.

Calisto and Melibea alongside Tristan and Isolde. The world of LC is one without redemption, as the author shows in a discussion of the amorous meetings in Melibea's garden and of Pleberio's lament.

926. VALENCIA GOELKEL, Hernando. "LC, acto nueve." *Tiempo* (Bogotá) (December 7 1975), Lecturas Dominicales, 1. A version also appears, under the same title, in his *El arte nuevo de hacer novelas* (Caracas: Fundarte, 1982), 143-49.

Act 9 is dead time in terms of the plot of LC, but is used well by Rojas in a narrative way that foreshadows Cervantes and, later, the late 19th and early 20th-century novel.

927. VALERA. Juan. "Nueva edición de LC," in *Obras completas. II. Crítica literaria* (3rd ed., Madrid: Aguilar, 1961), 1025-29.

A review (originally published in 1900) of Krapf's ed. of the TCM. Its valuations of the literary qualities of LC are of historical interest still.

928. VALIS, Noël M. "'El triunfo de Celestina': The Go-Between and the Penal Code of 1870." *Cel* 5, i (May 1981), 35-40.

The 19th-century source article uses Celestina to illustrate a contemporary case of adultery as a legal problem.

929. VALLATA, Johannes. *Poliodorus (comedia humanística desconocida)*. Introd., study and transcription by J. M. Casas Homs. Madrid: CSIC, 1953. 273p.

Has an interesting commentary (pp. 151-65) on the relationship of Vallata's work to the LC in terms of its genre, its characterization and literary development.

a. *Latomus* 13 (1954), 448-51, E. González
b. *Anales de la Universidad de Chile* 114, no. 100 (1955), 161-62, R. Oroz
c. *Les Etudes Classiques* 23 (1955), 99, J. Deleuze
d. MLR 50 (1955), 348-49, P. E. Russell
e. *Revue Belge de Philologie et d'Histoire* 33 (1955), 101-03, L. Bakelants
f. *Symposium* 9 (1955), 182-85, D. W. McPheeters
g. HR 24 (1956), 153-54, J. E. Gillet
h. LR 10 (1956), 115-17, J. Horrent
i. NRFH 10 (1956), 415-39, M. R. Lida de Malkiel

930. VALLE LERSUNDI, F. del. "Anotaciones a LC." *El Diario Vasco* (August 5 1958), 8; (August 8 1958), 8.

Two parts of a series (I could find no others) occasioned by a staging of LC in San Sebastián. States that Rojas was the sole author of the work. The references in Act 12 to the curate of San Miguel and to Mollejas 'el hortelano' link the text to the real life Rojas. The second part of the article uses books by Diego de San Pedro and Cota that were in Rojas' library to show the likelihood of Rojas' paternity of LC.

931. VAN BEYSTERVELDT, Antony. "La adulteración del amor cortés en LC." *LaC* 4, i (1975), 17-18.

An abstract of a paper read in May of 1975. The paper makes two points. One is that Calisto abandons *amor cortés* formulas when he hires Celestina. The other is that Melibea never considers her virginity as anything but a symbol of a social value, which she rejects when she succumbs to Calisto's amours.

932. _____. "Nueva interpretación de LC." *Segismundo* 11 (1975), 87-116.

A long study which illuminates socio-literary attitudes of the 15th-century *cancioneros* and how they enter into an interpretation of LC. Rojas, a 'converso', adopted an anti-courtly stance because its social stratification did not favor his caste and, in LC, was seeking to restore some measure of equality by showing a corrupt social system.

933. _____. *Amadís. Esplandián. Calisto. Historia de un linaje adulterado*. Madrid: Porrúa, 1982. xv + 281p. (Studia Humanitatis)

A generous portion of this study (pp. 114-271) focusses on "la celestinesca" as a reflection of an authentic cultural reality of the late 15th century. Through a study of the transformations in the affective culture of this important period, the author maintains that individual liberties of expression had reached an all-time low even as LC was being written. Frustration leads to hypocrisy and the interiorization of social conflict (as in the case of Rojas). Rojas lashed out against this repression, caused both by Church and State, with corrosive irony: the so-called didacticism of LC is merely a veil covering the protest against prevailing social injustice. Rojas work is uniquely Spanish, seen in this light. One unusual claim made is that Rojas fabricated the entire matter of the "autor primitivo."

a. BHS 61 (1984), 522, D. S. Severin
b. *Le Moyen Age* 90 (1984), L. Chalon

934. VARELA, José Luis. "Lope recibe a Celestina." *ByN*, no. 2638 (1962), n. p.; rpt. in his *La palabra y la llama* (Madrid: Prensa Española, 1967), 25-33.

On Fabia and Gerarda from, respectively, Lope's *El caballero de Olmedo* and *La Dorotea*.

935. _____. "Calisto no adora a Melibea," in his *La palabra y la llama* (see preceding entry), 17-24.

Calisto not as a heretic but as a true 'loco enamorado'.

936. VECCHIO, Frank. "El 'antifeminismo' de Sempronio." *Proceedings of the Pacific Northwest Conference of Foreign Languages* 16 (1965), 115-18, and, with a slight title variation, in *RomN* 9 (1967-68), 320-24.

LC is not antifeminist. In the work, attitudes shift from character to character and any such debate is rendered meaningless. Sempronio's famous speech in Act 1 is mere posturing.

937. VILARDELL VINAS, Teresa. "Aspectos de la brujería en LC de Fernando de Rojas." Thesis (Tesina). Univ. of Barcelona, 1962. M. de Riquer. (*)

938. VILLALOBOS, Miguel Angel. "El personaje de la pícara

en la literatura española.'' Diss. Florida State Univ., 1978. 287p. DAI 39/03, 1627A. No. 78-15488. D. L. Hoffman.

The female figure in the LBA, LC, *La lozana andaluza* and other, later works.

939. VILLEGAS, Juan. ''La estructura dramática de LC.'' BRAE 53 (1974), 439-78.

A detailed scheme of the divisions and sub-divisions of major themes through the progress of the action, showing how they are carefully dovetailed to produce a work of magnificent structural density. The relations between action and structure are LC's central nervous system and the source of its dynamic artistic concept.

940. VINDEL, Francisco. *El arte tipográfico en Burgos y Guadalajara durante el siglo XV*. Madrid: Dirección de Relaciones Culturales, 1951.

Facsimiles are reproduced (pp. 291-96) of the Burgos 1499(?) copy in the library of the Hispanic Society of America. The data will not support the definite assignment of this copy to the year 1499; Vindel thinks 1501 is a more likely date for this exemplar, and that Toledo 1500 is the earliest known edition of the CCM. (See also entry 637.)

941. VOLKENING, Ernesto. ''LC enfocada desde otro ángulo.'' *Eco: Revista de la Cultura de Occidente* (Bogotá) 16 (1967-68), 140-60.

In Celestina there is expressed a subconscious myth of power seeking to find an outlet, a power which knows how to join that which has been sundered. This is one element in LC's eternal appeal.

942. VON RICHTHOFEN, Erich. ''Alfonso Martínez de Toledo und sein *Arcipreste de Talavera*, ein kastilisches Prosawerk des 15. Jahrhunderts.'' ZRP 61 (1941), 417-537.

The relevant section on the close relationship between this work and LC is found on pp. 522-29.

943. _____. ''El *Corbacho*: las interpolaciones y la deuda de LC,'' in *Homenaje a Antonio Rodríguez-Moñino* 2 (Madrid: Castalia, 1966) 115-20; rpt. in his *Tradicionalismo épico-novelesco* (Barcelona: Planeta, 1972), 241-48.

Rodrigo de Cota and Rodrigo de Reinosa are two writers who continue the spirit of *Corbacho* and who could also be candidates for authorship of LC's Act 1. Two similarities of Martínez de Toledo's work and Rojas' are the moralizing and the cosmetic catalogue (which has its precedent in the *De casibus virorum illustrium* of Boccaccio.

944. _____. ''Lo de la 'abuela con el ximio': otra expresión humanística y caballeresca (de LC)?'' *Cuadernos para Investigación de la Literatura Hispánica*, no. 5 (Madrid: Fundación Universitaria Española-Seminario 'Menéndez Pelayo', 1983), 133-34.

Given that there are other poor readings of sources in LC, the author suggests that 'ximio' might have originally been 'eximius'. Then the allusion would be to a grandmother who, like Calisto, could have been a member of the lower nobility, but who became the lover of an aristocrat.

W

945. WARDROPPER, Bruce W. ''Pleberio's Lament for Melibea and the Medieval Elegiac Tradition.'' MLN 79 (1964), 140-52.

Pleberio's lament is also directed to himself (as well as to Melibea). The themes summarize those of the earlier action, and the anguish caused by the world's disharmonies is not lessened by the consolations of faith.

946. WEBBER, Edwin J. ''Tragedy and Comedy in LC.'' *Hispania* 35 (1952), 318-20.

Assesses these twin concepts as Rojas must have understood them. Also explores similarities of LC to Senecan tragedies.

947. _____. ''LC as an *Arte de amores*.'' *Modern Philology* 55 (1957-58), 145-53.

Similarities in equating the CCM with a manual on love would include its title, language, moral aim, the love affairs themselves, the recourse to a third party and, finally, the tragic denouement.

948. _____. ''Hispano-Italian Renaissance Drama: Notes on Opportunities and Problems.'' *Renaissance Drama* 7 (1964), 151-57.

In the Salamanca of Rojas' times there was great interest in the humanist drama of Renaissance Italy, which also mixed tragedy and comedy and had ties with Seneca, Plautus and Terence. LC surely was shaped in part by this interest.

949. _____. ''CCM como *Arte de amor*.'' ACTAS: 31-34.

By demonstrating that it presents a genuine case of 'loco amor', the author feels that LC could be thought of as an *Ars amoris*.

950. WEBBER, Ruth House. ''Pedro Manuel de Urrea y LC.'' ACTAS: 359-66.

Outlines the celestinesque content of three of Urrea's works: *Egloga de Calisto y Melibea* (c. 1513), *Penitencia de amor* (1514), and a pastoral eclogue. The influence of LC is not so much a direct one as it is a shared interest in the art of love. These works often feature a servant who acts as the procurer of love: this modification becomes a mainstay in several imitations of LC.

951. WEBER DE KURLAT, Frida. ''Relaciones literarias: LC, Diego Sánchez de Badajoz y Gil Vicente.'' *Philological Quarterly* 51 (1972), 105-22.

Influence of LC on the pre-Lopean dramatists through an examination of spell-casting and conjurations in Diego Sánchez and Gil Vicente.

952. WEINBERG, F. M. "Aspects of Symbolism in LC." MLN 86 (1971), 136-53.

Examination of the symbolism of places, objects and even of the figure of Celestina. Also the garden, Calisto's house and Melibea's girdle.

953. WEINER, Jack. "Adam and Eve Imagery in LC." *Papers on Language and Literature* 5 (1969), 389-96.

The allusion in Sempronio and Calisto's first dialogue in Act 1 prepares for the presentation of Woman as responsible for the Fall of Man (reflected in Calisto's fall from the garden wall). Celestina is the serpent in this pattern of images.

954. WEST, Geoffrey. "The Unseemliness of Calisto's Toothache." *Cel* 3, no. 1 (May 1979), 3-10.

The toothache, which is a cover for the lovesickness of Calisto (Act 4), has long been associated with the pain of frustrated carnal love, a fact documented here with examples. Melibea's quick acceptance of the feint by Celestina (which solves her own problem with sexual frustration) shows how sharp was Rojas' intuition of human psychology and motivation.

955. WHINNOM, Keith. "The Relationship of the Early Editions of the *Celestina*." ZRP 82 (1966), 22-40.

More than a review of Herriott's book (1964), this study proposes a different scheme of filiation for the early eds. of LC.

a. RFE 51 (1968), 320-21, A. Llorente Maldonado

956. _____. *Spanish Literary Historiography: Three Forms of Distortion.* Exeter, England: Exeter University Press, 1967.

It is hard to see the LBA as a source for LC; a more likely source is Petrarch, as his humanist ideas would bind him to a personality like Rojas'. LC is but one part of this interesting essay.

a. BHS 46 (1969), 52-54, E. M. Wilson
b. MLR 64 (1969), 198-99, C. A. Jones

957. _____. "'El plebérico corazón' and the Authorship of Act I of LC." HR 45 (1977), 195-99.

Opposes the interpretation of Ruiz Ramón (entry 792), who argues for single authorship of LC based on this phrase. There is evidence that Rojas made emendations in the text of Act 1 and he may also have inserted the adjective.

958. _____. "'La Celestina', 'The Celestina', and L₂Interference in L₁." *Cel* 4, ii (Fall 1980), 19-21.

Advocates the abolition of the definite article 'la' from the *title* of Rojas' work (and 'the' from the English title as well). It is a modern solecism not justified by any of the early printings.

959. _____. "The Problem of the 'Best-Seller' in Spanish Golden-Age Literature." BHS 57 (1980), 189-98.

LC is the leader in eds. of the various works of fiction published in the 16th century, but the whole question of what was and was not popular in the Spanish Golden Age needs serious re-evaluation, as the author proves with pertinent examples.

960. _____. "Dr. Severin, the Partridge, and the Stalking Horse." *Cel* 4, ii (Fall 1980), 23-25.

Two additional notes on the identification of *perdices* in LC and Renaissance hunting methods. See also Severin (entry 838) on the 'falso boezuelo'.

961. _____. "Interpreting LC: The Motives and the Personality of Fernando de Rojas." *Medieval and Renaissance Studies on Spain and Portugal in Honour of P. E. Russell*, ed. F. W. Hodcroft et al (Oxford: SSMLL, 1981), 53-68.

A series of speculations on Rojas as man and writer. This dual vision results in a balanced perspective: without demythifying either LC or its author, both are perceived as having flaws. The discussion and exemplification take many critical views into account.

962. _____. "The *Historia de duos amantibus* of Aeneas Sylvius Piccolomini and the Development of Spanish Golden-Age Fiction," in *Essays on Narrative Fiction in the Iberian Peninsula in Honour of Frank Pierce,* ed. R. B. Tate (Oxford: Dolphin, 1982), 243-55.

Notes similarities between the works of Piccolomini and Rojas (and others); also contrasts their use of the narrative techniques for, respectively, omniscient author present and absent.

963. _____. "Miguel Marciales, a Necrology." *Cel* 5, ii (Fall 1981), 51-53; a Spanish translation by J. Gregorio Lobo appears in *Hoy Domingo* (May 30 1982), Suplemento, p. 14.

Eulogizes Marciales (d. December 23 1980) rightly as a distinguished *Celestina* scholar whose works, when posthumously published, will give new impetus to LC studies. See entry 579.

964. WILHITE, John F. "Fernando de Rojas' Pármeno: The Making of a Pícaro." *South Atlantic Bulletin* 41, no. 2 (1976), 137-44.

Celestina's psychological *brujería* assists Pármeno to discover the level of inner passion that converts him from loyal to reprobate servant. His progress reflects contemporary changes in servant-class attitudes towards the nobility.

965. WISE, David O. "Reflections of Andreas Capellanus' *De reprobatio amoris* in Juan Ruiz, Alfonso Martínez and Fernando de Rojas." *Hispania* 63 (1980), 506-13.

A recapitulation of the evil effects of love and the evils of women from Andreas in three works which highlight the opposition of the ecclesiastical tradition to the tenets of courtly love. The

Reprobatio was a compendium that served many authors well in drawing a negative picture of worldy love.

966. WOLFENSTEIN, Alfred. "Der jüdische Poet aus Burgos." *Jüdische Revue* (Mukacevo) (April 1937), 218-19.

On the meaning of LC to one who for the first time is presenting it on stage in a German adaptation.

967. WRIGHT, Leavitt O. *A Study of the History of the -ra Verb Form in Spain*. Berkeley: Univ. of California Press, 1932. (UCPMP, 15)

On pages 67-68 and in Appendix B, the author offers evidence that Act 1 differs from the remaining acts of LC respecting the use of the forms of -ra (indicative vs subjunctive); also -ra as opposed to -se forms.

Y

968. YNDURAIN, Domingo. "Un aspecto de LC," in *Estudios sobre el Siglo de Oro: Homenaje a Francisco Yndúrain* (Madrid: Ed. Nacional, 1984), 521-540.

The aspect studied is the use of contrast—at all levels—which allows the alert reader to perceive the moral message underlying LC as well as to enjoy the literary experience of the reading. Contrasts organize the work: the idealized practices of courtly love do not work in the civilian setting of Celestina's town; Melibea's parents, in guarding their daughter, provide the incentive for the family dishonor; attitudes about things are theoretically sound but impractically put into service; fancies and dreams are constantly being punctured by the thorns of reality, and so on.

969. YNDURAIN, Francisco. "Una nota a LC." RFE 38 (1954), 278-81.

On popular and erudite sources of LC. One of the latter seems to have been the Latin "Poema del gallo." The deepest permanent values of LC are rooted in Rojas' deft mixing of the two levels.

Z

970. ZALAZAR, Daniel E. "La misión de Celestina," in his *Ensayos de interpretación literaria* (Buenos Aires: Nuevas Ediciones Argentinas, 1976), 11-26.

Calisto and Melibea are known to each other before the action begins, but Zalazar rejects the idea that Melibea's anger is rooted in any aspect of courtly love, of which Melibea is doubtless ignorant, since her own replies to Calisto are not in that mold, nor does she heed any of its recommendations. Celestina's mission is to allow Melibea to express her sexuality without feeling guilt, which is tantamount to a mental seduction.

971. ZAMBRANO, María. "Los sueños en la creación literaria: LC." PSA 29 (1963), 21-35; rpt. in her *El sueño creador (los sueños, el soñar y la creación por la palabra)* (Xalapa: Univ. Veracruzana: 1965), 113-30, with another title: "LC: una semitragedia."

Melibea's situation compared to an initation dream of virginity-love-death, and Calisto's as one of virility-love-death.

972. ZARATE, Armando. "La poesía y el ojo en LC." CA 164, no. 3 (1969), 119-36.

A consideration of visual aspects of LC: seeing and being seen; love at first sight;and Celestina's projection of a seduction scene that 'seduces' Pármeno. All the voluptuous visions are followed by severe punishments.

973. ZELSON, Louis G. "The *Celestina* and Its Jewish Authorship." *The Jewish Forum* (New York) 13 (1930), 459-66.

Notes on the formation of the TCM and on Rojas' Jewishness. Cota, who was also a Jew, may have written Act 1. The author looks ahead to future investigations of Jewish sources for LC.

974. ZERTUCHE, Francisco M. "La *Comedia* o *Tragicomedia de Calisto y Melibea*." *Artes y Letras* 3, no. 6 (June 30 1946), 1, 5.

A brief presentation of some external data about LC: fate, stages of the formation of the text, biography of Rojas, and locale (Salamanca).

II. Translations and Adaptations of Rojas' *Celestina*

In this section both kinds of works are included because they are often—in the foreign languages—one and the same. Also, it is not infrequent that a staging is based on a particular translation and this information is usefully recorded in the same place. The first division lists the Spanish adaptations since technically these are not really translations. This grouping is followed by an alphabetical-by-language listing of translations and adaptations from the non-Hispanic world. A final grouping combines all the miscellaneous items: these are mostly creative works inspired by *Celestina*.

All sections and sub-sections follow a roughly chronological course which allows all stagings, say, of a particular production to be listed together. When entries can be identified as related (separate productions of the same theatrical adaptation, for example), the adaptation—in whatever language—is assigned a whole number and a '1' (e. g., 888.1). The separate arrangements retain the main number and a sub-class number (e. g., 888.2, 888.3 and so on). This makes indexing of entries and available reviews a more accurate procedure. Any potential problems caused by this arrangement are eliminated by this volume's two indices.

I have made every attempt to place here all the reliable information that I have been able to collect. Many data have come to me from colleagues and other LC enthusiasts from around the world. While I must assume that this list is far from complete, it seems to me that nowhere else is so much data on theatrical performance of LC printed together. This section should serve to stimulate further study of LC on stage; after all, the stagings do represent particular readings of Rojas' work in our century and these, too, need to be explored seriously. These readings of LC are the most ephemeral since, often, so few written reminders of them remain. What there is—reviews, programs with notes, typescripts (when printings of the adaptation have not been made), and the like—I have attempted to document as well, when possible. For articles that treat of these matters, consult the Subject Index at the end of this volume.

Adaptations in Spanish

975.1. LC, in the version of Tomás Borrás. Opened in Madrid, at the Teatro Español, on November 13 1940, directed by Felipe Lluch Garín, with Julia Delgado in the role of Celestina.

975.2. The same production, directed by Lluch Garín, was reprised in 1955 by the Teatro Popular Universitario of Madrid and taken to the Tercer Festival Internacional del Teatro (Parma, Italy) where it took first prize in April.

975.3. Later in 1955, it was put on outdoors in Cáceres and

broadcast on Spain's Radio Nacional. Directed by Salvador Salazar, it featured, in the cast, Blanquita Sendino, Pablo Vázquez, Amalia Oyonarte, Marcelo Arroito Jáuregui and Luis Morris.

a. ABC (May 1 1955), n. p., J. Cortes Cavanillas
b. *Indice*, no. 180 (June 1955), 14, Anon.
c. ABC (June 24 1955), 53, A. Marquerie

976.1. LC, in a theatrical version by José Ricardo Morales. Santiago de Chile: Ed. Universitaria, 1958. 79p. (Biblioteca Hispana, 13). The most recent printing is 1983, Col. Los Clásicos.

This version is based on the CCM, has 4 acts, music, and adds a few extra characters (*alguaciles*).

976.2. Opened in Montevideo's Teatro Solís October 28 1949, with Margarita Xirgu both directing the company, Comedia Nacional de Uruguay, and playing Celestina. Also Alberto Candeau as Sempronio, Enrique Guarnero as Pármeno, Concepción Zorrilla as Melibea, Horacio Preve as Calisto, Cotina Jiménez as Alisa and Miguel Moya as Pleberio. See entry 647.

a. *Número* 1 (1949), 356-58, J. Sorondo.

976.3. Produced in Santiago's Teatro Municipal in 1949, directed by the adapter, J. R. Morales, for the Teatro Experimental of the Univ. de Chile. Brisolia Herrera was Celestina, Domingo Tessier was Calisto, with María Maluenda and Marta Huneeus alternating as Melibea. Roberto Parada played Sempronio and Pedro Orthous—who would later condense this version for other stages—played Pármeno.

a. *La nación* (28 November 1949), A. Romera Múñoz

976.4. This production was taken to Buenos Aires in 1956, put on by the Comedia Nacional de Uruguay and directed again by Margarita Xirgu, who played Celestina in the production.

a. *El Día Médico* (May 1956) (*)

976.5. Morales' version was restaged in Chile in 1972 by the company "Teatro del Angel," and directed by Gustavo Meza. This time the principal roles were taken by Bélgica Castro (Celestina), Alejandro Sieveking (Calisto), Jael Unger (Melibea), Lucho Barahona (Sempronio), and Jaime Azócar (Pármeno).

976.6. Morales' adaptation was made into a "Celestina en Cámara" by its original Pármeno (see above 976.3), Pedro Orthous. It starred Bélgica Castro as Celestina. In various forms, this production toured several Latin American countries in 1974-1975 (see, for example, entries 991.1-3).

976.7. In 1976 a student version, directed by Juan Pablo Donoso for the Theatre Department of the Univ. of Santiago, featured a male in the role of Celestina: Andrés Pérez.

976.8. In 1977, another production with a male as Celestina (Oscar Vigoroux) was staged by the Teatro de la Universidad de Antofagasta (Chile) and directed by Omar Galarce. On this occasion, Manuel Lattus was Calisto, Brenda Gijón was Melibea, Félix Alcayaga was Sempronio and José Santander was Pármeno.

976.9. In 1981, the Compañía Teatro Joven, with Elsa Poblete as Celestina, presented Morales' version of LC in the Sala Bulnés. Omar Gutiérrez appeared as Calisto and Eliana Rodríguez was Melibea. It was directed by Alejandro Castillo.

976.10. The Morales version was restaged in February 1982, opening in Santiago de Chile's Teatro La Serena. The director was Edgardo Bruna. Sets were by Guillermo Ganga and costumed by Patricio Solavera. The Compañía de Teatro Itinerante's cast was headed by Mares González as Celestina, both in Santiago and, later, on tour throughout Chile. Omar Gutiérrez and Eliana Rodríguez repeated their roles from the 1981 production. Mario Bustos was Sempronio (and Pleberio!) while Max Corvalán appeared as Pármeno.

a. *El Mercurio* (January 3 1982), p. E8, Anon.

976.11. Morales adaptation of LC was published complete in *Cuadernos de Teatro*, no. 7, March 1983 (Santiago de Chile: Dept° de Extensión Cultural del Ministerio de Educación, 1983. 95p. Paper. Illustrated.

This publication contains the text (first ed. 1958) and commemorates the restaging of LC (Santiago, Teatro Itinerante, 1982). The adapter, J. R. Morales, contributes a prologue (5-9). There is a brief history of seven stagings of this adaptation (13-18) illustrated in both color and in black and white: these latter are of programs, casts of characters, and photos of some of the performances.

977. LC, in a production in the theatre of the Univ. of Puerto Rico (1958). The director was Nilda González; the production was notable for its use of pantomime.

978.1. LC, in an adaptation by Alvaro Custodio. Mexico: Ed. Teatro Clásico de México, 1966. 134p. Illustrated with photographs. Custodio's prologue is "Adaptaciones teatrales de LC."

a. RHM 33 (1967), 132, A. G. Mier
b. *RPh* 21 (1967-68), 606-07, K. V. Kish

978.2. Custodio's adaptation had its opening in 1953, in Mexico City's Sala Molière and, until its prohibition in 1960, was seen over 300 times. The adaptation is fairly faithful to the CCM and features a divided set: the three houses of Calisto, Melibea, and Celestina. Amparo Villegas starred as Celestina, with Miguel Maciá as Calisto, Pilar Crespo as Melibea, Ofelia Guilmain as Elicia, Alma Margarita Pliegot as Areúsa, Ignacio López Tarso as Pármeno, Guillermo Orea as Sempronio, Lina Catalán as Lucrecia and Alfredo W. Barrón as Pleberio. Direction was by Alvaro Custodio, sets by Antonio López Mancera, music by Christian Caballero and costumes by Blanca Chacel.

López Tarso won an award for his acting and Custodio for his directing in this 1953 staging.

a.*Novedades* (August 9 1953), n. p., Marís y Campos (*)
b. *México en la Cultura*, no. 229 (August 9 1953), 2, M. Guardia
c. *Revista de Revistas*, no. 2275 (October 18 1953 [see *infra*]), 89, F. Mota

978.3. In 1954, the Custodio production was taken to the provinces and seen in Cuernavaca, Guadalajara (Teatro Degollado), San Luis Potosí(Teatro de la Paz), Tépic and in Mexico City again (Teatro Reforma).

978.4. The production was restaged in Mexico City's Teatro del Caballito in November of 1957 but not without censorship problems. Amparo Villegas again was Celestina. Others were Ofelia Guilmain, J. de Campo, María Idalia, Miguel Córcega, Rosenda Monteros and Sergio Ramos.

a. *Claridades* (December 1 1957), 2nd section, 8, A. de las Bárcenas
b. *Revista Mexicana de Cultura*, no. 558 (December 8 1957), 12, A. Magaña Esquivel (*)
c. *México en la Cultura*, no. 456 (December 15 1957), 10, M. Guardia

978.5. In January of 1958 LC moved to the Teatro Trianón. In the 1957-58 season there were more than 150 performances given.

978.6. In 1960 Custodio's LC was being prepared for a revival at the Teatro Fábregas in Mexico City when it was prohibited as 'indigna', a ban that lasted eight years. However, the Act 9 banquet scene was restaged in 1963 in a special evening celebrating the tenth anniversary of the Teatro Clásico de México (September 9, Teatro Xola). Amparo Villegas appeared as Celestina, Ofelia Guilmain as Elicia, Guillermo Orea as Sempronio, Sergio Ramos as Pármeno, and Lilia Juárez and Alicia Quintos as Elicia and Areúsa.

a. *Examen*, no. 10 (Jan.-Feb. 1960), [2], M. Gómez Mayorga et al

978.7. One other time before the ban was lifted did parts of Custodio's LC appear on stage. The 1965 inauguration of the Teatro Jiménez Rueda in Mexico City included an aging Amparo Villegas in a recreation of some of her scenes as Celestina from past productions.

978.8.   Custodio prepared again his LC for staging in 1968, this time as for a "corral" and with the addition of some 15th-century musical pieces. It was seen from January to April at the Teatro Reforma, with Virginia Manzano as Celestina. Sets by David Antón and costumes by Isabel Richart. Others in this cast were: Juan Ferrara as Calisto, Alicia Bonet as Melibea, Miguel Córcega as Sempronio, Mauricio Herrera as Pármeno, Lourdes Guerrero as Lucrecia, Mercedes Pascual as Elicia, Belinda Corel as Areúsa, Enrique Gilabert as Centurio [the scenes with Centurio are an addition with this staging; they had not been part of earlier productions], and Tomás Bárcenas as Pleberio.

978.9.   This production was also invited to play before audiences in attendance at the summer Olympic Games in Mexico City. A handsome 24-page program was produced with nineteen black and white photos from this production at the Teatro Reforma.

a. *Excélsior* (May 25 1968), n. p., F. Baguer
b. *Impacto* (February 19 1968), Lya Engel
c. *Heraldo de México* (January 17 1968), Suplemento Literario, J. M. de Mora
d. *Jueves de Excélsior* (February 8 1968), M. Villalta
e. *Mañana* (February 17 1968), J. Sánchez Sosa
f. *El Sol de México* (February 13 1968), F. Durán M.
g. *El Universal* (February 4 1968), J. H. Cardona
h. *Heraldo de México* (February 13 1968), J. A. Alcaraz
i. *El Fígaro* (February 25 1968), Anon.

978.10.   Custodio's LC was produced by the Teatro Estudiantil Universitario of Oakland Univ. (Michigan, USA) in April 1975. It played five performances under the direction of William C. Bryant, and was later that month taken to Kalamazoo College (Michigan). Music used in the production was by Juan del Encina, Antonio de Cabezón, Cabanilles, Fuenllana, Mucarra and Millán. Appearing as Melibea was Ivy Corfis; Calisto was portrayed by Frank Liegghio, and Celestina was played by two actresses: Ann Schultz and Isabella Klecun. The production is preserved on videotape.

979.1.   LC, in the adaptation by Luis Escobar and Huberto Pérez de la Ossa. Madrid: Artes Gráficas 'Arges', 1959. 109p. With a prologue by José M. Ruiz Morales. Based on the CCM.

a. *Indice Cultural Español* 14 (1959), 847-48, Anon.
b. *Hispania* 44 (1961), M. E. Barrick

979.2.   The opening took place in Madrid's Teatro Eslava on May 10 1957, with Irene López Heredia as Celestina and Javier Escribá as Calisto. It was directed by Luis Escobar and featured multi-level sets with scaffolding.

a. ABC (Airmail edition, May 16 1957), 22-23 (*)
b. *Insula*, no. 126 (1957), 11, R. Vázquez Zamora
c. *Ciervo* (Barcelona) 6, no. 56 (1957), 7, F. Sitja (*)

979.3.   This production was taken to Paris in 1958 for the second season of the Théâtre des Nations and opened at the Sarah Bernhardt April 8 of that year. An introductory speech delivered by the Director General of [Spanish] Cultural Relations, which is the prologue to the printed version of the adaptation (see 979.1), was also printed—accompanied by several review citations—in the *Spanish Cultural Index* (October 1 1959), 956-63.

a. *La Revue de Paris* 65 (1958), 147, Th. Maulnier
b. *Insula*, no. 140 (1958), 11, J. Corrales Egea

979.4.   The production was also a hit at the Primer Festival Internacional de Danza, Música y Teatro (San Sebastián, 1958), where it was seen on August 1 in the Plaza del 18 de Julio. The Compañia Teatro de Lope de Vega directed by José Osuna and led by Irene López Heredia as Celestina was much praised. Others taking roles were Asunción Sancho as Melibea, Fernando Guillén as Calisto and Carlos Lemos as Sempronio. Sets were by José Tamayo and music by Cristóbal Halffter.

a. *El Diario Vasco* (August 1 1958), 8, Anon.
b. *El Diario Vasco* (August 2 1958), 4, T. G. de A.

979.5.   A production of this version was performed in 1967 at the Univ. of Havana, directed by Ramón Valenzuela.

979.6.   See also below, entry 1002.

980.   LC [scenes from] and other dramatic works from the 16th century and later. Selected and presented by Manuel Collado under the title *El bolulú, ayer y hoy*. Opened at Madrid's Teatro de la Comedia, November 28 1960.

981.   LC, given in a Spanish version at Westhampton College (Richmond, Virginia) April of 1960, with R. Merritt Cox as Calisto.

982.1.   LC, in an adaptation by Alejandro Casona. *Obras completas*, vol. 2 (Madrid: Aguilar, 1962), 1188-1262. Based on the CCM.

982.2.   A production of this version enjoyed great success at the XXIV Bienal de Teatro held in Venice at the Teatro di La Fenice. The company was Madrid's Teatro de Lope de Vega and Milagros Leal was a triumphant Celestina.

a. *Nuova Antologia*, no. 495 (1965), 415-16, M. Miserocchi

982.3.   On July 15 1965, this same company took LC to Barcelona, under the direction of José Osuna, with sets by Emilio Burgos. This production emphasized throughout the figure of Celestina with all other players relegated more or less to a secondary plane. Milagros Leal, who played Celestina here, was awarded the "Premio Nacional de Teatro y de la Crítica de Barcelona." She also was given the "Minerva de Plata" by the Círculo de Bellas Artes. Performed at the Teatro Griego de Montjuich.

982.4.   The Madrid opening at the Teatro de Bellas Artes took place in October. With Milagros Leal appeared José Rubio as Calisto, Asunción Sancho as Melibea, Ramón Durán as Sempronio and Antonio Medina as Pármeno. The magazine *Primer acto* presented the production with its "Premio Larra."

   a. ECV (for October 11 1965), 126-31, F. Alvaro [This is a pastiche conversation produced by juxtaposing "questions" from Alvaro and snippetsof "answers" from reviews that appeared in ABC, *Madrid, El Alcázar, Arriba, Informaciones, Ya* and *Pueblo*.]
   b. *Reseña*)Madrid) 2 (1965), 360-62, F. Segura
   c. *Arbor* 61 (1965), 231-32, J. L. Santaló
   d. CHA, no. 192 (1965), 584-96, R. Doménech
   e. *Est Lit*, no. 329 (1965), 14, J. E. Aragonés
   f. *Miscellanea Barcinonensia*, no. 11 (1965), 177-78, M. D. Iglesias Barba
   g. *Primer Acto*, no. 69 (1965), 55-56, R. Doménech

982.5.   In addition to being seen in the two capitals in 1965, the company took LC on tour to 32 smaller provincial cities and towns, among them Albacete, Bilbao, La Coruña, León, Lérida, Málaga, Mérida, Orense, Palencia, Salamanca, Tarragona and Vigo.

982.6.   In 1967, with Casona deceased, Milagros Leal's company, under the direction of Salvador Soler Marín, restaged LC at the Teatro Reina Victoria in Madrid. Leal again acted the role of Celestina, and was supported by María José Goyanes, Emilia Rubio, Jaime Blanch, Ricardo Alpuente, Ana María Méndez and Elena Rubí. Shortly after its run here, it moved to the Teatro Cómico.

982.7.   In 1968, Milagros Leal's company went to the provinces where LC formed a popular part of the repertory. At this time, it was calculated that Casona's version had passed 2,000 performances.

982.8.   In 1969, LC was again included in the provincial tour made by Leal's company.

982.9.   In 1974, at the end of October, and with a final-scene modification, the Casona adaptation was given a student-faculty production at Madison, Wisconsin, in the University's Union Theatre, under the direction of Roberto G. Sánchez. It had four performances.

983.1.   MELIBEA (Versión celestinesca en dos actos), by Manuel Criado de Val. *Teatro Medieval* (Madrid: Taurus, 1963), 109-54.

   a. *Segismundo*, no. 1 (1965), 176-78, A. Roldán

983.2.   This loose version of LC was performed June 30 1962 at Hita. Melibea is the focus of this version which accentuates the lyricism even as it emphasizes the moral lessons to be gleaned from the tragedies caused by the excesses of 'loco amor'.

984.   LC, in a version by José Estruch. It was performed by "Grupo 65" in the Teatro Odeón of Montevideo in 1966.

985.   LC, Act 19. Presented in 1966-67 by the company La Carreta of Douglas College and Rutgers Univ. Directed by A. M. Gil. Performed both at Douglas and the Univ. of Pennsylvania. Gil was Calisto, Michele Guerrini was Melibea, Hadassah Weiner was Lucrecia, with Ford Bacigalupo as Tristán and Carlos Chaves as Sosia.

986.   CALIXTO Y MELIBEA. Tragicomedia razonadamente atribuida a Fernando de Rojas. Adaptación a la escena en tres actos por Domingo González. Madrid: Escelicer, 1967. 104p. Paper (Alfil, Col. Teatro, 530). There is both a forward and an afterward by the adapter.

987.   LC; TRAGICOMEDIA DE LA ESPAÑA RENACENTISTA. Nueva adaptación teatral en dos partes. Version by Edma Ottelenghi, with the collaboration of a group of students. Montreal: Loyola College, [1972]. 52p.

988.1.   LC, in a new version by Ricardo López Aranda. Madrid: Ed. Prensa Española, 1974.

988.2.   The company Tirso de Molina, directed by Manuel Manzaneque, performed this adaptation while on tour of various cities in Spain. It had María Guerrero as Celestina, Gloria Cámara as Melibea and Arturo López as Calisto.

988.3.   CALISTO Y MELIBEA (Tragicomedia de Fernando de Rojas). In a new free version by Ricardo López Aranda.

   This production, which had previously played in the provinces, had its Madrid opening February 6 1980, directed by Manuel Manzaneque again, at the Teatro Espronceda 34. In the cast were María Guerrero as Celestina, José Sancho as Calisto, Inma de Santy as Melibea, Ramón Pons as Sempronio, María Vidal as Elicia, Araceli Conde as Lucrecia and José María Esquer as Pleberio. Sets were designed by Javier Artiñano and music was orchestrated by Angel Arteaga

   a. *El País* (February 7 1980), 27, Anon.
   b. *Ya* (February 7 1980), J. Parra [interview with María Guerrero]
   c. *El País* (February 10 1980), E. Haro Tecglen
   d. ABC (February 10 1980), L. López Sancho
   e. *ByN*, no. 3537 (February 13-19), 52-53, A. Prego
   f. ECV 23 (1981), 217, F. Alvaro

989.   LC. I have a notice of a production of February 1974, in Spanish, at the Greenwich Mews Theatre (New York), directed by Andrés Castro.

990.1.   LC. In an adaptation by René Buch. The Compañía de Teatro Repertorio de Nueva York opened with this production in the Grammercy Arts Theatre on March 1 1974,with sets by Robert Federico and direction by René

Buch. The action, based on the CCM, is in two parts (LC, acts 1-7 and 8-16). Taking the major roles were Ofelia González as Celestina, Phyllis Barzaretti as Melibea, María Norman as Elicia, with some shared roles as follows: Vivian DeAngelo or Graciela Más as Areúsa, Roberto Antonio or José Rodríguez as Calisto, Braulio Villar or Tony Díaz as Pármeno (the one not performing as Pármeno did Sempronio), and either Alfonso Manosalvas or Fernando Miyares as Pleberio. The other characters from Rojas' LC do not appear in this version.

990.2.   This version was well-received in a series of places while on tour in 1974, among them Northwestern Univ. and St. Louis. It was also on display in 1974 at the II Festival Internacional Cervantino in Guanajuato, Mexico.

990.3.   In 1976 this production was entered in the competition at the Festival de Teatro del Siglo de Oro at El Chamizal (El Paso, Texas), where it won a prize.

990.4.   On another tour in 1977, the Buch production was seen in several places on the West Coast, among them at Berkeley (Univ. of California). At this time Ofelia González was seen again as Celestina, Nelson Landrieu as Calisto, Mirtha Cartaya as Melibea, Mateo Gómez as Sempronio, Braulio Villar as Pármeno, Virginia Rambal as Areúsa, Nereida Mercado as Elicia and Alfredo Manosalvas as Pleberio. Performances at Berkeley took place on November 21 and 22.

a. *Cel* 2, i (May 1978), 31-33, A. S. Mandel

990.5.   Basically the same cast performed the play at the Univ. of Kansas, November 7 1978, with the substitution in the role of Elicia of Elizabeth Pena.

990.6.   In 1980, the production again went on the road after a revival in New York.

a. *The New York Times* (March 3 1980), R. Shepard

990.7.   The company was in San Antonio (March 15-16 1980) and made another appearance at El Chamizal. Ofelia González repeated as Celestina, with Yolanda Arenas as Melibea, Frank Robles or Omar Torres as Calisto, and Mateo Gómez and Juan Carlos Giménez as Sempronio and Pármeno.

a. *Cel* 4, ii (Fall 1980), 39-40, E. W. Hesse
b. LATR 13, ii (Spring 1980), 82, A. Pérez y R. Rodríguez

990.8.   Later in 1980, the show was performing at the Teatro Darío in Managua, Nicaragua.

a. *La prensa literaria* (October 12 1980), 6, S. Bonilla Castellón
b. *La prensa literaria* (October 26 1980), 6, G. Ramírez de Espinoza

991.1.   LC EN CAMARA (versión muy condensada para

cinco actores). Performed in May of 1974 in San José, Costa Rica, at the Teatro Castella. It was produced by a Chilean Company and starred Alejandro Sieveking, Bélgica Castro, Lucho Barahona and Dionisio Echeverría.

991.2.   This company returned permanently to Costa Rica in September of 1974 and, towards the end of that year, presented an expanded version of its LC at the Teatro Nacional. After a stay there, it passed to the Teatro de la Compañía Nacional de Teatro.

991.3.   A third and even more expanded version had its opening June 20 1980 in San José's Teatro del Angel, presented by the same company. Directing was Alejandro Sieveking (he also designed the costumes). Sets were the work of Lucho Barahona. Bélgica Castro appeared as Celestina, Lizbeth Quesada as Melibea, Lenín Vargas as Calisto. Others were Ana Istaru and Alejandro Rueda.

a. *Ancora/La nación* (San José, Costa Rica) (June 22 1980), 6-7, N. Loaiza

992.1.   ¿OS ACORDAIS DE CELESTINA ... LA VIEJA ALCAHUETA? Version of LC prepared by Manuel Criado de Val. Text in ACTAS: 491-520, with an introd. explaining how the adaptation came into being.

992.2.   A performance of this version was seen in Hita during the summer of 1974. It is based on TCM and gives considerable emphasis to the theme of vengeance, e.g., the *Tratado de Centurio* section. Its opening was designed to coincide with the Primer Congreso Internacional Sobre La Celestina (June 17-22). In three acts, it was performed at night outdoors. Luisa de Córdoba appeared as Celestina, Sagrario Sala as Melibea, Carlos Manet as Calisto, Carmen Maura as Areúsa and Pepe Ruiz as Centurio. Music was provided by Cristóbal Halffter. Eugenio García Toledano directed.

a. *Est Lit*, no. 544 (1974), 38, J. E. Aragonés

993.   LA INMORTAL CELESTINA (juego musical en torno al tema de Fernando de Rojas). A musical comedy of Enrique Llovet which had its première at Buenos Aires' Teatro Municipal General San Martino in June of 1974.

a. ABC (June 27 1974), 95, P. Massa
b. *Hispania* 58 (1975), 383 [a brief note], J. W. Díaz

994.   LC. THE SPANISH BAWD. Spanish adaptation and direction by Alvaro Custodio. English translation by Carmen Zapata and Alan Stark in collaboration with Custodio. Bilingual production sponsored by the Bilingual Foundation of the Arts (Los Angeles, California).

This bilingual production ran from October 6 to November 12 1978 (the Spanish and English versions alternating) at the Inner City Cultural Center. Sets designed by Estela Scarlata, costumes fashioned by Frances Acosta, and lighting designed by José López. Music was by Mark Elson. The roles were taken (in both languages) by David Estuardo as Calisto, Julio Medina as Sempronio, James Victor as Centurio, Don Cervantes as Crito and Irene de Bari as Areúsa. Other cast members worked in one language only as follows (Spanish language first): Rose Ramón/Victoria Richart as Melibea, Haydée du Barry/Lillian Adams as Celestina, Ilka Tanya Payán/ Ivonne Coll as Elicia, Alfredo Rodríguez/Robert Dunlap as Pármeno, Irma García/Denise Capitano as Lucrecia and Carlos Petrel/Frank Hill as Pleberio.

a. *Los Angeles Times* (October 10 1978), Section 4, p. 9, S. Drake
b. *Cel* 2, ii (Fall 1978), 37-38, A. S. Mandel
c. *Neworld*, no. 2 (February-March 1979), 30-31, L. Anderson

995.1. LC. Modern Spanish version by Camilo José Cela. Barcelona: Destino, 1979. 263p. (Áncora y delfín, 540)

995.2. The Compañía Teatro Lope de Vega, under the direction of José Tamayo, performed this version in Madrid, opening January 31 1978 at the Teatro de la Comedia. Scene design by Andrea d'Odorico, costumes by Miguel Barros, music by Antón García Abril. Irene Gutiérrez Caba was Celestina and Teresa Rabal appeared as Melibea, with Joaquín Kremel as Calisto, Paco Guijar as Sempronio, Pep Munné as Pármeno, Terele Pávez as Elicia, Salomé Guerrero as Areúsa, Julio Oller as Pleberio, Gaby Alvarez as Alisa, Angel Farreras as Tristán, Primitivo Rojas as Sosia, Amaya Curieses as Lucrecia, Tito García as Centurio, Manuel Brun as Crito and Macarena Sánchez as a maid.

Irene Gutiérrez Caba was honored with the "Premio Miguel Mihura" for her portrayal of Celestina.

a. *ABC* (February 6 1987), 29, P. Corbalán
b. *El País* (February 9 1978), 31, E. Llovet
c. *Est Lit*, no. 630 (February 15 1978), 31, J. E. Aragonés
d. *Reseña*, no. 113 (March 1978), 23-24, S. Martín
e. *CHA*, nos. 337-338 (1978), 230-32, S. Martín
f. *RyF* 197 (1978), 318-22, J. Paulino
g. *ECV* 21 (1979), 41-48, F. Alvaro et al
h. *Hispanic Journal* 5, ii (1984), 66, P. W. O'Connor

996.1. LC, adaptación nueva por Juan Guerrero Zamora para Radio Nacional de España. Madrid: Ministerio de Cultura, 1980. 79p. 2 cassettes. Stereo. Vol. 2 of "Teatro Clásico Español".

This has two parts: a libretto with the text of this version, together with an introd. to the work by the adapter and director of the production (Guerrero Zamora), and two cassettes (= Diapason 13,9047-48). The voice of Celestina is Mary Carrillo's; María del Puig is heard as Melibea and Luis Porcal as Calisto. Running time is about two hours.

996.2. Guerrero Zamora apparently took this version on tour in 1982 and it was seen on many provincial stages in Spain.

996.3. A somewhat modified version of Guerrera Zamora's production appeared on Spanish television (TVE) in three segments, corresponding to the three acts of his adaptations. It played as part of the 10:05 p. m. offering of the Primer Programa the evenings of October 4, 11, and 18, 1983.

a. *ABC* (20 October 1983), 109, anon.

997. LC, in a version by Miguel Bilbátua, who directed its performances June 26-29 1980 in the Cloister of San Pedro Mártir in Toledo. Co-director was Manuel Gutiérrez Aragón. Appearing in the production were Julia Martínez, Gabriel Llopart, Patricia Adriani, Maite Brik, Agustín Poveda, Mario Pardo, Vicente Cuesta, Lola Mateo, Virginia Mataix, Emilia Mellado and Vicente Gisbert. [See *Guía del ocio* (June 22-29 1980), 8.]

998. LC, performed three times in the Teatro Palenque in Talavera de la Reina on October 29-31 1980 by the Compañía Teatro Libre of that city. It commemorated the return of Rojas' mortal remains to Talavera.

999.1. TCM. Performed by the Compañía Teatro del Aire of Madrid in the new adaptation by Angel Facio, in 43 Spanish cities from August 1981 to May 1983.

A very free adaptation with scaffolds, nets, ropes, webs, all projecting symbolic meaning onto the action of the play. Public reception was cool. Celestina (Asunción Sancho) was garbed as a nun, and an additional character, the Grand Inquisitor, furnishes a level of interpretation Rojas did not intend (performed by Santiago Ganuza). The action ends with a tableau featuring all the dead principals (Celestina's corpse remains on stage, as do those of the hanged servants, after they are executed). There are frequent references to Judaism, there is substantial nudity and emphasis on sexual nuance throughout.

Charo Amador was Melibea and Fernando Romo played Calisto. Others in the cast included: Paco Menéndez as Sempronio, David Alvarez as Tristán, Lola Casamayor as Elicia, Gloria Villalba as Areúsa, Cristina Vázquez as Lucrecia and Daniel Moreno as Pármeno.

999.2. The production played in Salamanca August 23 1981 to poor audience response. The director, Facio, met with the public after the performance to discuss the play, a custom he continued on tour in the US.

a. *El Adelantado* (August 23 1981), 'Temas de Actualidad,' Pollux

999.3. The play was seen in the USA in several places in early 1982, at Hunter College in New York City, Wellesley College (Massachusetts), the University of Chicago and the Lisner Auditorium of The George Washington University in Washington, D. C.

a. *Cel* 6, i (May 1982), M. S. de Cruz-Saenz

999.4. Angel Facio's adaptation appeared in printed form, Madrid: Círculo de Bellas Artes, 1984, 190p. Paper (Col. Teatro, 214). Illustrated.

999.5. Facio's LC was selected to inaugurate the newly created Sala Fernando de Rojas in Madrid's Círculo de

Bellas Artes and had its debut in October of 1984, exactly 75 years after its first staging ever (also in Madrid). Several public events were held in association with this production (see entry 427), which ran until December 1984. Facio's dialogue is a re-ordering of Rojas' own (condensed) and is his own modern interpretation of its dramatic message. Facio also helped in the stage setting and directed the production as well. The cast of characters is reduced for this version, and one new character—the Grand Inquisitor—is added (played by Juan Carlos Lavid). Celestina was portrayed by Dora Santacreu, Melibea by Charo Amador and Calisto by Angel Pardo. Ernesto Ruiz was Pármeno, Paco Torres was Sempronio, Aurora Herrero played Elicia and Blanca Paza was Areúsa. Lucrecia was Cristina Vázquez and David Alvarez completed the cast as Tristán.

a. *El público* (October 1984), 20-21, illus., A. F. L.
b. *El País* (11 October 1984), 26, R. T.
c. *El País* (13 October 1984), Artes II, illus., Anon.
d. *Ya* (13 October 1984), 32, J. P. G.
e. *El País* (17 October 1984), 36, illus., E. Haro Tecglen
f. ABC (17 October 1984), 71, L. López Sancho
g. *Ya* (17 October 1984), 34, illus., J. Arroyo
h. *Guía del ocio* (22-28 October 1984), 39, illus.,J. C. Avilés
i. *Cambio 16* (29 Oct-5 Nov 1984), 132-35, illus., M. Bayón
j. *El público* (November 1984), 12-14, illus., J. L. Vicente M.
k. *Cel* 8, ii (Fall 1984), 45-46 [J. T. Snow]
l. *Reseña* XXI, no. 154 (Jan-Feb 1985), n. p., illus., J. L. Veza
m. *Cel* 9, i (May 1985), 56-62, E. Gurza

1000. LC. TCM. Adapted by Tina FRENCH and Salvador GARCINI. The latter also directed this production at Mexico City's Teatro 'Julio Prieto'. It premiered July 23 1982 under the auspices of the Teatro de la Nación I. M. S. S.

This production emphasizes the diabolic and perverse nature of Celestina, here played by Ofelia Guilmain. Calisto and Melibea are Roberto Ballesteros and Luz María Jérez; Sempronio and Pármeno are Ernesto Yáñez and Alejandro Camacho; Elicia and Areúsa are played by Gabriela Araujo and Patricia Bernal; Tristán and Sosia by Josafat Luna and José Antonio Morales; Lucrecia by Stasia de la Garza, Centurio by René Campero and Pleberio (Alisa is cut from this adaptation) by Eduardo Liñán.

a. *Cel* 6, ii (Fall 1982), 25-26 [J. T. Snow]
b. *Cel* 7, ii (Fall 1983), 32-33 [J. T. Snow]

1001.1. Alfonso Sastre. *Tragedia fantástica de la gitana Celestina*. Publication of final Spanish version in *Primer Acto* no. 192 (Jan-Feb. 1982), 63-102.

A free adaptation by the polemic Spanish dramatist. It had already been staged in Italian and German (see entries 1074 and 1062). On pp. 46-62 of the same number of *Primer Acto* there is an interview with and an appreciation of Sastre by F. Caudet.

1001.2. The Spanish production of Sastre's version of LC was staged at Barcelona' Sala Villarroel, April 30 1985. This was a co-production of the Centre Dramàtic de la Generalitat and the Grupo de Acción Teatral of

L'Hospitalitet. It was directed by Enric Flores. Maria Josep Arenós was Celestina: others in the cast were Minerva Alvarez, Teresa Vilardell, Inma Alcántara, Ramón Teixedor, Pere Vidal, Pepe Miravete, Tomás Vila and Alfons Flores.

a.*El País* (2 May 1985; Barcelona ed.), 28, J. de Sagarra

Arabic

1002. ROJAS, Fernando de. LC. Traducida al árabe por Mahmud Sobh. Madrid: Instituto Hispano-Arabe de Cultura, 1977. xvi + 148p. (Clásicos hispanos, 4)

This is a translation of the stage adaptation of Luis Escobar and Huberto Pérez de la Osa (See 979.1., above.) from 1959. There is a brief introd. in Spanish by Felisa Sastre Serrano.

a. *Informaciones* (May 4 1977), 22, J. Goñi

Croatian

1003. _____. *Celestina ili Tragikomedija o Kalistu i Melibeji*. Translation and notes by Vojmir Vinji. Zagreb: Zora, 1957. 303p.

According to RL 20 (1961), 468, this translation was done by Vinji under the inspiration of some verses by Drago Ivanisević.

Czech

1004. _____. *Celestina*. Translation by E. Hodousek. Prague: SNKLHU, 1956. 391p.

A production of *Celestina* (this translation ?) was seen in Prague during the 1963 season, in a short stage run.

Danish

1005. _____. *Ruffersken fra Toledo* (The Bawd of Toledo), tr. by Team Teatret. Grasten: Forlaget Drama, 1975.

Dutch

1006. _____ LC. Translation and introd. by Albert Helman (pseudonym of Lou Lichtveld). Amsterdam: Contact, 1954; 2nd ed., 1961. lx + 245p.

1007.1. _____ *De Spaanse Hoer* (Toneelstuck naar LC van F. de R.). A stage version by Hugo Claus. Amsterdam: Contact/De Bezige Bij, 1970. 146p. (Literaire Reuzenpocket, 322).

In 22 scenes. There are some characters new to LC who are given little or nothing to say.

1007.2. A production using this translation/stage version opened January 1 1970 in Eindhoven's Stadsschouwburg,in performances by the Toneelgroep Globe company. Ton Lutz directed with the staging and sets of Nicolaas Wijnberg. It opens with Celestina's entrance: she is singing. A revolving stage was used and a chorus was introduced to accentuate the action. In the principal roles were Ank van der Moer as Celestina, Mart Gevers as Claudina, Femke Boersma as Areúsa, Kitty Janssen as Elicia, Jeroen Krabbé as Calisto, Jérôme Reehuis as Sempronio, Eric Schuttelaar as Pármeno, Pleuni Touw as Melibea, Heleen van Meurs as Alicia [sic], Ineke Cohen as Lucrezia [sic] and Henk Molenberg as Centurio.

English

1008. _____ *Celestina; or the Tragicke-Comedy of Calisto and Melibea*. Englished from the Spanish of F. de R. by James Mabbe, anno 1631. This is a reprint, Valencia: Ed. Castalia, 1949. 199p.

1009.1. _____. *Celestina*. The Ashley Dukes adaptation which, in turn, is based on a German version by Alfred Wolfenstein. Dukes' adaptation, from 1931, was also called *Matchmaker's Arms* and is notably free in its conception.

1009.2. It was produced in 1951 at London's Embassy Theatre by Mary Morris and opened January 9th. Some of the stars and their roles: Mary Ellis as Celestina, Clement McCallin as Calisto and Maxine Audley as Melibea. Other roles in the play—to show how free this adaptation is—include those of Jerome, Laura, a sergeant and a captain.

1010. _____. LC. A radio broadcast by the British Broadcasting Company. Adapted from the Mabbe translation by Peter Duval Smith, it was heard twice, March 18 and 20 1954. In the cast were Flora Robson as Celestina, Cyril Cusack as Calisto, Carol Marsh as Melibea, Laurence Payne as Pármeno, Anthony Jacobs as Sempronio, Maxine Audley as Elicia, Daphne Anderson as Areúsa and Oliver Burt as Pleberio. (See also, below, entry 1021),

1011. _____. *The Celestina. A Novel in Dialogue*. Translation of the CCM by Leslie Byrd Simpson. Berkeley and Los Angeles: Univ. of California Press, 1955; 2nd printing 1959. x + 162p.

a. *Hispania* 38 (1955), 377-39, J. E. Keller
b. *American Scholar* 25 (1955), 126, R. P. Sebold
c. *The New York Times* (July 10 1955), Section 7, 6, R. Sender

d. *El Universal* (Caracas) (June 18 1955), Suplemento, R. Sender
e. BHS 33 (1956), 174-75, A. E. Sloman
f. MLN 71 (1956), 234-35, B. W. Wardropper
g. MLR 51 (1956), 464-65, A. I. Watson
h. *Quarterly Journal* (London), no. 18 (1956), 20-21, P. H. Robinson
i. *RPh* 10 (1956-57), 367-78, J. H. Herriott
j. HR 26 (1958), 241-43, L. S. Poston, Jr.
k. *The New Vida Hispánica* (London), no. 3 (1966), 12-16, J. Chapman

1012.1. _____. LC. Translation of the TCM by Mack Hendricks Singleton. Madison: Univ. of Wisconsin Press, 1958. xiv + 299p.

Besides the sprightly translation, there is a select bibliography prepared by Cándido Ayllón.

a. *Indice*, no. 129 (1959), 19, H. T. Young
b. BA 33 (1959), 463, M. D. Triwedi
c. HR 28 (1960), 368-72, M. Morreale
d. MLR 55 (1960), 288-90, A. I. Watson
e. *Hispania* 43 (1960), 298-99, E. J. Webber
f. BHS 37 (1960), A. E. Sloman

1012.2. A reading version of this translation under the direction of Roberto G. Sánchez, with the aid of Art Beringer and Erna Berndt[-Kelley], was performed at the Play Circle of the Univ. of Wisconsin, November 29 1954. Margot Herriott was Celestina, Peter J. Lunardini was Calisto, Virginia Burdick was Melibea and the translator, M. H. Singleton, was Pleberio. The program notes indicate that "so far as we know, this is the first time LC has ever been given in any form in the United States."

1012.3. Another reading version in three acts was given, with a focus on Melibea's story and based on the Singleton translation, in Wisconsin's Play Circle, September 8-10 1957. It was again directed by Roberto G. Sánchez. Margot Herriott was Celestina, Carol Cowan was Melibea and Don Robinson was Calisto.

1013. LC. Using the translation by James Mabbe, an adaptation was staged at the Theatre Royal in Stratford, England, with a première on February 21 1958. It was directed by Joan Littlewood and was taken, later that same year, to a London theatre. In it were seen: Murray Melvin as Calisto, Olive McFarland as Melibea, Eileen Draycott as Celestina, Marguerite Stone as Elicia, James Booth as Sempronio, Robin Chapman as Pármeno, Anna Korwin as Areúsa and Joan Littlewood as Alisa. Una Collins designed the costumes and John Bury the sets.

1014. LC. Translation of the TCM by Phyllis Hartnoll. London: J. M. Dent/New York: E. P. Dutton, 1959. xii + 212p. (Everyman's Library, 100)

a. TLS (June 19 1959), 368, Anon.
b. BHS 37 (1960), 37-40, A. E. Sloman
c. HR 28 (1960), 368-72, M. Morreale
d. MLR 55 (1960), 288-90, A. I. Watson

e. *Hispania* 43 (1960), 298-99, E. J. Webber

f. *The New Vida Hispánica* (London), no. 3 (1966), 12-16, J. Chapman

g. RLC 45 (1971), 222-28, G. Martínez Lacalle

1015.　LC, or the Tragi-comedy of Calisto and Melibea. Stage adaptation in five acts, based on Mabbe's version, by Eric Bentley. *Six Spanish Plays* [= vol. 3 of *The Classic Theatre*, ed. Eric Bentley] (New York: Doubleday, 1959), 1-95.

a. *Américas* 16 (1959-60), 412-13, V. R. B. Oelschläger

b. *Hispania* 43 (1960), 127-28, N. P. Sacks

c. *Arbor* 48, no. 184 (1961), 549-51, A. Valbuena Briones

d. RHM 27 (1961), 57-58, A. Agostini de del Río

1016.　LC. There was a curious adaptation by George Christopolous that was seen in New York in 1960. It was updated to Tarpon Springs, Florida in the 1940s and the characters all had Greek names, in keeping with the Hellenic spirit in which the venture was conceived.

1017.1.　ROJAS, Fernando de. *LC: The Spanish Bawd.* Translated by J. M. Cohen. Harmondsworth, England: Penguin, 1964 (Penguin Classics L142); also New York/London: New York Univ. Press, 1966. 247p.

a. TLS (February 25 1965), 149, Anon.

b. *Choice* 2 (July 1965), 304, Anon.

c. *Modern Language Journal* 50 (1966), 293, M. E. Barrick

d. *The New Vida Hispánica* (London), no. 3 (1966), 12-16, J. Chapman

e. RLC 45 (1971), 222-28, G. Martínez Lacalle

1017.2.　This translation was reproduced with acquatints by Dodie Masterman in the ed. of the London Folio Society of 1973. 205p.

1018.　[Anon.]*An Interlude. Showing the Beauty and Good Properties of Women* (Commonly known as *Calisto and Melibaea*), in *Early English Dramatists. Six Anonymous Plays,* First Series, ed. J. S. Farmer (London, 1905; rpt. New York: Barnes and Noble, 1966), 47-87.

The play, adapted from Rojas and printed by John Rastell (c. 1525), is thought by Farmer to be the work of John Heywood (p. 237). Some facsimile pages from the unique Bodleian Library exemplar are included.

1019.　_____. *Celestina, or the Tragick-Comedy of Calisto and Melibea.* Englished from the Spanish of F. de R. by James Mabbe, anno 1631. Being a rpt., with the introd. by James Fitzmaurice-Kelly, of the 1894 London edition. New York: AMS Press, 1967. xxxvi + 287p.

1020.1.　_____. LC. Adapted for the stage and translated by David Castillejo. *Plays*, vol. 2 (London: Ladbroke, 1969), n. p. This is a very reduced ed. of just twenty copies.

1020.2.　This adaptation was apparently used in a production in London's Southwark in March 1965.

1021.　LC. A 1969 radio broadcast by the British Broadcasting Company featured an arrangement of the James Mabbe translation by Terence Miller (see also, above, entry 1010). This new broadcast was heard on January 24 and again, later, in February. The roles were taken by: Nicolette Bernard as Celestina, Robert Rietty as Calisto, Patricia Gallimore as Melibea, Trader Faulkner as Pármeno, Michael Deacon as Sempronio, Carol Marsh as Elicia (she was the Melibea of the 1954 broadcast version), Elizabeth Proud as Areúsa and Peter Williams as Pleberio.

1022.　_____. LC. Tragicomedy of Calisto and Melibea. Translated from the Spanish by Wallace Woolsey. New York: Las Américas, 1969. 235p.

1023.　*The Beauty and Good Properties of Women . . . Otherwise Calisto and Melebea, c. 1530.* Being a rpt. of the 1909 London/Edinburgh facsimile edition. New York: AMS Press, 1970. This work is also known as the *Interlude of Calisto and Melebea*, often attributed to John Rastell, who was its printer.

1024.　Rojas, Fernando de. *Celestine; or, the Tragick-Comedy of Calisto and Melibea.* Translated by James Mabbe and now edited by Guadalupe Martínez Lacalle, London: Támesis, 1972. xiv + 268p. (Serie B - Textos, 14)

The introd. studies LC in England, the life and works of Mabbe, the manuscripts (the newly-discovered Alnwick Castle one is the basis of the new ed.), and the characteristics of the text. There is, in addition, a useful select bibliography.

a. MLR 70 (1975), 202-03, K. Whinnom

b. HR 43 (1975), 422-25, K. V. Kish

c. CL 27 (1975), 374-77, C. F. Fraker, Jr.

d. NRFH 25 (1976), 407-12, D. E. Eisenberg

e. BHS 54 (1977), 50-52, P. E. Russell

1025.　_____. *Celestina, the Spanish Bawd, or the Tragicomedy of Calisto and Melibea.* This is an adaptation of the Mabbe translation for the stage by Laurence Senelick, who also directed the performances by a theatre group of Tufts Univ. (Massachusetts, USA) in collaboration with the company, Pen, Paint and Pretzels. It has 2 acts. It ran November 19-23 1974. The frame is Melibea's remembrance of the action, told in flashbacks as she stands on her fateful tower. Danny White played Celestina, Susan Middeleer was Melibea, Robert Kulow was Calisto and Donald T. Wangel played Pleberio. There is a program printed in *Prologue* 30, no. 2 (November 1974), 2-3.

1026.　_____. *Celestina.* This is another adaptation of Mabbe, this time by Sir Charles Lewsen, who directed the production seen at the Crucible Theatre (Sheffield, England) from September 27-October 14 1978.

In the speaking roles were Antonia Pemberton as Celestina, Pamela Stephenson as Melibea, Malcolm Sinclair as Calisto, Bill Stewart as Sempronio, David McGaw as Pármeno, Souad Faress as Elicia, Catherine Hall as Areúsa, Helen Cooper as Lucrecia, Martyn Hesford as Tristán, David Sassieni as Sosia, Christopher Guinee as Pleberio, Sylvia Barter as Alisa and Terry Gilligan as Traso. The sets were the work of Roger Glossop, the costumes were by Anne Sinclair, lighting by Mick Hughes and sound effects by Alan Stretch.

a. *The Daily Telegraph* (September 29 1978), E. Shorter
b. *The Times* (October 2 1978), 7, N. Chaillet
c. *Plays and Players* 26, no. 2 (November 1978), 22, H. Rorrison
d. *Drama: The Quarterly Theatre Review*, no. 131 (Winter 1979), 65-66, E. Shorter

1027. _____. *Celestina*. See above, the Spanish section (entry 994), for the bilingual productions in Los Angeles (1978) of Alvaro Custodio, director of both the Spanish and English adaptations.

1028. CELESTINA. In an adaptation by Edward Senior and Wendell Phillips. Presented in San Francisco, California by the StageGroup Theatre Company in late 1979.

Presented on weekends in, apparently, two runs, one in August and September, the other in November and December. A free adaptation that gives emphasis to the prostitution (even adding scenes). Major surgery has been done to the original: the opening encounter is eliminated; Celestina is much younger and rather more vigorous than oft imagined; Calisto is impaled on Centurio's sword; Melibea commits suicide using Calisto's dagger; Alisa mourns Melibea at the play's end; and a chorus of infernal voices is used to emphasize the tragic overtones of the production. Celestina was portrayed by Maureen Mileski.

a. *Cel* 4, ii (Fall 1980), 38-39, G. Dardón Tadlock

1029. AXTON, Richard, ed. *Three Rastell Plays: Four Elements; Calisto and Melebea; Gentleness; and Nobility.* Cambridge, England: D. S. Brewer/Totowa, N. J.: Rowman & Littlefield, 1979. 169p. (Cambridge Tudor Interludes, 1)

The best available general introd. (pp. 15-20), text (69-96) and notes (140-52) to this earliest English adaptation of LC, written for six players [c. 1525], possibly by John Rastell, its printer.

a. *Comparative Drama* 15 (1981), 176-78, D. Bevington

1030. CELESTINA. Prof. Hugh Richmond adapted LC in an abbreviated English version in 1981 with a view to capturing the similarities of Rojas' work to Shakespeare's *Romeo & Juliet*. He produced a videotape record of a performance, with student actors garbed in Renaissance style. The action has both indoor and outdoor locations on the Berkeley campus. Running time is about 55 minutes. Available from The Educational Television Office of the University of California.

a. *Cel* 9, ii (Fall 1985), J. T. Snow

1031. THE FRUITS OF LOVE. An adaptation by David Gilmore from the Mabbe translation of 1631. Unpublished mimeographed typescript. 55p.

Basically the CCM in three acts. First performed at the Nuffield Theatre in Southampton (England), February 3-19 1983. Directed by John Ginman, with Patsy Large doing the sets, Glenn Willoughby the costumes and Richard Caswell the lighting. Eight characters appear (missing are Crito, Alisa, Pleberio, Tristán, Sosia and Centurio [the latter is, however, an offstage presence]). Major alterations include: Lucrecia admits Celestina directly into Melibea's unmonitored presence; Melibea admits Calisto into her house on the evening of the first tryst; Lucrecia announces the news of the deaths of the servants to the lovers in the garden; Calisto is tricked out of the garden by a faked call for help from Elicia and Areúsa, and run through by the sword of Centurio (offstage); Calisto returns to the garden, mortally wounded, to speak of his love for Melibea; and at the end of the action, Lucrecia goes off to church to seek comfort in the pursuit of heaven.

Sheila Burrell was Celestina, with Paul Clarkson as Sempronio and Gary Powell as Pármeno. The lovers were played by Jason Carter and Edita Brychta. Samantha Bond, Adrienne Thomas and Helena Little were, respectively, Elicia, Areúsa and Lucrecia.

a. *Southern Evening Echo* (Southampton), (29 January 1983), 20, A. King
b. *Southern Evening Echo* (8 February 1983), A. King

1032. CELESTINA. This was a cut version of Mabbe's 1631 translation into English, directed by Christopher FETTES and performed by final-year students of London's Drama Centre, November 27-30 1984.

This production had several memorable innovations: Irish accents, a black Celestina, and the Brechtian device of out-front narrators (who spoke LC's ''argumentos'' and performed other stage business; they were played by members of the cast). Public response was enthusiastic.

Juanita Waterman was Celestina, with Mark Schofield and Helen Parkinson as the doomed lovers. Pármeno and Sempronio, respectively, were Dominic Arnold and John Wagland, while their paramours, Areúsa and Elicia, were played by Kate Gartside and Sarah Huntley. Tristán and Sosia were Andrew Latham and Brian Fearne, Centurio was James Burton, and Lucrecia was Emma D'Inverno. Bas van Dam made a brief appearance as Crito, and Alisa and Pleberio were portrayed by Yvonne Orengo and Stephen Caro.

a. *Cel* 9, i (May 1985), 51-53, D. Hook
b. *Cel* 9, i (May 1985), 53-54, J. London
c. *Cel* 9. i (May 1985), 54-55, C. Ludden, A. Taylor and M. Strickland

French

1033. COPEAU, Jacques. *L'Illusion* [d'après *L'Illusion comique* de Pierre Corneille et (inspirée de) LC, de Rojas]. Unedited but c. 1929. There is a manuscript in the collection of Mme. Marie-Hélène Dasté [This information comes from the *Répertoire bibliographique des traductions et adaptations françaises du théâtre étranger du XVe siècle a nos jours*, vol. 4 (Paris: Centre National de Recherches Scientifiques, 1961), p. 65.]

1034. ROJAS, Fernando de. LC, Tragi-comédie imitée de l'espagnol. Adaptation de Fernand Fleuret et Roger Allard. Paris: Ed. du Trianon, 1929. 120p. (Le Bocage des Plaisirs, 3)

> Limited ed. of just 325 copies; illustrated with four copper engravings by Constant Le Breton. Toward 1928 this version was in rehearsal by the company "Les Copiaus", led by Jacques Copeau, but was never performed.

1035. _____. LC. An adaptation by Albert Camus was staged during the season of 1937 (December 5-?) in Algeria, at the Théâtre de l'Equipe.

1036.1. _____. *La Célestine. Tragi-comédie de Fernando de Rojas (1492)*. Adaptation en 8 tableaus de Paul Achard. Paris: Odette Lieutier, 1942. A 3rd ed. is 1946. 101p. (Collection Masques)

1036.2. Published to commemorate the production's one-hundredth performance (the première was February 20 1942) at the Théâtre Montparnasse-Gaston Baty in Paris. It was performed that year by the Compagnie d'Art Dramatique under the direction of Jean Darcante. Stage direction was by Jean Meyer and sets were by R.-Ph. Couallier, with costumes designed by Rosine Delamare. The principal roles were taken by Marcelle Géniat as Celestina, Hélène Constant as Melibea, Jean Darcante as Calisto, René Dupuy as Pármeno, André Bervil as Sempronio, Ariane Borg as Areúsa, Yvonne Galli as Elicia, Marie Servane as Lucrecia, Germaine LeDoyen as Alisa, Lefèvre-Bel as Pleberio, Louis Salou as Centurio and Michel Gudin as the 'sereno', an addition of Achard's.

> From this theatre it then went on to the Théâtre de la Renaissance (1942-43) and, a few seasons later to the Palace (1945-46). Darcante's company performed them all and he was each time the Calisto, as was Marcelle Géniat Celestina. There was a different Melibea on each occasion. This LC was performed more than 700 times.

> a. *Finisterre* 2 (1942), 206, E. Serrano
> b. BH 45 (1943), 98-100, G. Cirot
> c. BH 45 (1943), 198-201, P. Verdevoye

1037. _____. (Same title as preceding entry). Adaptation complète de Paul Achard. Illustrations de Maurice L'Hoir. Paris: Ed. de la Nouvelle France, 1943. 288p.

> A small ed. of 187 copies. The "Avant-propos" by Achard documents the process of his adaptation's many revisions (no less than seven) in search of dramatic unity. The first version (entry

1036.1) contained eight scenes and this one contains eleven. Illustrated.

1038. _____ (Pièce en 8 tableaus). D'après l'oeuvre célèbre de F. de R., par Paul Achard. Paris: O. Lieutier, 1946. 112p. Also in the first volume of *Paris-Théâtre* (Paris: Georges Lang, 1947), 1-50.

1039. _____. LC. Reproduces the translation of Germond de Lavigne (1841). Introd. by Maurice Lacoste. Paris: F. Sorlot, 1942. 276p. (Les Maîtres Etrangers)

1040. _____. *La Célestine, tragi-comédie de Calixte et Melibée*. Introd. by E. Martinenche [written in 1920]. Paris: M. Daubin, 1946. (Les Chefs d'Oeuvre Étrangers, 2).

> This is a partial ed. of the 1841 Germond de Lavigne translation, which Martinenche had published in 1920 (Paris).

1041. _____. LC. Translation of A. Germond de Lavigne. Paris: Les Compagnons du Livre, 1949. 264p. New ed. of the 1841 translation. Frontispiece by Jean Mohler.

1042. _____. *La Célestine: Tragi-comédie de Calixte et Melibée*. Translation of Germond de Lavigne. Two volumes. Paris: Les Bibliophiles de France, 1949-50. 155, 151p. This bibliophile's ed. is illustrated with lithographs by Maurice Lalan.

1043. _____. *La Célestine: Comédie tragique de Calixte et Melibée*. This is the Germond de Lavigne translation revised and presented by René-Louis Doyon. Paris: Club Français du Livre, 1952. xxvi + 325p. (Le Club Français du Livre, Théâtre, 9)

1044. _____. A French adaptation was presented in Paris 1955 by Jean Anouilh. [Information from ECV (October 11 1965), 128, F. Alvaro.]

1045. _____. LC. A French version by Hicter and Prévot was presented in Belgium in 1958.

1046.1. _____ LC (together with *Don Juan*). Adaptation by Georges Brousse. Paris: Denoël, 1961. 277p. (Collection Jaune. Théâtre)

> This adaptation was performed in 1960 at Montaubon, France, at the "Festival du Langedoc". It was directed by François Maistre and featured Maria Mériko as Celestina.

1046.2. According to *The Best Plays of 1966-67*, ed. O. L. Guernsey (New York: Dodd Mead, 1967), p. 140, this adaptation was also done in Paris, season of 1966-67, with Maria Mériko recreating her Celestina.

1047. _____. LC (together with *La Chanson de Mon*

Cid and *Le Comte Lucanor*). Lausanne: Ed. Rencontres, 1961, 287-555. (Sommets de la Littérature Espagnoles, 1)

A rpt. of the Germond de Lavigne translation with the preliminary material and the concluding verses at the end of the text. Jean Cassou provides a general introd. (vii-xix). There are no notes, vocabulary, or illustrations in this volume. The basis for the Lavigne translation was the TCM.

1048. _____. LC. Translation, introd. and notes by Pierre Heugas. And with an "Avant-propos" by Marcel Bataillon. Paris: Aubier, 1963. 560p. (Collection Bilingue des Classiques Etrangers). Rpt. Paris: Aubier-Montaigne, 1980. (Collection Bilingue Poche, 67-68)

Heugas' extensive introd. (9-97) and end notes (arranged by act) make this bilingual French-Spanish LC very useful. The Spanish text is that of Criado de Val/Trotter (1958, etc.). For the acrostic verses, Heugas has adopted the translations of Germond de Lavigne.

a. *Segismundo* 3 (1966), 204-05, E. Rull

1049. BRAULT, Gerald J., ed. *"Célestine": A Critical Edition of the First French Translation (1527) of the Spanish Classic "LC" with an Introduction and Notes.* Detroit: Wayne State Univ. Press, 1963. vii + 264p. (Humanities Studies, 12)

a. *Cultura Neolatina* 23 (1963), 296, E. Scoles
b. BHS 41 (1964), 125-26, G. D. Trotter
c. *Neophilologus* 48 (1964), 132, J. A. van Praag
d. RLR 76 (1964), 132, J. L. Flecniakoska
e. RR 55 (1964), 120-21, C. F. Fraker, Jr.
f. *RPh* 18 (1964-65), 251-52, L. Picoche
g. *Notes & Queries*, New Series, 12 (May 1965), 197-98, A. D. Deyermond
h. HR 33 (1965), 332-34, J. H. Herriott
i. *Neuphilologische Mitteilungen* 66 (1965), 406-07, E. V. Kraemer
j. ZRP 82 (1966), 241-50, K. Baldinger

1050.1. ROJAS, Fernando de. LC. An adaptation by Jean Gillibert, who also designed the sets. It had its première in Chateauvallon, France, at Le Centre de Rencontres on July 20 1972. María Casares played the title role. The adaptation is not faithful to the text of Rojas but instead aims to project a mythic concept of sexuality.

1050.2. Gillibert's version played at the TOP theatre in Paris until February 10 1973. Created in Chateauvallon, it came to Paris with María Casares as Celestina, Gerald Robard as Calisto, Monique Fabre as Melibea, François Chodat as Sempronio, Claude Aufaure as Pármeno, Juliette Brac as Elicia and Danièle Sabbagh as Areúsa.

a. *Le Monde* (February 11-12 1973), 19, C. Godard
b. *Le Nouvel Observateur*, no. 432 (February 19-25 1973), 71, G. Dumur

1051. DRYSDALL, Denis L., ed. *LC in the French Translation of 1578 by Jacques de Lavardin.* A Critical Edition with Introd. and Notes. London: Támesis, 1974. x + 266p. (Serie B - Textos, 18).

a. YWMLS 36 (1974), 271, A. K. G. Paterson
b. RJ 26 (1975), 375-78, P. Heugas
c. *Studi Francesi* 19 (1975), 136. F. Simone
d. MLR 71 (1976), 195-96, G. Martínez Lacalle
e. *Revue d'Histoire Littéraire de la France* 76 (1976), 998-99, R. Zuber
f. RR 69 (1978), 349, A. Alcalá
g. *XVIIe Siècle*, no. 131 (April-June 1981), 212-14, M. Lazard
h. *RPh* 36 (1982-83), 490, D. S. Severin

1052.1. ROJAS, Fernando de. LC. Version scénique de Pierre Laville. *L'avant-scène*, no. 566 (June 15 1974), 9-45.

The definitive form of the text also published in the 'Collection du Répertoire, 6' by the Comédie-Française (Paris, 1975, 168p.). There are throughout many photographic illustrations of scenes from the stage version, as well as —at the end—some excerpts from reviews.

1052.2. The première of this adaptation took place at Paris' Théâtre Marigny on January 23 1975, in a production by the Comédie Française. It was directed by Marcel Maréchal. Emphasizes the farce, the humor, and the ludic aspects of the action, as well as the unchained primitive passion which, in the view of adapter and director, is at the heart of LC.

Appearing in the leads were Denise Gence as Celestina, Catherine Chevallier as Melibea, Bruno Devoldere as Calisto, Jean-Paul Roussillon as Sempronio, Patrice Kerblat as Pármeno, Catherine Samie as Elicia, Christine Fersen as Areúsa, and Michel Etcheverry as Pleberio. There is a new character, a beggar; there is mixed music from operas and sambas and a few other popular rhythmic pieces, all arranged by Bernard Ballet. Sets and costumes by Jacques Angeniol.

1052.3. In June and July of 1981, Laville's *Célestine* was presented to audiences in the garden of Paris' Petit-Palais. The version is a revised one, but based on the one directed earlier by Marcel Maréchal, and produced for the Comédie Française [1975]. It was this time directed by Jean-Claude Amyl with set design by Jean-Guy Lecat and Hortense Guillemard. The latter also designed the costumes. The performance of Judith Magre as Celestina was widely acclaimed. Others in the cast were: Michel Robbe as Calisto, Monique Brun as Melibea, François Clavier as Sempronio, Emmanuel Dechartre as Pármeno, Catherine Hubeau as Areúsa, Sylvie Orcier as Elicia and Emmanuèlle Stochl as Lucrecia. After the summer performances in Paris, the production travelled to festivals at Sarlat and Carcassonne.

a. *Cel* 5, ii (Fall 1981), 54, J. Joset

1053. _____. LC. There was a French adaptation staged in Madrid's Teatro Alfil from August 30 to September 4 during the 1977-78 season. It was performed by the company, 'Le Théâtre du Hangar' of Paris directed by Fernando de Cobos (who also appeared as Celestina). The stage direction was by Fernando Cobos, *hijo*,. This version featured most of the first 12 acts of the CCM and a resumé of the rest. Elisa Chicaud appeared as Melibea, Alain Heril as Calisto, Denis Chabroulet as Sempronio, Tom Michel as Pármeno and, as Areúsa, Lucrecia and Elicia, the actresses Paloma Cobos, Leila Djitli and Françoise Soavi.

a. *ABC* (September 1 1977), 40, L. López Sancho
b. *Hojas del lunes* (Madrid) (September 5 1977), n.p.
c. *Cuadernos para el diálogo* (September 17 1977), 8, M. B.
d. ECV 20 (1977), 208-10, F. Alvaro et al

1054. _____. LC. In a French adaptation by Liliane Wouters. This version was staged in Brussels, at the Théâtre du Parc, from January 15 through February 8 1981. It was directed by Jean-Pierre Dusseaux. Sets were designed by Raymond Renard. In the principal roles were: Jacqueline Bir (Celestina), Catherine Robillard (Melibea), Emmanuel Dessablet (Calisto), Raymond Avenière and Léonil McCormick (Sempronio and Pármeno), Suzanne Colin and Martine Vlaemynck (Elicia and Areúsa), Catherine Sombreuil (Lucrecia), Léon Dony (Centurio), Bobette Jouret (Alisa) and Ralph Darbo (Pleberio).

a. *Porquoi pas?* (January 22 1981), J. Bertrand

1055. LC, in *Théâtre espagnole du XVIe siècle*, under the direction of Robert Marrast, with an introd. by Jean Canavaggio (Paris: Gallimard, 1983), 3-198. (Bibliotheque de la Pleiade)

The translation used is Heugas' (1963: see entry 1048) to which is added a brief and useful historical overview of LC's place in theatrical history (xxv-xxxvii) and a study of its origin and literary qualities (823-46) by Canavaggio. Heugas' extensive notes, variants and bibliography are on pp. 846-79.

1056. CELESTINE. This staging of LC took place in Créteil (France) at the Maison des Arts André Malraux in November of 1983. It was directed by Petrika Ionesco and featured Tsilla Chelton in the role of Celestina.

a. *Le nouvel observateur*, no. 995 (2 December 1983), G. Dumur

German

1057.1. _____. LC. *Celestina: Tragikomödie von Ritter Calisto und der Jungfrau Melibea* Translated by Egon Hartmann and F. R. Fries. Introd. by Fritz Schalk. Bremen: Schünemann, 1959. xxvii + 302p. Also Leipsig: Dieterich, 1959; 2nd ed. 1961, 3rd ed. 1971. Illustrations. A rather faithful translation of the Criado de Val/Trotter edition (entry 1116).

a. *Insula*, no. 168 (1960), 11, C. Bravo-Villasante
b. LR 15 (1961), 196, P. Groult
c. *Humboldt* 3, no. 11 (1962), 76, Anon.

1057.2. A staging based on this translation took place in East Germany, at Weimar in 1970. The adaptation was by F. Bennewitz. Christa Lehmann was Celestina. It was also seen on television.

1058. _____. LC (together with works by Lope, Tirso and Calderón). In *Spanische Meisterdramen* (Basel: Desch, 1961), 11-142. Translation by Eugen Ortner in 3 acts.

1059.1. _____.LC. With Karl Paryla directing and Grete Wurm as Celestina, a German performance of LC was staged in Cologne in 1966. It emphasizes the comic aspects of the action and the social gap between rich and poor. There was also a mix of old and modern music.

1059.2. The same production was revived in Berlin 1967.

1060. _____. There was a stage version of LC produced in Göttingen in 1971 at the Stadttheater.

1061. _____. LC. German adaptation by Karl Mickel. It was staged at Berlin's Berliner Ensemble theatre towards the end of 1974. It had a strong satirical tone and focussed on ambition, greed and gain, even injecting the shadow of the Inquisition to deepen the sombre mood of the production. It was directed by J. Pörschmann and G. Schmidt, and featured Erika Pelikowsky as Celestina, Jutta Hoffmann as Melibea, Jaecki Schwarz as Calisto, Michael Gerber as Sempronio, Hans-Joachim Frank as Pármeno and Annemone Hase as Elicia. The sets and costuming were by L. Scharsich.

a. *Nürnberger Nachrichten* (January 8 1975), J. Beckelmann (*)
b. *Theater der Zeit* (Berlin), no. 4 (1975), 19-20, K. Lennartz
c. *Die Deutsche Bühne* (Cologne) (March 1975), A. W. Mytze (*)
d. *Insula*, no. 349 (December 1975), n. p., A. C. Isasi Angulo

1062. A German version of Alfonso Sastre's free version of LC (see entry 1001.1) was seen in East Germany in the early 1980s. It was directed by Irmgard Lange and Wolfgang Bellach.

Hebrew

1063. _____. LC. *Selestina*. Hebrew translation by Yaakov Yisrael Fink. Tel Aviv: Mahbarot Lesifrut, 1962. 182p. Illustrated.

Hungarian

1064. _____. LC. A stage version, based on the French one of Achard (1942), was produced in the theatre of the Univ. of Budapest in both 1970 and 1971.

1065. _____. LC. Based, like the University production, on the French version of Achard, this staging was mounted at Budapest's National Theatre in 1972.

1066. There was a broadcast of LC on Hungarian Radio in 1977.

1067. _____. LC. *Celestina: Calisto és Melibea Tragikomédiája*. The original translation of Károly Sándor was reworked and completed by Ferenc Szönyi. Illustrations are by Károly Feledy, with a postcript essay by Katalin Kulin. Budapest: Európa Könyvkiadó Ed., 1979. 389p.

Italian

1068.1. _____. LC. Italian translation by Corrado Alvaro. Milan: Bompiani, 1943. (Col. Corona) This translation of the TCM is accompanied by a preface by the translator.

1068.2. _____. LC. This is a rpt. of the Alvaro translation (his preface is retained), re-edited and prefaced with a new introd. by Cesare Segre. Milan: Bompiani, 1980. 245p. Paper (Nuovo Portico, 15).

   a. *RPh* 35 (1981-82), 557, D. S. Severin

1069. _____. LC. Translation by A. Gasparetti. Milan: Rizzoli, 1958. 351p. (Biblioteca Rizzoli, 1361-64).

1070.1. _____. LC. Tragicommedia di Fernando de Rojas. Free translation and reduction by Carlo Terron. *Il dramma* 38, no. 307 (April 1962), 5-47. Contains seven photographs from the original production.

1070.2. The original production opened March 14 1962 at Milan's Teatro Nuovo. The performances were staged by the Compagnia del Teatro Stabile di Torino. Stage direction was by Gianfranco De Bosio, aided by Mischa Scandella who did the sets, Eugenio Guglilminetti who designed costumes and Sergio Liberovici who prepared the music.

   The diabolic Celestina of this version was Sarah Ferrati, with Alberto Terrani as Calisto, Cecilia Sacchi as Melibea, Renzo Giovampietro as Sempronio, Franco Parenti as Pármeno, Didi Perego as Elicia, Maria Fiore as Areúsa, Bob Marchese (Sosia), Alessandro Esposito as Tristán, Giulio Oppi as Pleberio, Isabella Riva as Alisa, Wilma D'Eusebio as Lucrecia, Mimino Craig as Centurio and Carlo Baroni as Crito.

   a. *Sipario* 17, no. 191 (March 1962), 4-5, 23-24, C. Terron

1070.3. According to Gerstinger (1968), this version returned to Milan in 1966.

1071. _____. LC: Commedia di Calisto e Melibea.

Translation by F. Capecchi. Florence: Sansone, 1966. 292p.

1072. KISH, KATHLEEN V., ed. *An Edition of the First Italian Translation of the "Celestina"*. Chapel Hill: Univ. of North Carolina Press, 1973. 320p. (UNCSRLL, 128)

   a. *RPh* 29 (1975-76), 349-51, C. Stern
   b. *Cultura Neolatina* 36 (1976), 129-37, B. Vignola
   c. BHS 54 (1977), 49-50, P. E. Russell

1073. ROJAS, Fernando de. LC. There was a stage version presented in Italian in July of 1976 in Milan, first at Villa Latti and then at Castello Sforzesco, by the company "Cooperativa Teatro Ancora". The translation and the adaptation are by Ettore Capriolo. Stage direction was by Serenella Hugony Bonzano. Playing Celestina was Delia Bartolucci. Dario Cipani was Calisto, Mariella Fonoglio was Melibea, Piero Sammataro, Sempronio and Giorgio Biavati, Pármeno.

1074.1. LC di Alfonso Sastre, a cura di Maria Luisa Aguirre d'Amico (translator). Rome: Officina Edizioni, 1979. 98p. Paper (Collana del Teatro di Roma, 6).

   Translated and revised from the Spanish text provided by Sastre. Sastre writes some personal notes (pp. 7-9) as does the director of the Rome production, Luigi Squarzina (pp. 11-14).

1074.2. LC (Tragicomedia de Fernando de Rojas), in an adaptation by Alfonso Sastre.

   The opening of this version took place on April 26 1979 in Rome. Sastre titled it: "Tragedia fantástica de la gitana Celestina, o historia de amooor [sic] y de magia, con algunas citas de la famosa tragicomedia de Calixto y Melibea." So it is an original re-creation and not a true adaptation. Calisto is seen as a disciple of Miguel Servet; he is a former monk pursued by the Inquisition when he meets, through the mediations of Celestina, the Mother Abbess (Melibea) of a convent for former prostitutes. It takes place in Salamanca in the second half of the 16th century, with a few scenes in c. 1978.

   This production was directed by Luigi Squarzina, with Anna Maestri as Celestina, Lisa Gastoni as Melibea and Ivo Garrani as Calisto. Others were Gianni Fenzi as Pármeno, Conchita Vázquez as Elicia, Vittorio Congia as Sempronio, Monica Ferri as Areúsa, Maria Grazia Tavolucci as Suor Lucrecia, Antonio Cascio as Centurio, Gabrielle Villa as Crito, Stefano Lescovelli as an Inquisitor's envoy, and with Maurizio Mattioli and Stefano Angelone in minor roles. Sets were designed by Lele Luzzati and music was scored by Benedetto Ghiglia. It played at the Teatro Argentina.

   a. *El País* (May 2 1979), J. Arias
   b. *ByN*, no. 3,497 (May 9-15 1979), 57, M. Pérez Cotorillo
   c. *Hispania* 64 (1981), 463.

Japanese

1075. LC. *Majo Celestina*. Translated into Japanese by Tadashi Oshimi. Kyoto: Gaikoko Bungakkai, 1975.

Polish

1076. _____. LC. Translation by Juliusz Gomulicki, from the French stage version of Achard (1942). It was presented in Lodz in 1947 in the Wojska Polskiego theatre. As Celestina, Jadwiga Chojnacka was a standout. Others in the cast were: Zdzilaw Szymanski, Andrzej Lapicki, Henryk Borowski and Kazimierz Dejmek. The production was directed by Léon Schiller.

1077. _____. LC. Polish translation by Kazimierz Zawanowski. Warsaw, 1962. Illustrated. A translation of the TCM.

Portuguese

1078. _____. LC *A Celestina*. Translation by Walmir Ayala. Brasília: Coordenada Ed., 1969. 124p.

1079.1. David Mourão Ferreira's Portuguese version of LC became the basis of the adaptation staged by José BLANCO-GIL and performed by the Teatro Ibérico de Lisboa at the VII Festival Internacional de Teatro Clásico (Almagro, September 1984). There were two performances on the 26th and 27th at the Claustro Dominicos at 10:30 p. m.

This version featured a black and white motif in order better to underscore underlying structures reflecting the importance of death and tragedy in LC; there was also a chorus to emphasize the tragic dimensions of the play. Domingo Morais composed special music and the scene and sets were a collaboration of the director and Antonio Filipe (who played Pármeno). Actors featured were Manuela Cassola (Celestina), Ana Santos (Melibea), Juvenal Garcês (Calisto), Francisco Soromenho (Sempronio), Arlete de Sousa (Elicia), Fernanda Policarpo (Areúsa), Teresa Monica (Lucrecia), Jorge Coelho and Paulo Guilherme Tomas (Sosia and Tristán), with Maria Rosa Lobato and Carlos Costa (Alisa, Pleberio).

a. *El público* (November 1984), 28-29, illus., J. Villán

1079.2. As part of the special theatre season, "Muestra de teatro español" in Lisbon, under the sponsorship of the Centro Dramático Nacional de Lisboa, Blanco-Gil's *Celestina* opened in October of 1984 with amplified sets and scenic effects in a larger arena and was favorably received, playing until March of 1985.

a. *El público* (December 1984), 15.

1079.3. With essentially the same cast, a more sharply-honed production of this *Celestina* was on display at the X Festival de Teatro del Siglo de Oro at El Chamizal (El Paso, Texas), where it won 9 of the 10 awards in the professional category (April 1985)

a. *Cel* 9, i (May 1985), 63-64, L. Fothergill-Payne

b. *Cel* 9, ii (Fall 1985), A. Madrigal (interview with José Blanco Gil)

Rumanian

1080. _____. LC. *Celestina: Tragicomedia lui Calisto şi a Melibeei*. Notes and translation by Nina Ecaterina Popescu and Lascar Sebastián. Bucharest: Ed. Univers, 1973. 305p. (Classicii: Literaturii Universale)

The preface-introd. is by Paul A. Georgescu (pp. 5-18).

Russian

1081. _____. LC. *Selestina*. Translated by N. Farfel. Introd. and notes by E. Lyssenko. Moscow: Gozlitizdat, 1959. 230p. Illustrated.

Miscellaneous Items

The following items are all miscellaneous by nature. They include poems, operatic works, a ballet, an exhibit, recordings. films, and imaginative pieces. What they all have in common is an inspiration in Rojas' *Celestina*. They are not properly catalogued anywhere else in this bibliography (or most other bibliographical works dealing with LC), so I have decided to create a special section here, since most are, in one way or another, in the spirit of "translations and adaptations."

1082. "Romance de Calisto y Melibea," in *Romancero hispánico*, vol. 2 (Madrid, Gredos, 1953), 67. This is not a text, but an allusion to a ballad composed, according to the author (Ramón Menéndez Pidal) around 1510. See also García Enterría, entry 339.

1083. XIMENEZ DE URREA, Pedro Manuel. *Egloga de Calisto y Melibea* (1513). See entry 436 for a modern edition.

1084. SEDEÑO, Juan de. A verse translation of LC first printed in 1540 (Salamanca: Pedro de Castro). Now it exists in a critical edition by Miguel Marciales (Mérida: Univ. de los Andes, Facultad de Humanidades, 1971), published in a multigraph format. Only a small number was printed.

1085. LARREA, Arcadio de. "Sobre LC (ópera de Pedrell)." *Arbor* 56, no. 213 (1963), 135-36.

A brief note which gives some details about Pedrell's opera (still unproduced in Spain) of 1903. For more information, see entry 875.

1086. *Argumento de LC: Tragicomedia de Calisto y Melibea.* Madrid: Ed. España, [1945]. 16p. (Col. Universo, Las Obras Más Famosas T15, no. 18)

This is an act-by-act summary of LC, of no critical value.

1087. GUILLEN, Jorge. *Huerto de Melibea (poema).* Madrid: Insula, 1954. 27p.

a. *Archivum* 5 (1955), 188-90, A. Alarcos Llorach
b. *Indice*, no. 84 (1955), M. Alfaro
c. PSA 2 (1956), 89-98, R. Gullón

1088.1. TESTI, Flavio. *LC: Opera in tre atti dalla tragicommedia omonima di Fernando de Rojas.* Libretto by Renato Prinzhofer. For voice and piano. [Milan]: Ricordi, [1961]. 387p.

A complete vocal and piano score for the entire operatic adaptation. There are twelve roles (Crito and Sosia do not appear). Filling in as choral participants are townspeople, processions, Celestina's "girls," and others (there is a Traso).

1088.2. LC. A musical piece based on Pedrell's opera and adapted for presentation by Flairo Testi in Florence's Teatro Maggio Fiorentino. This took place in 1963. The Italian lyrics are by Angelo Bignotti and are contemporary with Pedrell's composing (c. 1903).

1089. CRIADO DE VAL, Manuel. *Polandria (Farsa celestinesca en tres actos)*, in *Teatro medieval* (Madrid: Taurus, 1963), 155-210.

1090. LEMAITRE ROMAN, Eduardo. *La aventura de Don Melón y Doña Endrina.* Farsa en cinco cuadros y un prólogo en prosa y versos. Sobre textos del LBA de Juan Ruiz y de LC de Fernando de Rojas. Bogotá: Revista Colombiana, 1968. 69p. Paper (Col. Populibro, 23). Rpt. in *Ifigenia y La aventura ...* (Bogotá: Inst. Colombiano de Cultura, 1973), 88-148. Paper (Biblioteca Colombiana de Cultura, Col. Popular, 93).

1091. LC. En forma de ballet "para dos bailarines y una cantante." Created by Alberto Cárdenas and danced in 1968 by Susana y José.

1092. LC. Versión cinematográfica de la inmortal obra de Fernando de Rojas. Por César F. Ardavin. Madrid: Aro Films, [1969]. 73p.

Photocopy of the screenplay at the Biblioteca Nacional [T-41723]. It is accompanied by six stills from the film. It takes place in Toledo about 1510. The text is compressed but it relies rather a lot on Rojas' language. The following actors played major roles: Amelia de la Torre as Celestina, Elisa Ramírez as Melibea, Julián Mateos as Calisto, Eva Guerr [sic] as Lucrecia, Gonzalo Cañas as Pármeno, Antonio Medina as Sempronio, Antonio Mancho as Sosia, Jaime Segura as Tristán, Hugo Blanco as Centurio, Heidelotte Diehl as Areúsa, Uschi Mellín as Elicia, Eva Lissa as Alisa and Konrad Wagner as Pleberio. This film was shown at the Moscow Film Festival in 1969, as a German-Spanish co-production.

a. *Variety* (July 30 1969), 6, Hawk
b. *Insula*, no. 279 (February 1970), 3, M. R. Alonso

1093. "A Celestina." Poem by León Felipe. It originally appeared as a dedicatory poem in 1970 (see entry 295) and was recently rpt. in *Cel* 6, ii (Fall 1982), 35-36.

1094. CALISTO & MELEBEA (ascribed to John Rastell). Disc recording directed by John Barton for the British Broadcasting Company (copyright 1970 by Dover Publications). Album commentary is by David Bevington.

A recording, with period music added, of the earliest English adaptation (c. 1525) of parts of LC. June Tobin plays Melebea, Peter Howell performs Calisto, Manning Wilson is Sempronio and Vivienne Chatterton is Celestina.

a. *Cel* 6, ii (Fall 1982), 31-33, J. T. Snow

1095. ROJAS, Fernando de. LC. Comentada por Enrique Llovet. New York: Simon & Schuster, 1970. (Spanish Literary Masterpieces LM-6)

A tape, thirty slides and a bilingual pamphlet of 16p. Serves to introduce the basics of LC to beginning students.

1096. HONIG, Edwin. *Calisto and Melibea.* Providence, Rhode Island: Brown Univ., Hellcoal Press, 1972.

A libretto by E. H. which was used for Jerome Rosen's opera produced in Davis, California (see entry 1098).

a. *Cel* 3, ii (Fall 1979), 32-40, J. T. Snow

1097. OURVANTZOFF, Miguel. *LC de Fernando de Rojas..* Illustrations. Madrid: Autor, 1972. 15 plates in a portfolio.

A limited edition of five sets of these deluxe illustrations inspired by LC, each signed by the artist, was made. The set I saw was at Madrid's Biblioteca Nacional. Taken together, they provide a very sensual "reading" of Rojas' celestinesque world.

1098. ROSEN, Jerome (composer). *Calisto and Melibea.* Libretto by Edwin Honig.

Opera in three acts and sixteen scenes which had its world première at the Univ. of California-Davis May 31 1979, directed by Jan Popper. It ran for eight performances over a two-week season. Major roles were sung by Patrick Neve as Calisto, Leonore Turner as Melibea, Gloria Blackburn as Celestina, Stephen Valentino as Sempronio, Jeannette Montineri as Elicia, Christine Moore as Lucrecia, Mark Marriott as Tristán and Ron Schuver and Bruce Turner as two 'alguaciles'.

a. *Davis Enterprise* (June 1 1979), A. Juncker
b. *Cel* 3, ii (Fall 1979), 27-30, R. Anderson

1099. MANTERO, Manuel. "Monólogo de Calisto ante las puertas de Melibea," in *Homenaje a Azorín*, ed. by Carlos Mellizo (Laramie, Wyoming: Department of Modern and Classical Languages, 1973), 85-89.

A poem of homage to Azorín inspired by Act 12 of LC.

1100.   TORO GARLAND, Fernando de. *Razón y pasión de enamorados* (Tragicomedia celestinesca en tres actos). Madrid: Escelicer, 1973. 56p.

> La Meli is the daughter of a silversmith; Carlos (= Calisto) is from a well-to-do family; and la Cele is a woman very like her go-between ancestor. In a modern staging—replete with telephones and birth control pills, Freud, Mary Worth and Sofía Loren—the adapter provides a main action which is parallel to that of LC, with language designed to be comparable.

1101.   MANTERO, Manuel. *Ya quiere amanecer* (poemas). Madrid, 1975. 80p. (Colección Dulcinea, 3)

Love poems whose epigraphs derive—as does the title of the volume—from the text of LC.

a. *Cel* 1, ii (Fall 1977), 29-32, C. Lee

1102.   ROJAS, Fernando de. LC. Bilbao: Ed. Cultura y Progreso, 1977; 3rd ed., 1980. 184p. (Literatura Universal, 9)

This is an abridged novelization of LC. It seems directed at a very young reading public. It carries six monochromatic illustrations by A. Ibarra. The novelization itself is not attributed.

1103.   CELESTINA (Los placeres del sexo). A film in color of 1979. Directed by Miguel Sabido.

> This film opened June 4 1979 in Madrid. The photography is by Miguel Garzón and the editing is by Federico Landeros. The film is fairly pornographic, emphasizing the sexual nuances of all aspects of LC. The film features Isela Vega (Melibea), Luigi Montefiore (Calisto) and Ofelia Guilmain (Celestina: she played Elicia in the early stage versions of Alvaro Custodio: 1953, etc). Others appearing include: José Galvez, Marcela López Rey, Ana de Sade and Martha Zavaleta.

a. *Cel* 4, ii (Fall 1980), 40, M.-A. Vetterling

1104. LC. A film from 1979, prepared by Televisión Española. Artistic supervision by M. Criado de Val. About 50 minutes. Distributed in the US by Films for the Humanities (Princeton), for either rental or purcahse.

1105.   ROJAS, F. de. *LC. Antología.* Presented by A. Labajo, C. Urdiales and T. González. Madrid: Coculsa, 1981. 47p. Paper (Literatura española, Col. Primera Biblioteca, 9).

A slim volume built around three short commentaries of selected passages from LC: 1) "El doble plano" (scenes from Acts 2 and 9); 2) "El valor dramático" (Acts 4 and 19 [one scene]); and 3) "El espíritu de la obra" (scene from Act 20). There is one illustration on p. 4 and, at the end, there are eight themes for student reports on the readings.

1106.   BENITO DE LUCAS, Joaquin. "Dos poemas de Amor: Calisto. Melibea." *Cel* 5, ii (Fall 1981), 55-56.

1107.   LOUREIRO, Angel. "Calixto en el jardín de Melibea" (poema). *Cel* 5, ii (Fall 1981), 56.

1108.   EVA Y DON JUAN. A play by Alvaro Custodio. It had its debut on December 26 1981 at the Teatro Real Coliseo Carlos III (El Escorial), performed by the Compañía Vocacional.

> A parade of real and fictional personalities in a satire of the myth of seduction. Texts by the original authors and by Custodio. One of the parts was Celestina, played on this occasion by María Calonge.

1109.   DARDON TADLOCK, Gisela. "El otromundo literario." *Cel* 6, no. 1 (May 1982), 41-44.

> A *sueño-querella* in which: Cervantes is made to confront Dorotea and Dulcinea; Rojas must handle complaints from Celestina; and Zorilla is denounced by many, among them Ana de Pantoja and Inés de Ulloa.

1110.   SNOW, J. T. "A *Celestina* Exhibit at Georgia." *Cel* 7, i (May 1983), 39-40.

> A brief report on a wide-ranging exhibit about the *Celestina* phenomenon, mounted in April 1983 at the Univ. of Georgia library.

1111.   *El carnaval de un reino.* The characters of Celestina and Claudina are prominently featured in this play by José Martín Recuerda about the life and times of Enrique IV. In it, they are young prostitutes and their characters are extrapolated from Celestina's memories as presented in LC. The play opened at Madrid's Centro Cultural de la Villa in October of 1983. The text was originally titled *Las conversaciones* and was published in 1981 (Murcia, Ed. Godoy).

a. ABC (23 October 1983), 75, L. López Sancho
b. *Cel* 7, ii (Fall 1983), 29-31 [J. T. Snow]

III. Editions

In this section I include facsimile editions produced (or reprinted) in the 1930-1980 time frame, as well as critical and popular editions of LC. These latter have been produced worldwide (in Spanish), and this compilation of them —for obvious reasons—can only approximate their number. I have often speculated on how many people have read LC in these modern—and often execrable—editions? It certainly must be, by now, in the millions. Most of the scholars writing today must have first been introduced to *Celestina* in one or another of them, and these editions do serve to keep the text in print and almost everywhere available and, thus, to provide ever new generations of readers with that first intimation of Rojas' artistic genius.

I have preferred here a chronological listing of these popular editions. Where it has been possible, I include information about the form (paper or cloth) in which it appeared, design, illustration, contents (if incomplete), and whatever items of scholarly apparatus (introductions, notes, bibliographies, vocabularies, etc.) that accompany the text.

A. Facsimiles

1112.   ROJAS, Fernando de. *Comedia de Calisto y Melibea.* Ed. facsímil de la primera ed., de Fadrique de Basilea, Burgos, 1499(?). Preparada por Archer M. Huntington. First printing 1909; rpt., New York: Hispanic Society of America, 1970. No pagination. Woodcuts at the beginning of most all the acts show the characters in stylized poses.

1113.   _____. *Comedia de Calisto y Melibea.* Facsímil de la edición de Toledo de 1500. Edited and introd. by Daniel Poyán Díaz. Cologny-Geneva: Bibliotheca Bodmeriana, 1961. 80 folios.

   Poyan's introd. presents a scheme for the evolution of the text until Toledo 1500, which copy he considers the *editio princeps* of the CCM.

   a. *Arbor* 54, no. 207 (March 1963), 362-65, J. Montero Padilla
   b. *Mapocho* (Santiago de Chile) 4 (1964), 253-55, M. Ferreccio Podestá
   c. QIA 5 (1960-65), 294-95, E. Caldera
   d. *RPh* 19 (1965-66), 142, M. J. Ruggerio

1114.   _____. *Libro de Calixto y Melibea y de la puta vieja Celestina.* This is a facsimile of what was thought at the time to be 'Seville 1502' but which has subsequently been shown by Norton (1966) to be c. 1518-20. Ed. Antonio Pérez Gómez. Valencia: Talleres de Tipografía Moderna, 1958. 65 folios. ('La fonte que mana y corre...')

   a. NRFH 13 (1959), 123-24, S. Gilman
   b. BH 62 (1960), 336-39, M. Bataillon
   c. RHM 26 (1960), 165-66, D. W. McPheeters
   d. HR 29 (1961), 144-47, E. J. Webber

1115.   _____. *Tragicomedia de Calisto y Melibea.* A facsimile ed. of Valencia 1514. With an introd. note by Martín de Riquer. Madrid: Espasa-Calpe, 1975.

   Reproduces the Biblioteca Nacional (Madrid) copy: R-4870. This is a not-for-sale copy designed as a gift for the collaborators of Espasa Calpe on the fiftieth anniversary of the publishing house.

B. Critical Editions

1116.   _____. *Tragicomedia de Calixto y Melibea, libro también llamado LC.* Ed. by Manuel Criado de Val and G. D. Trotter. Madrid: CSIC, 1958; 2nd corrected ed. 1965; 3rd corrected ed., 1970 [rpt. 1984]. 322p. (Clásicos Hispánicos, 2-3)

   The Seville base text used is not 1502 as believed (see Norton: 1966), but rather c. 1517-18. The notes to this ed. record the variants from Burgos, 1499(?) and Seville 1501.

   a. BH 61 (1959), 119-20, A. Rumeau
   b. BHS 36 (1959), 177-78, F. Street
   c. *Hispania* 62 (1959), 134, G. Edberg
   d. TLS (June 19 1959), 368, Anon.
   e. BA 34 (1960), 388, A. Adler
   f. *Boletín de la Facultad de Filología* (Santiago de Chile) 12 (1960), 259-71, M. Ferreccio Podestá
   g. RHM 26 (1960), 165-66, D. W. McPheeters
   h. LR 15 (1961), 196, P. Groult
   i. RL 26 (1964), 210, R. Esquer Torres
   j. RHM 33 (1967), 149-50, L. Mades
   k. ZRP 83 (1967), 696, W. Mettmann
   l. *Universidad Pontífica Bolivariana* (Medellín) 29 (1967), 267, L. B.
   m. HR 37 (1969), 315-20, J. H. Herriott

1117.   _____. *Comedia de Calisto y Melibea.* Edited by Jerry R. Rank. Chapel Hill, North Carolina: Estudios de Hispanófila, 1978. 243p. (See also entry 662.)

   A critical ed. of the unique copy of Seville 1501 from Paris' Bibliothèque Nationale, with complete variant lists from the other two *Comedias*, Burgos 1499(?) and Toledo 1500 in the notes (pp. 209-43). The detailed introd. (11-83) provides considerable information on the textual filiation of the early editions and establishes the importance (shown in examples and stemma charts) of Seville 1501 in the early TCM text tradition.

1117bis.   See also entry 579.

C. Popular & Student Editions

1118.   _____. LC (together with the *Segunda comedia de Celestina* of Feliciano de Silva). Madrid: [Librería Bergua], [1930]. 624p. Paper (Biblioteca de Bolsillo, 15).

A 2nd ed. is identical to this one: Madrid: Ed. Ibéricas, [1945?]. Cloth. A third printing (with Lope's *La Dorotea*) is Madrid: Ed. Ibéricas, 1957. 498p. (Biblioteca de Bolsillo).

This edition carries a short Prologue by J. B. Bergua as well as the Azorín essay, "Las nubes." The *Auto de Traso* is included. Cover is illustrated.

1119. _____. LC. TCM. Madrid: Espasa-Calpe, 1936; rpt., 1942. 364p. (Col. Universal 565-58)

This reproduces exactly the text of the Calpe ed. of 1922, with the same introd.

1120. _____. LC. TCM. Madrid: Ed. Cultural, [1938?]. Also produced in Paris the same year (Paris: Viuda de C. Bouret, [1938]) in the Clásicos Bouret collection. The introd. is signed 'Zeda'. Previous printings of this ed. are recorded for 1910(?), 1912(?) and for 192? 'Zeda' was the producer-director of a 1909 Madrid production of LC, in which the young Amparo Villegas played Melibea (for her later roles as Celestina, see entries 978.1 through 978.7).

1121. _____. LC. Introd. by Pedro Henríquez Ureña. Buenos Aires: Losada, 1938. (Las cien obras maestras de la literatura y del pensamiento universal, 4). A 2nd ed. is 1941. There is a new ed. in 1965 by Losada, in the Col. Biblioteca Clásica y Contemporánea, with 217p. This reached its own 7th reprinting in 1975 and has a 'viñeta' on the cover signed by Baldessari.

The editor's introd. was rpt. in his *Plenitud de España: estudios de historia de la cultura* (Buenos Aires: Losada, 1940) 139-43; 2nd expanded ed., 1945, pp. 153-57. It was also utilized in the program notes for the 1953 Mexico City production of LC by Alvaro Custodio (entry 978.2).

1122. _____. LC. TCM. Buenos Aires: Araujo Hermanos, 1940. 244p. (Col. Leda)

1123. _____. LC; o la TCM. Buenos Aires: Sopena Argentina, 1941. 142p. (Biblioteca Mundial Sopena). Later eds. are 1944 and 1958. This series has an introd. by Ramón Villasuso. A 6th printing (1963) restores a prologue by Juan Mateos (originally written in 1918) and some notes. Contains all the preliminary and posliminary materials but no bibliography. This had also been published in Barcelona by Sopena in 1925.

Another ed. is Barcelona: Ramón Sopena, 1967, 248p, with rpts. in 1972 and 1975. Paper (Biblioteca Sopena, 581). The cover is illustrated.

1124. _____. LC. Madrid/Buenos Aires: Espasa-Calpe, 1941. 178p. Paper (Col. Austral, 195).

No introd., notes, or illustrations. Seems to be the same as the Calpe text of 1922, used for the Col. Universal printing of 1936 as well. The Austral ed. saw a 19th reprinting in 1981. 146p.

1125. _____. LC. TCM. Barcelona/Buenos Aires: Ed. Molino, [1942?]. 240p. Paper (Col. Literatura Clásica, 19).

Brief prologue by José Mallorquí Figuerola. Very few notes. Each act has small woodcut illustrations at beginning and end and the cover reproduces the Titian portrait of Maria Templegang. No bibliography.

1126. _____. LC. A cura di Corrado Alvaro. Milan: Bompiani, 1943. 2 vols. (Col. Corona, 1920). [See also entries 1068.1 and 1068.2.]

Bilingual ed. (Italian-Spanish).

1127. _____. LC. Madrid: Ed. Mediterráneo, 1944. 319p. Paper (Col. de Clásicos, 2). Another printing is 1952.

Modernized Spanish. None of the LC preliminary materials is included, although the final verses appear. No introd., notes, bibliography, or illustrations.

1128. _____. LC. Madrid: Aguilar, 1944. 496p. Leather (Crisol, 72). With a "Nota preliminar" by F. C. de Sainz Robles. A 2nd printing is 1951, and a 4th (1960) appears in reduced-size format and has as its frontispiece the *portada* of Barcelona: C. Amoros, 1529. The 7th printing is 1968 (reproduced again in 1975) and is in the Col. Crisol Literario, 41. It has the *Auto de Traso*. No notes or bibliography.

1129. _____. LC. Ed. by Julio Cejador y Frauca. 3rd ed. Madrid: Espasa-Calpe, 1945 (Clásicos Castellanos 20 and 23). The original printing was 1910-1913, in the collection "La lectura". An 11th rpt. is 1984.

The text of the CCM (Burgos 1499?) is in roman and the added material of the TCM is in italic type fonts. Valencia 1514 is used as the base text for the TCM interpolations.

1130. _____. LC. TCM. Prologue by José María Pemán. Original illustrations by José Segrelles and Luis Enríquez de Navarra. Valencia: Castalia, 1946. 350 folios plus 4 engraved pages and 8 plates. Cloth.

Valencia 1514 is the base. Gothic typefont is used. Red initials and other nice printing touches. Pemán's introd. emphasizes the romantic view of LC.

1131. _____. LC. Buenos Aires, 1946. Edited by W. M. Jackson. (Col. Grandes Novelas) (*)

1132. _____. LC. Edited and with an introd. by A. Millares Carlo and J. I. Mantecón. Mexico: Universidad Autónoma de México: 1947. xxiii + 328p. Illustrated by Ramón Gaya. A later ed. (1964), 300p., carries almost the same introd. but adds a chronology and a summary bibliography.

a. *Revista de la Universidad de México* 18, no. 11 (1963-64), 31, C. V.

This ed. was also printed in Mexico by Ed. Leyenda [1947] as one of their series "Obras maestras de la literatura amorosa," with 248p. There are both black and white and color illustrations throughout by Miguel Prieto (the 8 in color illustrate erotic themes).

1133. _____. LC. TCM. Barcelona: Argos, 1948. 241p. Cloth.

Limited ed. of 160 copies on folio size paper, beautifully bound. There are 27 plates, 10 in color, all by Manuel Humbert. Valencia 1514 is the base text (following Krapf, 1899-1900). It is very elegantly produced.

1134. _____. LC. Ed. and prologue by Adolfo Bioy Casares. Buenos Aires: Estrada, 1949. 334p. (Col. Clásicos Castellanos) (*)

1135. _____.LC. Edited with a prologue, notes and vocabulary by Pedro Bohigas. Barcelona: Montaner y Simón, 1952. xlv + 332p. Cloth. There is a printing also in 1958.

The introd. is extensive and covers the LC text and critical problems well for its day and now could use updating. The CCM is printed, with separate sections reserved for the interpolations of the TCM, and for the *Auto de Traso*.

1136. _____. LC (with the *Lazarillo* and *Buscón*). Barcelona: Ed. Exito, [1952]. x + 399p. (Grandes Novelas de la Literatura Universal, 3)

LC is on pp. 1-211. Modernized Spanish. Uses brackets to enclose the additions of the TCM. Has the entire text. There is a brief anonymous "nota preliminar" but no text notes or illustrations. It uses the text of W. M.Jackson (1948) and is printed a 2nd time in 1961.

1137. _____. LC. Ed. by Jesús M. Alda. Zaragoza: Ebro, 1955. 215p. Paper (Biblioteca Clásico Ebro, Clásicos Españoles, Serie Prosa, 31-32). A 7th rpt. is 1976. It is expurgated and plagued with typographical errors. A brief bibliography and a few illustrations.

a. BHS 33 (1956), 236-37, G. D. Trotter

1138. _____. LC. TCM. Barcelona: Fama, 1955. 257p. Paper (Serie Junco).

There is no introd. and no annotations; however, the edition appends the *Auto de Traso*. Not illustrated. Modernized Spanish.

1139. _____. LC; o TCM. Nueva transcripción y notas por Pilar G. Moreno. Notas prologales (v-xvi) de Emiliano M. Aguilera. Barcelona: Ed. Iberia, 1958; another ed. is 1966. xvi + 232p. (Col. Obras Maestras)

There are approximately 100 notes, No bibliography or illustrations.

1140. _____. LC. In *Teatro Clásico Español* (Buenos Aires: Ed. 'El Ateneo', 1958), 15-234. (Col. Clásicos Inolvidables)

The text of the TCM with the excision of the verses of Proaza at the end. The prologue (pp. 9-12) is by R. Menéndez Pidal. There is one illustration by B. Kriukov.

1141. _____. LC. Mexico: Ed. Nacional, 1958. 288p. (Col. Económica) (*)

1142. LC. TCM. Mexico: Novaro-México, [1959]. 313p. (Col. Nova-Mex) (*)

1143. _____. *LC y Lazarillos*. Ed., prologue and notes by Martín de Riquer. Barcelona: Vergara, 1959. 811p. Cloth (Clásicos del Mundo).

The "notas prologales" (pp. 7-78) are generous. The text is the TCM in the ed. of Criado de Val/Trotter (1958), and includes the *Auto de Traso*. Ample notes (oriented to vocabulary). Illustrations in color by J. Palet and Lorenzo Goñi. Rpt. in 1962 and 1966.

a. BH 62 (1960), 339-40, M. Bataillon

1144. _____. LC (with other texts), in *Novela picaresca* (Madrid: Taurus, 1960), 15-157. Rpt. in 1965 and 1967.

This is the CCM text, with only slight modernizations, with all the preliminary materials but only one of the final stanzas. The introd. by Joaquin del Val is used in later Taurus eds. No illustrations or notes.

1145. _____. LC. Barcelona: Augusta, 1961. 454p. (*)

1146. _____. LC. Barcelona: Maucci, 1961. 454p. Cloth (Clásicos Maucci, Literatura Medieval). Six illustrations by Chico Prats.

The complete TCM. Pages 9-12 contain a "retrato biográfico" and a full-page plate of Fernando de Rojas.

1147. _____. LC. TCM. Mexico: Ateneo, 1961. 213p. (*)

1148. _____. LC. Ed., prologue and notes by Martín de Riquer. Barcelona: Vergara-Círculo de Lectores, 1962. 381p. Cloth. Frontispiece.

This is the TCM, but the ed. carries the same prologue as the Vergara 1959 printing of the CCM (see above). Includes the *Auto de Traso*. The ed. was redone in 1966 and 1969 more elegantly. 427p. Cloth. No illustrations or bibliography. The 1981 rpt. has 432p. and carries the long-outdated 1959 prologue (not signed).

1149. _____. LC; o TCM. Barcelona: Zeus, 1962. 302p. Paper (Col. Literaria Zeus).

This is the full text, following Cejador, with a brief six-page introd. The initial verses are missing, Rojas' prologue is gone as are the acrostic verses. The final verses are here, as is the *Auto de*

Traso. No notes, bibliography, or glossary. Punctuation and orthography are modernized.

1150.   LC. Buenos Aires: Tor, [1962?]. Paper (*)

1151.   _____ LC. TCM. Mexico: Herrero Hermanos Sucesores, 1963. viii + 249p. (Col. Clásicos 'Herrero') (*)

1152.   _____. LC. Buenos Aires: La Mandrágola, 1963. 157p. (Bolsiclásicos, 3) (*)

1153.   _____. LC. TCM. Madrid: Ed. Bullón, 1963. 265p. Paper (Col. Generaciones Juntas, 10).

   Modernized text. There is a preliminary essay on pp. 7-21 (anonymous). The TCM interpolations are in italics. The frontispiece is by Julián Grau-Santos. Does not include the *Auto de Traso*.

1154.   _____. LC. TCM. Havana: Consejo Nacional de Cultura, 1963. 297p. Paper (Biblioteca básica de literatura española).

   With a very brief introd. All the TCM but no *Auto de Traso*. No notes, bibliography or illustrations.

1155.   _____. LC. Madrid-Caracas: Mediterráneo, 1964. 153p. Paper (Col. de Bolsillo Edimé, 5). A 6th printing is 1980.

   No introd., no notes. The *Auto de Traso* is included but Proaza's end verses are not. Has a cover illustration.

1156.   _____. LC, o TCM. Barcelona: Mateu, 1964. 268p. Paper (Todo Para Muchos, 111). Another printing is 1973.

   Modernized spelling. Base ed. is Criado de Val/Trotter (1958 etc.). No introd., notes or glossary. The cover art is by Acosta Moro and depicts Celestina and Melibea.

1157.   _____. LC. Havana: Ediciones 'R', 1964. (*)

1158.   _____. LC. TCM. In *Las diez mejores obras inmortales*, vol. 1 (Barcelona: Ed. Ahr, 1964), 1509-1729. Cloth.

   The selection and notes are by F. C. Sainz de Robles and he reprints here the text he prepared in 1944. The *Auto de Traso* is included. No glossary, bibliography, illustrations.

1159.   _____. LC. TCM. Madrid: EDAF, 1965. Paper (Biblioteca EDAF, 46).

   There is another printing in 1969 which is clothbound and contains eight color illustrations by J. Picà (these do not appear in a later 1976 printing). A 1979 rpt. is 275p. The series has an anonymous "nota prologal" and few notes. The Spanish is modernized. The *Auto de Traso* is absent. Later printings in the collection (e. g., 1981) have a prologue by Francisco Alonso. 267p.

1160.   _____. LC. Barcelona: M & S, 1966. 282p. Paper (Col. Eterna, 10).

   The cover has an unsigned illustration, and there is a frontispiece illustration as well. No introd., no notes or glossary. Does not include the *Auto de Traso*. The preliminary materials are absent, but the end verses are included.

1161.   _____. LC; o TCM. Introd. and notes by B. V. Ayala Gauna. Buenos Aires: Huemul, 1966. 280p. Paper (Col. Clásicos Huemul, 41). A 5th printing is 1975. Huemel issued a new edition in 1984 (see entry 1241).

   Contains all the preliminary materials and all but Proaza's end verses. The introd. relies heavily on Menéndez y Pelayo, and brings out the witchcraft aspect as vital. There is less emphasis on the other topics treated: authorship, plot, characterization, style or language. There are 225 notes (pp. 265-73) and a vocabulary (275-80). Cover art by M. Waray.

1162.   _____. LC. TCM. Estudio preliminar y bibliografía seleccionada de A. Cardona de Gisbert. Barcelona: Bruguera, 1967. 332p. Paper (Col. Libro Clásico, 1). A 13th printing is 1983.

   Follows the text of Criado de Val/Trotter, 2nd ed. (1965). Includes the *Auto de Traso*. Minimal notes. Cover illustration varies with the printings. This same ed. appears clothbound in the same publishers' 'Libros Selección-Clásicos' in 1971.

1163.   _____. LC (and *Lazarillo*). Dirección literaria y prólogo de J. García Pérez. Versión de M. Torello. Barcelona: Ed. Ferma, 1967. 439p. Cloth (Col. Clásicos Ferma).

   A two-page prologue. Prints the TCM (but not the *Auto de Traso*). No illustrations and only a very few notes.

1164.   _____. LC. TCM. Ed., introd. y notas por J. del Val y María A. Merino. Madrid: Taurus, 1967. 309p. Paper (Col. Temas de España, 53). Later printings are 1969 and 1980.

   The introd. is pp. 7-33. Notes are scattered. There is a thematic bibliography. Edition follows Cejador's. The cover is illustrated with an early woodcut, a detail from Valencia 1514. The interpolations are in italics. The *Auto de Traso* is appended.

1165.   _____. LC: TCM. Text modernized by M. Criado de Val. Introd. and notes by Juan Alcina Franch. Illustrations by Jaime Azpelicueta. Barcelona: Juventud/New York: Las Américas, 1967. 238p. Cloth (Col. Obras Maestras de la Literatura Universal); Paper (Libro de Bolsillo 'Z', 192). A 3rd ed. is 1982.

   The introd. is brief and general (pp. 5-13). There are 530 notes on vocabulary, mostly. An appendix prints the *Auto de Traso*.

   a. *Universidad Pontífica Bolivariana* 29 (1967), 267, L. B.
   b. *Indice Cultural Español* 22 (1967), 371, N. N.

1166.   _____. LC. TCM. Introd. and notes by Antonio

Prieto. Avila: La Muralla, 1967. 389p. Paper (Col. Literatura Año 2000, 2).

The introd. is comparatist in nature and extols the creation of Celestina, Calisto and Melibea. The text follows Criado de Val/Trotter (entry 1116) and appends the *Auto de Traso*. On the cover is a reproduction of an engraving from the 1520 German translation of LC. The work is further divided into scenes by the editor. Notes—about 750 of them—are generous.

1167. _____. LC. Prologue by M. de Ezcurdia. Mexico: Porrúa, 1968. xxxii + 173p. Paper ("Sepan cuantos ...", 88). A 9th printing is 1981.

With a chronology and two glossaries. The full TCM text.

1168. _____. LC. TCM. Prologue by M. Criado de Val. Bilbao: Moretón, 1968. 252p. Cloth (Biblioteca de Divulgación Cultural, 45; Mil Joyas de la Literatura Universal-15)

About ten pages of prologue cover general items as well as textual problems and authorship theories. No notes or glossary.

1169. _____. LC. Antología. Prologue by Trinidad González Rivas. Madrid: Coculsa, 1968. 48p. (Col. Primera Biblioteca) A new printing is 1981.

For young audiences, a selection from LC.

1170. _____. LC. TCM. Introd. by Antonio Prieto. Preparation of text and notes by M. Smerdou Altolaguirre. Madrid: Magisterio Español, 1968. 344p. Paper (Col. Novelas y Cuentos, 16). A 4th printing is 1981.

The introd. situates the work around Toledo in 1500 and focuses on the transitional times in which it was written. The text follows Criado de Val/Trotter, with modernized orthography. The cover is illustrated and there is one photograph of a frontispiece from 'Sevilla 1502'(= Seville c. 1518). The *Auto de Traso* is absent from this ed.

1171. _____. LC. Adaptation and prologue by Antonio Prieto; critical text by M. Criado de Val. Barcelona: Marte, 1968. xx + 219p. (Col. Pliegos de Cordel)

This ed. is richly illustrated with 60 drawings in color by F. Ezquerro, often full-page size. The printing ran to 3,000 copies. The text is the complete TCM. No *Auto de Traso*, no notes, no bibliography. Modernized orthography.

1172. _____. LC. TCM. Madrid: J. Pérez de Hoyo, 1969. 192p. Paper (Col. Cien Clásicos Universales, 13). The cover carries an unidentified woodcut from an early edition.

Prints only the 21 acts and the "Concluye el autor". Everything else is lacking. No introd., notes or glossary. No bibliography or illustrations. Modernized orthography.
This same ed. appears together with R. L. Stevenson's *Treasure Island* and N. Hawthorne's *The Scarlet Letter* in a

clothbound ed. from the same publisher in 1969, in the series 'Obras Maestras Universales.'

1173. _____. LC. TCM. Ed. and notes by Dorothy S. Severin. Introd. by Stephen Gilman. Madrid: Alianza, 1969. 274p. Paper (Col. El Libro de Bolsillo, 200). An 11th printing is 1985.

The base edition is Valencia 1514 (and 1518), corrected with earlier eds. of the CCM, and the TCM of Zaragoza 1507, which makes this the most dependable of the editions in circulation. The notes are useful. Gilman's introd. is a Spanish version of an essay already published in English (see entry 381). This ed. has the full text (does not append the *Auto de Traso*) and two appendices: one with variants from the three CCM eds.; the other with a chronology of literature, culture and history in Rojas' times.

a. QIA 5 (1970), 116-17, B. Damiani

1174. _____. LC. Prologue, notes and new revision of the text by F. C. de Sainz Robles. [Madrid]: Ed. del Arce, [1969]. 309p. Cloth.

Prepared for El Círculo de Amigos de la Historia (sold by subscription). (Identical to an edition published by Amigos do Livro [Lisbon], n. d., but around the same time.) The editor revised his old introd. of 1944 (for Espasa) for this special ed. There are four photographs by way of illustration. It claims to follow Seville 1501 but prints the TCM (minus some of the end verses), closely following Cejador. Another printing is 1973.

1175. _____. LC. TCM. Barcelona: Ed. Vosgos, 1969. 200p. Paper (Col. Grandes Maestros, 26). A 5th printing is 1975.

The full text with all the preliminary material and the closing verses. Some notes. No introd., glossary or illustrations.

1176. _____. LC. TCM. Version, introd., and notes by J. Costa Clavell. Barcelona: Rodegar, 1969. 255p. Cloth (Col. Grandes Obras).

Text follows Criado de Val/Trotter (1958 etc.); modernized orthography. Only one item in the short bibliography was published outside Spain. The cover art is by Barreda Soligo. Rpt. by the same publisher in the collection 'Obras Inmortales' in 1973.

1177. _____. LC. Barcelona: De Gassó, 1969. 256p. Paper. Identical in content to the LC of the preceding entry, except for format. No illustration. A second printing is 1973. Another is 1977.

1178. _____. LC. Buenos Aires: Centro Editor de América Latina, 1969. 163p. (*)

1179. LC. TCM. Madrid: Susaeta, 1969. 246p. Paper (Clásicos Universales, 21).

Lacking are all the preliminary materials and the closing verses. No introd., notes, glossary, bibliography or illustrations. Modernized orthography.

1180. _____. LC (together with *La Lena* of A. Velázquez de Velasco). Pamplona: Ed. Larraiza, 1970. 432p. Cloth. Another printing is 1974.

The anonymous introd. of 20 pages seems not to know of recent investigations into the textual tradition of LC. No illustrations, notes, glossary or bibliography. Proaza's verses are part of the preliminary materials! LC on pp. 31-257.

1181. _____. LC. Adaptation of the text by A. Jiménez-Landi Martínez. Madrid: Aguilar, [1970]. 117p. Cloth (Iniciación Literaria, Col. El Globo de Colores).

For young audiences. Expurgated. With 42 illustrations by the adapter of the text. It is a series of scenes from LC linked by narrative paragraphs, designed to stress the moral message.

1182. _____. LC. Version and prologue by E. B. Sánchez Pascual. Barcelona: Petronio, 1970. 234p. (Col. Clásicos Petronio) (*)

1183. _____. LC. TCM. Ed., prologue and notes by M. Criado de Val. Barcelona: Salvat [and Alianza Ed.], 1970. 187p. Paper (Biblioteca Salvat de Libros RTV, 75). Also [Estella]: Salvat, 1971. Appends the *Auto de Traso*.

1184. _____. LC (with *La lozana andaluza* and *La pícara Justina*). Introd. and notes by Luis. P. de los Reyes. Madrid: J. Pérez de Hoyo, 1971. 566p. Cloth. Only the text of the 21 acts. No introd. worthy of the name. No notes, glossary or illustrations.

The same year, this ed. was published (without *La lozana andaluza*) by the same publisher. 394p. Cloth. In 1975, this publisher reprinted its LC (this time with *Justina*). It repeats the short prologue by L. P. de los Reyes, not taking into account the different content. Cloth. 310p.

1185. _____. LC. TCM. Barcelona: Ed. Juventud, 1971. 240p. Half leather.

This is a special ed. for the members of Discolibro, with a brief general introd. accentuating the humanistic nature of the work. The entire TCM is here with, appended, the *Auto de Traso*.

1186. _____. LC. Río Piedras, Puerto Rico: Edil, 1971. (*)

1187. _____. LC. *Calixto y Melibea*. Mexico: Orion, 1971. 196p. (Col. Lit. Cervantes.) (*)

1188. _____. LC. Bilbao: Ed. Vasco Americana, 1971. 184p.

There is a brief biographical note on Rojas as sole prologue to this modernized and abridged version. Proaza's end verses are omitted. Six color illustrations by A. Ibarra.

1189. _____. LC. TCM. Barcelona: Bruguera, 1972. 332. (Clásicos Bruguera).

This is a special ed. containing eight illustrations by Lozano Olivares. Rpt. in 1974. In all other ways, it is identical to the same publisher's ed. of 1967 (see above). The bibliography needs updating.

1190. _____. LC. Madrid: J. Pérez de Hoyo, 1972. 262p. Cloth (Escritores Universales).

This is the same text the publisher has used in combination with others before (see above for 1971, etc.). The preliminary materials are restored but the final verses of Proaza are still missing from this TCM.

1191. _____. LC. Barcelona: Ed. Petronio, 1972. 288p. Cloth (Col. Obras Clásicas). Version of the TCM by J. Ribera.

No introd., notes, glossary, bibliography or illustrations.

1192. LC. Lima: Ed. Universo, 1972; rpt. 1976. Prólogo de Enrique Carrión Ordóñez. xi + 220p. (Col. Autores Clásicos, 40) (*)

1193. LC. Medellín, Colombia: Bedout, [1972?]. (*)

1194. LC. Mexico: Iztaccihuatl, [1972?]. (*)

1195. LC. Lima: Peisa, [1972?]. (*)

1196. _____. LC. Barcelona: Nauta, 1973.

Reproduces the Barcelona: Mateu , 1964 text. The introd. is full of errors about the early history of the LC text tradition.

1197. _____. LC. Mexico: Organización Editorial Novaro, [1973]. 263p. Paper (Col. Arco Iris, 15).

This is the TCM unaccompanied by a study, notes, or glossary.

1198. _____. LC. TCM. Ed. by Bruno Damiani. Madrid: Cátedra, 1974. 302p. Paper (Letras Hispánicas, 4). A 6th printing is 1979. Uses Valencia 1514 as base text.

a. *Segismundo*, nos. 19-20 (1974), 366-67, F. Abad Nebot
b. *La Torre*, nos. 89-90 (1975), 198-200), J. L. Laurenti
c. QIA, nos. 45-46 (1973 [1975]), 320, J. V. Ricapito
d. MLN 92 (1977), 361-63, S. B. Vranich

1199. _____. LC. TCM. Ed. by Martín de Riquer. Madrid: Alfaguara, 1974. 250p. Cloth. Contains 19 lithographs by Lorenzo Goñi.

Follows Criado de Val/Trotter's text (1958 etc.). A printing of just 1,000 copies. Beautifully bound. No introd.

1200. _____. LC. TCM. Barcelona: Jaimes Libros, 1974. 232p. Cloth (Clásicos Universales).

No introd., notes or glossary.

1201. LC. With a critical study and analysis of the text by

Lucía Fernández Echeñique. Santiago de Chile: Delfín, 1974. 302p. (Col. Biblioteca Clásica, 6) (*)

1202. _____. LC. Barcelona: Columna, 1975. 304p. Leather. (*)

1203. _____. LC. TCM. San Antonio de Calonge (Barcelona): Hijos de José Bosch, 1975. 500p. Paper (Col. Aubi, Clásicos y Ensayos, 6).

The introd. is by A. Cardona de Gisbert. Text by Manuel Criado de Val. The modern transcription and the notes are the work of J. B. Caselles Llena. There is a selected bibliography (pp. 82-97) which follows a good general introd. (which has been rewritten for this ed. (the original, in use for a long time, was written for the 1967 Bruguera ed.). A bilingual format is used, the original Spanish on the left, the modern on the right. There are 325 notes at the end of the text. Also there are two illustrations from early texts of the CCM. The *Auto de Traso* is appended.

1204. _____. LC. Santiago de Chile: Gabriela Mistral, 1975. (Fondo Escolar) (*)

1205. _____. LC (plus *Lazarillo*). Madrid: Emiliano Escolar, [1975]. 283p. (Col. 'Cultura Clásica')

Has a brief introd. by E. E. V. This is the full TCM text but without notes, glossary or illustrations. Rojas' introd. and the acrostics are in an Appendix. Proaza's end verses are omitted.

1206. _____. LC. San José de Costa Rica: EDUCA, 1976. 276p. (Col. Clásicos) (*)

1207. _____. LC. Madrid: EDAF, 1976. 275p. Paper (Col. Baca, EDAF Bolsillo). (*)

1208. _____. LC. In *Las Celestinas* (the *Segunda Celestina*, *Tercera Celestina* and *Lisandro y Roselia* as well as LC). Barcelona: Planeta, 1976. Leather (Col. Clásicos Planeta).

Prints the TCM. The introd. study is by M. Criado de Val and José María Valverde.

1209. _____. LC. CCM. São Paulo: Nautilus, 1976. 368p. (Clásicos Nautilus).

A 4-page introd. is signed D. A. It is claimed that this is a pirated text of a nineteenth-century ed. (see Montañes Fontenla, entry 639)

1210. _____. LC (with *La lozana andaluza*). Madrid: R. Rico Sastre, 1976. 310p. Leather (Clásicos Espãnoles). The text is borrowed from Madrid: J. Pérez de Hoyo, 1971 (see entry 1084).It also appeared in a cheap paper ed. in the same year (1976) with a cover illustration by F. Coronado. a 1975 paper ed. of 300p.] (*)

1211. _____LC. TCM. Ed., introd. and notes by Humberto López Morales. Madrid: Cupsa, 1976. 254p. Paper (Col. Hispánicos Planeta).

Another useful modern ed. It is complete and has a large number of annotations.

a. *Cel* 1, i (May 1977), 21-22, J. F. Schneider

1212. _____. LC. TCM. Ed. de Román Oltra Costa. Barcelona: Columna, 1976. 324p. Cloth (Clásicos Columna, Literatura).

No illustrations or introd. At the end there is a glossary of 30p.

1213. _____. LC. TCM. Havana: Ed. Pueblo y Educación, 1977 (a 4th ed.). 363p. (*)

1214. _____. LC. Barcelona: Verón, 1977. (Col. Scriba) (*)

1215. _____. LC. In *Picaresca española*, vol. 4. Madrid: Círculo del Bibliófilo, 1977. Leather (Col. Clásico).

This set is of facsimiles of early printings of a variety of texts. LC shares the last vol. with the second half of *Guzmán de Alfarache*

1216. _____. LC. TCM. Barcelona: Mundo Actual de Ediciones, 1977. 385p. Cloth (Col. Grandes Clásicos). With an anonymous introd. (pp. 7-19). A 3rd printing is 1981 (in Discolibro).

This is the text copyrighted by Ed. Juventud (1967). No illustrations, notes or bibliography. The *Auto de Traso* figures as an Appendix.

1217. _____. LC. TCM. Barcelona: Acervo. 1977. 268p. Paper (Col. Gaudeamus, Clásicos Españoles, 10). Another printing is 1978.

Has a brief prologue and notes supplied by J. M. Mundet Gifre. The text is modernized and based on Criado de Val/Trotter (1958 etc.). No bibliography or illustrations. No *Auto de Traso*.

1218. _____. LC. TCM. Buenos Aires, Kapelusz, 1977. 278p. Paper (Col. GOLU). Estudio preliminar y notas de Elena Huber y María Sílvia Delpy.Another printing is 1982.

The complete TCM, amply annotated. The introd. gives an overview of the usual topics in LC studies. The Spanish is modernized and the base text is Criado de Val-Trotter (1958 etc.). A glossary and a brief bibliography are included.

1219. _____. LC. Ed. prepared by M. Criado de Val. Madrid: Ed. Nacional, 1977. 280p. Paper (Biblioteca de la Literatura y el Pensamiento Hispánicos, 23).

A phonological ed. of LC. In his introd., Criado expounds on the phonological situation of Spanish at the end of the 15th century and prints the LC text with spelling and symbols designed to help the reader (and actor) to approximate the sound of LC.

1220. LC. Panama: ENLACOMEX, 1977. 218p. (Clásicos Universales, 9)

This is the text of the CCM, lacking all the opening and closing materials. Celestina's name is left out of the cast of characters. The introd. is weak. No notes, bibliography, or illustrations.

1221. _____. LC. TCM. Madrid: Club Internacional del Libro, 1978. 254p. (Clásicos Universales de la Literatura Erótica)

A brief introd. is supplied by I. G. Sanguinetti. A bibliography contains eight entries to 1965. The *Auto de Traso* is appended. No notes, no illustrations.

1222. _____. LC. Buenos Aires: El Cid, 1978. 173p. (*)

1223. _____. LC. London-Madrid: S. A. de Promoción y Ediciones, 1978. 256p. Leather (Col. Clásicos Universales de la Literatura Española). (*)

1224. _____. LC. Barcelona: Ed. Argos-Vergara, 1979. 456p. Ed. and notes by Martín de Riquer. Ten illustrations by J. Palet and L. Goñi. Another printing is 1980. (Biblioteca de Literatura Universal)

The same text was used for a joint edition (with *Lazarillo*) in 1959. The complete TCM plus the *Auto de Traso*. No bibliography. Riquer's prologue, from the 1959 ed., is not included.

1225. _____. LC. Barcelona: Producciones Editoriales, 1979. 320p. (Col. Clásicos). (*)

1226. _____. LC. TCM. Prologue and ed. of Pedro M. Piñero Ramírez. Madrid: Espasa-Calpe, 1980. 360p. Paper (Selecciones Austral, 73).

A long 75-page introd. makes this an attractive ed. for students. It covers most all the critical areas that concern the LC as literature, as text (with its problems of authorship, genre, and formation), and as literary history. There are useful notes and several woodcuts from the Valencia 1514 TCM. An index brings together all the words and expressions treated in the notes.

1227. _____. LC. Barcelona: Planeta, 1980. 296p. Paper (Col. Clásicos Universales Planeta, 13). A 3rd printing is 1982.

The introd. is by Juan Alcina Franch, and the ed. is by H. López Morales (see entry 1211). The bibliography lists only items in Spanish. The prologue explores the basic problems of the text and anticipates the first enjoyment of the text and characters (for the new reader).

1228. _____. LC. Ed., prólogo y pedagogía de Rosendo

Roig. Bilbao: Mensajero, 1980. 304p. Paper (Col. Bolsillo, 75).

The complete TCM with all preliminary and end materials. Lightly annotated. This student ed. uses Valencia 1514 as a base text. There is a chronology for Rojas' period, and some light commentary based on Siebenmann, whose 1975 bibliography (see entry 859) is the basis of the shorter one offered here. There is, finally, a list of themes and essays for the student.

1229. _____. Madrid: Salma, 1980. 212p. Paper (Col. Lecturas Universales, 2). In a version by M. Criado de Val.

Introd., notes and text by M. Criado de Val. Contains a 27-page, wide-ranging introductory study, four pages of select bibliography, and a fully annotated text of the TCM. The *Auto de Traso* is included at the end of the text. No illustrations.

1230. _____. LC. Castellón: Plon, 1981. 192p. Paper. (Col. La Palma Viajera, 25)

A single introd. page, and one and a half of bibliography. All the preliminary materials are lacking and most of the end verses as well. The text is the TCM, modernized. No critical apparatus. The cover has a color illustration.

1231. _____. LC. Introd. by Javier Huerta Calvo. Madrid: Playor, 1981. 220p. Paper (Col. Clásicos Comentados Playor, 6). A 2nd printing is 1982.

Special student ed. with black and white illustrations by Arturo Rodríguez. It is the complete TCM with all additional materials preserved. The ed. has 400 notes on language, allusions etc. The pedagogical part is extensive and useful. The introd. focuses on the kind of world into which LC was thrust in 1499. Other features are: a chronology; a summary of the work; a list of important themes and situations; notes on characterization; and a lengthy analysis of LC (pp. 197-211). There is a helpful onomastic index. The bibliography is short and of limited value.

1232. _____. LC. TCM. Introd. and notes by Juan Alarcón Benito. Madrid: Fraile, 1981. 221p. Paper (Col. Clásicos Fraile, 5).

Complete TCM with all the preliminary and end materials preserved. Brief introd. and a bibliography of just 14 entries.

1233. _____. LC. Mexico: Ed. Mexicanos Unidos, 1981. 206p. Paper (Col. Literaria Universal, Clásicos, 8).

The complete TCM with all additional materials. The introd. highlights characterization and types of discourse, but seems a bit dated on questions of authorship. A bibliography is promised in the *Indice* but is missing.

1234. _____. LC. 2 vols. Elda (Alicante): Nueva Generación, 1982. 94, 96p. Paper (Biblioteca de la Familia, Colección Arahal, 21-22).

The complete TCM. Modernized Spanish. No notes, bibliography, or illustrations.

1235. _____. LC. Managua: Ed. Nueva Nicaragua, 1982. 304p. Paper.

This is Cejador (with his introd. and notes) but in a different format from the Clásicos castellanos ed. There is also the "Prólogo a la edición cubana" (5-15), an essay by Adolfo Martí titled "El renacimiento y LC" (no date but post-1965).

1236. _____. LC. Madrid: Fascículos Planeta, 1983. 251p. Paper (Col. Aula, Biblioteca del Estudiante).

The complete TCM with text and notes of H. López Morales (see 1211) and a brief prologue by Lázaro Lucas. Cover art by F. Ezquerro.

1237. _____. LC. Edition, notes and prologue by M. Criado de Val. Barcelona-Madrid: Salvat/Alianza, 1983. 187p. Paper (Biblioteca Básica Salvat, 52).

The complete TCM plus the *Auto de Traso*. The text is lightly modernized, and is accompanied by a brief prologue. Notes are limited to the clarifications deemed essential. No illustrations.

1238. _____. LC (with *La lozana andaluza*). Madrid: Elección Ed., 1983. 312p. Cloth.

A reissue of the 1971 (rpt. 1975) ed. of these two works (see entry 1184). It preserves an introd. for an ed. which also included *La pícara Justina*! This is—although the cover doesn't even mention the *Lozana*—identical in all ways to the 1976 printing of the two texts (see entry 1210), with the exception of the cover illustration (now missing).

1239. _____.LC. Ed. de Dorothy S. Severin. Barcelona: Ed. Orbis & Ed. Origen, 1983. Cloth (Historia de la Literatura Universal, 59).

This is identical to Severin's Alianza ed. (entry 1173). Gilman's introd., however, has been omitted.

1240. _____. LC. Ed. prepared by Bonifacio Valdivia. San Sebastián: Haranburu, 1983. 144p. Paper (Colección Pedagógica—Textos Clásicos, 4).

A school text. Contains a chronological chart for the period and has an introd. highlighting the socio-political background of Rojas and LC. One section summarizes the changes made from the CCM to the TCM. In addition to the 21 acts, only the "Carta" remains of the added materials. There are textual notes and questions (131 in all) printed at the bottom of the page. The ed. is completed by a section of "documentación temática," a selection of three critical passages from works by Goytisolo (entry 402), Maravall (577) and Gilman (391).

1241. _____. LC. Estudio preliminar, notas y vocabulario de Regula Rohland de Langbehn. Buenos Aires: Ed. Abril, 1984. 309p. Paper (Clásicos Huemul, 41).

Huemul's new replacement edition (see entry 1161) for students, with more than 670 explicative notes. There is, in the preliminary study, information about the author(s) controversy, sources, and structural elements in the work. Also a brief bibliography and a useful glossary. The language has been modernized. No illustrations. The complete text of the TCM.

a. *Cel* 9, i (May 1985), 49-50, J. T. Snow

1242. _____. LC. Barcelona: Antalbe, 1984. 203p. Paper (Clásicos El Toboso).

Complete text of the TCM. Some notes, but little other critical apparatus; no bibliography or illustrations. The prefatory note speaks of two *Lazarillos* that do not appear in the volume!

1243. _____. LC. Madrid: Alba, 1984. 174p. Paper. (*)

1244. _____. LC. Ed. de Joaquín Benito de Lucas. Barcelona: Plaza y Janés, 1984. 382p. Paper (Clásicos Plaza y Janés—Biblioteca crítica de autores españoles, 6).

Based on Criado de Val-Trotter (entry 1116). The introd. (13-50) will be very useful for the student of LC. In addition to the text of the TCM, there is a Glossary (329-37), an Index of Proper Names (338-52), an explication of a passage from Act 12 (355-63), four excerpts from later celestinesque works (364-75) and suggestions for written themes. The text has been modernized. Notes tend to explain difficult lexical items and certain of the proverbs in LC. The bibliography has just fifteen entries. The cover art is by Jordi Sánchez but there are no textual illustrations.

Subject Index

In order to increase the effectiveness of this bibliographical survey, this Subject Index has been created as a complement to the Index of Names. It is a reference guide to the entries themselves, and principally to the accompanying annotations. These annotations were made over a period of time extending in a few cases back to 1976; they are either longer or shorter, detailed or succint, according to the intention of the moment and the nature of the item being abstracted. In all cases, I have attempted to extract the maximum number of pertinent "keywords and key phrases" with a view to user needs. In this fashion certain subjects, themes and concepts, and topics related to LC can be located with relative ease. The user needs to be reminded, however, that many of the entries in this bibliography treat a far greater range of themes than were possible to record in the annotations to them and, for that reason, this Subject Index is far from being a complete compendium of all matters treated by the works surveyed or even of the themes and topics listed here.

In preparing this listing, I have tried to be as general in my coverage as possible in making the Index a useful guide. It can be used profitably by anyone initiating a study of a particular aspect of LC studies and it will be an additional way in which to locate items about certain themes and topics when the author's name cannot be recalled. It will stand, too, in part, as a small reminder of the wealth of thematic materials with which the author(s) of *Celestina* endowed this Spanish classic. In fine, this Subject Index, the Index of Names, and the additional cross references used in many of the entries themselves should, when combined with user knowledge, intuition and curiosity, give to all scholars and students of *Celestina* a reliable reference tool for pursuing individual interests.

A Celestina [poem] (Felipe) 1093
Aboab, I. 603
Abravanel, Judás 615 bis
Achard, Paul 5, 212, 222, 275 (see also Stage adaptations)
Acrostic verses in LC: interpretation of 234, 638, 662
Act 01 6, 58, 79, 107, 151, 164, 261, 321, 334, 405, 410-411, 622, 629, 737, 791, 824, 855, 857, 885, 887, 896-897, 910-912, 936, 954, 957, 973
Act 01, adapted 112
Act 01, compared to rest of CCM and TCM 910
Act 01, scene i 27, 90, 173, 209, 239, 289, 346, 374, 409, 509, 548, 756, 793, 795, 874, 881, 884, 892, 897, 970
Act 01, source of the Comedia 113
Act 02 509, 1105
Act 03 164, 202, 320, 392, 737, 886
Act 04 27, 46, 61, 154, 653, 854, 1105
Act 06 318
Act 07 243, 387, 654, 737, 799, 885
Act 09 73-74, 294, 660, 737, 926, 1105
Act 10 432, 854

Act 11 465-466
Act 12 74, 99, 164, 294, 509, 1244
Act 13 437
Act 14 503, 509, 561, 673, 799, 889
Act 16 606, 805
Act 17 889
Act 19 35, 164, 243, 302, 509, 886, 911, 925, 1105
Act 20 857, 1105
Act 21 149, 152, 242, 270, 327, 361, 413, 462, 621, 770, 857, 925, 945
Adam and Eve 953
Aeneas (commentaries of Servius) 628
Alchemy in LC 128
Alexis, Saint 770
Alfonso X, el Sabio 810
Alfonso, Pero (Petrus Alfonsus) 418
Allegory in LC 177, 378, 562, 603, 814, 910-911
Allegory in LC imitations 324
Almenara de la luz (Aboab) 603
Amadís de Gaula (Anon.) 162, 548, 814, 933
Amantes de Teruel (Hartzenbusch) 790
Amarita, León 734
Ambiguity in LC 398, 741, 753
Analogs of LC 266, 526, 867, 882, 907
Analogs of LC: 20th century 715
Analogs of LC: Arabic 729
Analogs of LC: Chinese 174
Analogs of LC: French fabliau 816
Anatomy of Melancholy (Burton) 225
Animal imagery in LC 852-853
Antecedents of LC 15, 29, 83, 93, 119, 148, 163, 172, 183, 221, 223, 225, 266, 318, 321, 323, 328, 331-332, 341, 380, 404, 418, 440, 522, 526, 590, 615 bis, 626, 786, 810, 816, 948, 956, 962, 965
Antecedents of LC: 15th century 419, 485, 683, 759, 942-943
Antecedents of LC: Arabic 273, 340, 494, 706, 899
Antecedents of LC: Jewish 760
Antecedents of LC: Latin 401, 416, 479, 515, 525, 625, 628, 632, 661, 969
Antifeminism in LC 265, 305, 316, 319, 362, 512, 864, 896, 936
Aphrodisiacs in LC 343
Apuleius 401
Aquinas, Saint Thomas 883
Archaisms in LC 320, 450
Ardavín, Cesar 1082
Aretino, Pietro 365, 882
Argumentos of LC 301, 375, 471
Aristotle in LC 841
Asinaria (Plautus) 401
Auberée (Anon.) 816
Aucassin 590
Authority and experience in LC 853, 857
Authorship problem 9, 12, 38, 79, 134, 167, 172, 191, 226, 269,

Index of Names

This Index is inclusive of all authors of studies, articles, chapters, books and monographs, bibliographies, poems and other creative works, including theatre, film and musical adaptations. It includes editors, translators, authors of introductions, dissertation directors, and annotators of editions. Also catalogued are reviewers of these items. Because certain actresses who played Celestina have achieved renown in that role I have systematically included in this listing all the names of those who have played Celestina: I have omitted the names, for the sake of economizing on space, of actors who appeared in all other roles; these, however, are listed—when known—in the appropriate entries. For similar reasons, I have not placed here the names of all the artists who have contributed to the iconography of *Celestina* for the period this bibliographical overview surveys. The curious should consult the SUBJECT INDEX, under 'illustrations' for this information. I have not included an entry for all the diverse anonymous contributions.   A whole number, e.g., 356, refers to a main entry listing and the name will be found there. A number plus letter, e.g., 356g, means that the name appears in a review (g), listed in a vertical column following the annotation for that number (356). A number and decimal, e.g., 356.2, will also correspond to a main entry, but one which has many divisions: an example would be a theatrical presentation with many different stagings.

A

Abad, M. 1
Abad Nebot, F. 1198a
Abbate, G. 2
Abrams, F. 3
Abruñeda, A. 4
Achard, P. 5, 1036.1, 1036.2, 1037, 1038, 1064, 1065, 1076
Adams, H. M. 669a
Adams, K. 230
Adams, L. 994
Adinolfi, G. 6
Adler, A. 1116e
Aguado, E. 162b, 813a
Aguayo Q. 52b
Aguilera, E. M. 1139
Aguirre, J. M. 7, 590e
Aguirre d'Amico, M. L. 1074.1
Agustini de del Río, A. 162c, 1015d
Alarcón Benito, J. 1232
Alarcos Llorach, A. 1087a
Albanese, P. 8
Albarracín Navarro, J. 609
Alborg, J. L. 9
Alcalá, A. 10, 11, 71f, 1051f
Alcina, J. 12
Alcina Franch, J. 1165, 1227
Alda, J. M. 1137
Aleixandre, V. 608

Alfaro, M. 1087b
Allard, R. 1034
Allison, A. F. 13
Almiñaque, C. B. 14
Alonso, A. 15
Alonso, D. 16
Alonso, F. 1159
Alonso, M. R. 1092b
Alonso Hernández, J. L. 17
Alpera, L. 458
Alvarez, G. 18
Alvaro, C. 1068.1, 1068.2, 1126
Alvaro, F. 982.4a, 988.3f, 995.2g, 1053d
Amezúa, E. 19, 20
Amícola, J. 21, 835a
Amyl, J.-C. 1052.3
Anderson, J. 486
Anderson, L. 994c
Anderson, R. 1098b
Anderson Imbert, E. 22
Andrachuk, G. P. 426h
Andrews, J. R. 377d
Angeles, J. 162d, 577h
Angulo Iñiguez, D. 23
Anouilh, J. 1044
Antolín, A. 26
Anton, K.-H. 27
Anzoátegui, I. B. 28
Aragonés, J. E. 982.4e, 992.2a, 995.2c
Araya, G. 584a
Arbea G., A. 29
Arciniegas, R. 30, 685
Ardavín, C. F. 1092
Arellano, J. 726a
Arenós, M. J. 1001.2
Ares Montes, J. 170c, 555a, 577e
Arias, J. 1074.2a
Ariza, M. 4
Armistead, S. G. 31-35
Arroyo, J. 999.5g
Artigas, M. 36
Artiles, Jenaro 37
Artiles, Joaquín 38
Asensio, E. 39
Asensio, M. 40-42
Asis, E. 426b
Astiazarán, G. C. 43
Austin, K. O. 44
Avalle Arce, J. B. 521a, 755d
Avilés, J. C. 999.5h
Axton, R. 1029
Ayala, W. 1078
Ayala Castro, M. C. 45
Ayala Gauna, B. V. 1161

H

Morales, J. R. 647, 648, 976.1-976.11
Morales, R. 608, 649
Morby, E. S. 82i, 377a, 522u
Moreno, P. G. 1139
Moreno Baez, E. 650, 651
Morgan, E. 652, 653
Moro, D. 654
Morón Arroyo, C. 412a, 426i, 655, 656
Morreale, M. 1012.1c, 1014c
Mortimer, R. 670e
Mörtinger-Grohmann, G. 657
Mourão Ferreira, D. 1079.1
Mota, F. 978.2c
Moya Trelles, M. 101b
Müller-Bochat, E. 79b
Mundet Gifre, J. M. 1217
Muñoz Calvo, S. 315
Muñoz Cortés, M. 658
Muñoz Garrigós, J. 658-661
Muñoz-Marino, E. 662
Murphy, A. F. 663
Mytze, A. W. 1061c

N

Nagy, E. 165, 664
Nallim, C. O. 237u
Naylor, E. W. 252a
Needham, P. 670b
Neiswender, R. 388a
Nelson, D. A. 222
Nelson, R. J. 256c
Nepaulsingh, C. 665
Newton, J. 666
Nichols Jr., S. G. 590a
Nieto, L. 667
Niveiro, E. 668
Norton, F. J. 669, 670

O

O'Connor, P. W. 995.2h
O'Connor, T. A. 671, 672
Oelschläger, R. B. 555e, 1015a
O'Kane, E. 673, 674
Okonska, A. 675
Oliva Martín, A. 676
Olson, P. R. 522g, 677
Oltra Costa, R. 1212
Onieva, A. 678
Oostendoorp, H. Th. 448e, 679, 680
Ophey, B. 786c
Orduna, G. 681
Orol Pernas, A. 682
Oroz, R. 929b
Orozco Díaz, E. 683, 684
Ortega, T. 685
Orthous, P. 976.6
Ortiz de Pinedo, S. 686

Ortner, E. 1058
Oshimi, T. 1075
Osmanova, A. G. 204a, 687
Osuna, J. 979.4, 982.3
Ottelenghi, E. 987
Ourvantzoff, M. 1097
Oyola, E. 688

P

P., M. 82a
Pabst, W. 689
Pagano, A. 690
Pageard, R. 741a
Palau y Dulcet, A. 691
Palmer, M. E. 692
Pane, R. 693
Parker, A. A. 162h, 577o, 643b, 695
Parker, M. A. 696
Parr, J. A. 697, 698
Parra, J. 988.3b
Paryla, K. 1059.1
Paterson, A. K. G. 455a, 655a, 825a, 1051a
Pauliello de Chocholous, H. 522ee
Paulino, J. 995.2f
Pavia, M. N. 699
Pedraza, F. B. 700
Peeters-Fontainas, J. F. 701
Peixoto da Fonseca, F. 702
Pelicaric, I. M. 703
Pelikowsky, E. 1061
Pemán, J. M. 608, 1129
Pemberton, A. 1026
Peña Prado, M. 704
Penney, C. L. 237o, 669e, 705
Pérez, A. 976.7, 990.7b
Pérez, J. B. 706
Pérez, L. C. 707
Pérez Blanco, L. 426f
Pérez Cotorillo, M. 1074.2b
Pérez de la Ossa, H. 708, 979.1
Pérez Estrada, F. 709
Pérez Gómez, A. 1114
Pérez Goyena, A. 710
Pérez Navarro, F. 711
Pérez Saenz, V. 712
Petriconi, H. 713
Pfandl, L. 163f
Phillips, K. K. 714
Phillips, W. 1028
Picoche, L. 1049f
Pierce, F. 797a
Piñero Ramírez, P. M. 1226
Poblete, E. 976.9
Pollux 999.2a
Popangea, E. 715
Popescu, N. E. 1080
Popper, J. 1098

Abbreviations

NOTE: In this compilation, I have not italicized journal and serials abbreviations entirely composed of capital letters. Additionally, some literary works and author surnames have occasionally been abbreviated in the annotations and do not appear here; these are readily understood from the main entry.

General

c., ca.	circa
CCM	*Comedia de Calisto y Melibea*
col.	column
diss.	dissertation
ed.	edition, edited, editor, Editorial
introd.	introduction
LBA	*Libro de buen amor*
LC	*Celestina*
MLA	Modern Language Association of America
MHRA	Modern Humanities Research Association
n. p.	no pagination used
rpt.	reprint, reprinted
TCM	*Tragicomedia de Calisto y Melibea*
transl.	translator, translated
Univ.	University
vol.	volume

Journals and Serials

ABC	*ABC* (Madrid)
ACTAS	*Actas del Primer Congreso Internacional Sobre LC* (Barcelona)
AEM	*Anuario de Estudios Medievales* (Barcelona)
AION-SR	*Annali dell'Istituto Orientali di Napoli-Sezione Romanza*
ASNS	*Archiv für das Studium der Neueren Sprachen und Literaturen*
BA	*Books Abroad*
BAAL	*Boletín de la Academia Argentina de Letras*
BBMP	*Boletín de la Biblioteca Menéndez Pelayo*
BCB	*Boletín Cultural y Bibliográfico* (Bogotá)
BH	*Bulletin Hispanique*
BHS	*Bulletin of Hispanic Studies*
BICC	*Thesaurus. Boletín del Instituto Caro y Cuervo*
BRAE	*Boletín de la Real Academia Española de la Lengua*
ByN	*Blanco y Negro*
CA	*Cuadernos Americanos*
CDI	*Cumulative Dissertation Index (1861-1972)*
Cel	*Celestinesca*
CHA	*Cuadernos Hispanoamericanos*
CL	*Comparative Literature*

CSIC	Consejo Superior de Investigaciones Científicas
DA	*Dissertation Abstracts*
DAI	*Dissertation Abstracts International*
DAI-C	*Dissertation Abstracts International-Foreign Series*
ECV	*El Espectador y la Critica*, ed. F. Alvaro (Valladolid)
Est Lit	*Estafeta Literaria*
ETL	*Explicación de Textos Literarios*
HR	*Hispanic Review*
JHP	*Journal of Hispanic Philology*
KRQ	*Kentucky Romance Quarterly*
LaC	*La coronica*
LATR	*Latin American Theatre Review*
LR	*Les Lettres Romanes*
MAe	*Medium Aevum*
MLN	*Modern Language Notes*
MLR	*Modern Language Review*
NRFH	*Nueva Revista de Filología Hispánica*
PMLA	*Publications of the Modern Language Association*
PSA	*Papeles de Son Armadans*
QIA	*Quaderni Ibero-Americani*
REH	*Revista de Estudios Hispánicos* (Alabama; Vassar College)
RenQ	*Renaissance Quarterly*
RF	*Romanische Forshungen*
RFE	*Revista de Filología Española*
RFH	*Revista de Filología Hispánica*
RHM	*Revista Hispánica Moderna*
RJ	*Romanistisches Jahrbuch*
RL	*Revista de Literatura*
RLC	*Revue de Littérature Comparée*
RLR	*Revue des Langues Romanes*
RO	*Revista de Occidente*
RPh	*Romance Philology*
RR	Romanic Review
RyF	*Razon y Fe*
SSMLL	Society for Study of Mediaeval Languages and Literatures (Oxford)
TLS	*Times Literary Supplement*
TRAMES	*Travaux et Mémoires de l'Université de Limoges*
UCPMP	*Univ. of California Publications in Modern Phililogy*
UNCSRLL	Univ. of North Carolina Studies in Romance Language and Literature
YWMLS	*THe Year's Work in Modern Language Studies*
ZRP	*Zeitschrift für Romanische Philologie*

Ysopete-Zaragoza, 1489

hic liber confectus est
Madisoni .mcmlxxxv.